Ancient Rome was one of the greatest cities of the pre-industrial era. Like other such great cities, it has often been seen as a parasite, a drain on the resources of the society that supported it. Rome's huge population was maintained not by trade or manufacture but by the taxes and rents of the empire. It was the archetypal 'consumer city'. However, such a label does not do full justice to the impact of the city on its hinterland. This book examines the historiography of the consumer city model and reappraises the relationship between Rome and Italy. Drawing on recent archaeological work and comparative evidence, the author shows how the growth of the city can be seen as the major influence on the development of the Italian economy in this period, as its demands for food and migrants promoted changes in agriculture, marketing systems and urbanisation throughout the peninsula.

Metropolis and hinterland

Metropolis and hinterland

*The city of Rome and the Italian economy
200 B.C.–A.D. 200*

Neville Morley

Lecturer in Ancient History
University of Bristol

CAMBRIDGE
UNIVERSITY PRESS

Published by the Press Syndicate of the University of Cambridge
The Pitt Building, Trumpington Street, Cambridge CB2 1RP
40 West 20th Street, New York, NY 10011–4211, USA
10 Stamford Road, Oakleigh, Melbourne 3166, Australia

First published 1996

Printed in Great Britain at the University Press, Cambridge

A catalogue record for this book is available from the British Library

Library of Congress cataloguing in publication data applied for

ISBN 0 521 56006 3 hardback

CE

Contents

Maps and figures

Preface

A great many people have assisted me in the writing of this book, and I wish to take this opportunity to thank them. Peter Garnsey was an exemplary supervisor of the Ph.D. thesis on which it is based, unfailingly providing encouragement, advice, ideas and obscure pieces of bibliography whenever appropriate; I am also grateful for his continued support since submission. As my examiners, Dominic Rathbone and Jeremy Paterson offered many invaluable suggestions as to how the thesis might best be turned into a book; it is undoubtedly much improved as a result of their comments.

I have benefited greatly from the opinions of people who have read sections of the work or heard versions of it in seminars. I particularly wish to thank John Patterson for his extensive comments and encouragement; Keith Hopkins, for necessary criticism of my grasp of demography and for lending me his unpublished piece on the city of Rome; Wim Jongman, for introducing me to recent work on early modern metropolitan cities and for the loan of another unpublished article.

The bulk of the work of revising the thesis for publication was carried out in the Department of Classics at the University of Wales, Lampeter; I wish to thank everyone there for their help and support, especially Geoff Eatough and Anne Gwilym. I am also very grateful to Pauline Hire at Cambridge University Press for all her encouragement and advice to a first-time author.

Finally, I must thank past and present members of the Graduate Common Room in the Faculty of Classics, Cambridge, for their support, friendship, extraordinary forbearance in the face of unrelenting pessimism, and innumerable cups of coffee; especially Sara Aguilar, Duncan Barker, Joanne Brown, Ray Clare, Penny Glare, Justin Goddard, Vedia Izzet, Richard Miles, Onno van Nijf, Rosanna Omitowoju, Lene Rubinstein, Gillian Shepherd and Natascha Zajac.

Abbreviations

Abbreviations used are those of *L'Année Philologique*, with the addition of the following.

Agr. Hist.	*Agricultural History*
Agr. Hist. Rev.	*Agricultural History Review*
Am. Anthr.	*American Anthropologist*
Amphores	*Amphores Romaines et Histoire Economique: dix ans de recherche*, Rome, 1989 (*CEFR* 114).
Ann. Rev. Anthr.	*Annual Review of Anthropology*
ArchMed	*Archeologia Medievale*
BAR Int. Ser.	*British Archaeological Reports International Series*
BEFAR	*Bibliothéque des écoles françaises d'Athènes et de Rome*
CA	*Current Anthropology*
CAH VII.2	Walbank, F.W., Astin, A. E., Frederiksen, M. W. and Ogilvie, R. M., eds., *The Cambridge Ancient History, Vol. VII.2: the rise of Rome to 200 B.C.*, 2nd edn, Cambridge, 1989.
CAH VIII	Astin, A. E., Walbank, F. W., Frederiksen, M. W. and Ogilvie, R. M., eds., *The Cambridge Ancient History, Vol. VIII: Rome and the Mediterranean to 133 B.C.*, 2nd edn, Cambridge, 1989.
CAH IX	Crook, J. A., Lintott, A. and Rawson, E., eds., *The Cambridge Ancient History, Vol. IX: the last age of the Roman Republic*, 2nd edn, Cambridge, 1994.
CEFR	*Collection de l'école française à Rome*
CIL	*Corpus Inscriptionum Latinarum*
Econ. Hist. Rev.	*Economic History Review*
HJAS	*Harvard Journal of Asiatic Studies*
Italie	*L'Italie d'Auguste à Dioclétien: actes du colloque international*, Rome, 1994 (*CEFR* 198).
MAAR	*Memoirs of the American Academy at Rome*

Mus. Afr.	*Museum Africum*
NSc	*Notizie degli Scavi*
Pop. Stud.	*Population Studies*
Tecnologia	*Tecnologia Economia e Società nel Mondo Romano,* Como, 1980.

Introduction: Rome and Italy

'Prima urbes inter, divum domus, aurea Roma.'

(Ausonius, *Ordo Urbium Nobilium* 1)

In praise of Rome

In the summer of A.D. 143, the Greek orator Aelius Aristides arrived in the imperial capital, having made a vow to the gods that, in return for safe passage, he would compose an address in praise of the Roman people:

But, since it was quite impossible to pledge words commensurate with your city, it became evident that I had need of a second prayer. It is perhaps really presumptuous to dare undertake an oration to equal such majesty in a city ... For it is she who first proved that oratory cannot reach every goal. About her not only is it impossible to speak properly, but it is impossible even to see her properly ... For beholding so many hills occupied by buildings, or on plains so many meadows completely urbanised, or so much land brought under the name of one city, who could survey her accurately? And from what point of observation?[1]

The inability of the orator and of oratory to do justice to the subject is a standard part of the prolegomenon to any panegyric, but Rome inspired similar reactions in other visitors. The emperor Constantius, visiting the city in A.D. 357, is said to have 'complained of Fama as either incapable or spiteful, because while always exaggerating everything, in describing what there is in Rome, she becomes spiteful'; one of his companions meanwhile remarked that 'he took comfort in this fact alone, that he had learned that even there men were mortal'.[2] When the city was sacked in 410, 'when the brightest light of the world was extinguished, when the very head of the Roman empire was severed', it was for Jerome as if the whole world had perished.[3] Even after its

---

[1] *Or.* 26.2, 6; translation and commentary in Oliver (1953).
[2] Amm. Marc. 16.10.16–17.   [3] *Commentary on Ezekiel*, prologue.

political eclipse, therefore, and despite the rivalry of Constantinople, Rome remained 'the greatest, most eminent and regal city'.[4]

Aristides' rhetorical portrait was designed to flatter; his views on certain topics – the beneficial effects of Roman imperialism, for example – can hardly be taken as typical of the majority of the inhabitants of the empire, although doubtless they conformed to the Romans' own beliefs. The themes he develops in describing and praising the city itself, however, are found in many other authors, not all of them so content with the Roman achievement. This set of ideas, of conventional responses, reflects not so much the reactions of visitors as the image of the city of Rome in the minds of people who may never have visited the place. Rome was known for certain things, and writers therefore tended to dwell on these themes. Nevertheless, in many cases the hyperbole of orators, historians and tourists was entirely justified.

The first theme is the sheer size of the city. Aristides declares that only some all-seeing Argus could adequately survey the place, and, borrowing the simile from Homer, he observes that:

Like the snow, she covers mountain peaks, she covers the land intervening, and she goes down to the sea ... And indeed she is poured out, not just over the level ground, but in a manner with which the simile cannot begin to keep pace she rises great distances into the air, so that her height is not to be compared to a covering of snow but to the peaks themselves.[5]

The elder Pliny, Strabo and Ammianus concentrate on the number and magnificence of the city's monuments (among which the first two count the 'veritable rivers' that supplied fountains and flushed out the sewers), but anonymous tourist guides like the *Notitia* and the *Curiosum*, dating from the fourth century, rely on sheer weight of numbers for their effect, listing the tens of thousands of houses as well as hundreds of bath houses, bakeries, brothels and warehouses.[6] According to the Talmud, 'the great city of Rome has 365 streets, and in each street there are 365 palaces. Each palace has 365 stories, and each storey contains enough food to feed the whole world.'[7]

The population of Rome at the time of Augustus is commonly estimated at around a million. Its nearest rival in the ancient Mediterranean world, Alexandria, contained perhaps half that number; Antioch was roughly the same size, according to Strabo, while Carthage, Pergamum, Ephesus and a few other eastern cities reached 100–200,000.[8] From a comparative perspective, too, Rome was exceptional. No other

---

[4] *Descriptio Totius Mundi* 55.   [5] *Or.* 26.6–8.
[6] Pliny, *HN* 36.101ff; Strabo 5.3.8; Amm. Marc. 16.10.13–15; Jordan (1871), 539–74; Nordh (1949); Hermansen (1978), 136–40.
[7] Talmud, *Pesahim* 118b.   [8] Duncan-Jones (1982), 260 n.4.

European city had a population of that size before London at the beginning of the nineteenth century, when dramatic changes in the structure of the English economy permitted a massive increase in urbanisation.[9] In the preceding centuries, only two European cities had passed even the half million mark.[10] Further to the east, Istanbul may have contained 700,000 people in the late sixteenth century.[11] Before the Industrial Revolution, cities of a million or more were to be found only in medieval China.[12] The hyperbole of ancient commentators on Rome seems to be entirely justified.

Aristides is equally impressed with the scale of Roman commerce:

Whatever the seasons make grow and whatever countries and rivers and lakes and arts of Hellenes and non-Hellenes produce are brought from every land and sea … Whatever is grown and made among each people cannot fail to be here at all times and in abundance … The city appears a kind of common emporium of the world. Cargoes from India and, if you will, even from Arabia the Blest, one can see in such numbers as to surmise that in those lands the trees will have been stripped bare and that the inhabitants of those lands, if they need anything, must come here and beg for a share of their own … Arrivals and departures by sea never cease, so that the wonder is, not that the harbour has insufficient space for merchant vessels, but that even the sea has enough, if it really does.[13]

A similar picture is painted in the Revelation of St John the Divine, describing the fall of Babylon (Rome is called a second Babylon by Christian writers from 1 Peter onwards).[14]

And the merchants of the earth weep and mourn over her, for no man buyeth their merchandise any more; merchandise of gold, and silver, and precious stone, and pearls, and fine linen, and purple, and silk, and scarlet … and wine, and oil, and fine flour, and wheat, and cattle, and sheep; and merchandise of horses and chariots and slaves; and souls of men … The merchants of these things, who were made rich by her, shall stand afar off for fear of her torment, weeping and mourning; saying, 'Woe, woe, the great city … for in one hour so great riches is made desolate.' And every shipmaster, and every one that saileth any whither, and mariners, and as many as gain their living by sea, stood afar off, and cried out as they looked at the smoke of her burning, saying, 'What city is like the great city?' And they cast dust on their heads, and cried, weeping and mourning, saying, 'Woe, woe, the great city, wherein were made rich all that had their ships in the sea by reason of her costliness.'[15]

Beside such apocalyptic rhetoric, the comments of writers like Strabo about the importance of the Tiber and the sea for the city of Rome seem remarkably tame, but all point towards the vast effort required to keep

[9] Wrigley (1967).   [10] de Vries (1984), 270–8.   [11] Braudel (1972), 347–8.
[12] Chao (1986), 56.   [13] Or. 26.11–12, 13.
[14] Mounce (1977), 321–35; Caird (1984), 221–32; 1 Peter 5.13; Augustine, De civ. D. 18.2.
[15] Revelation 18.11–19.

such a city adequately provided with the necessities of life.[16] A million people require a minimum of 150,000 tonnes of grain per annum for subsistence; the actual figure for imports must have been significantly higher.[17] Equally vast quantities of staples like wine, oil, vegetables and fruit were needed, to say nothing of more luxurious foodstuffs like meat and spices, of wood for fuel and building work, of marble and of innumerable other commodities.[18] Rome drew these supplies from a vast area; from its empire – as Aristides observed, 'your farms are Egypt, Sicily and the civilised part of Africa' – and from the furthest corners of the world. The grain trade alone required a massive infrastructure of ships, sailors, dock workers and merchants; well might those who made their living from the sea mourn the loss of such a market.

Rome was immensely rich. Ausonius describes the city as *aurea*, golden, which has connotations of both wealth and decadent luxurious-ness.[19] The passage of the Talmud cited above envisages Rome as a place of superabundance, with each building containing enough food to feed the whole world. Another passage observes: 'ten *kabs* of wisdom descended to the world: nine were taken by Palestine and one by the rest of the world ... Ten *kabs* of wealth descended to the world: nine were taken by Rome and one by the rest of the world.'[20] The source of this wealth is equally plain: the empire. Aristides claims that 'if one looks at the whole empire and reflects how small a fraction rules the whole world, he may be amazed at the city, but when he has beheld the city herself and the boundaries of the city, he can no longer be amazed that the entire civilised world is ruled by one so great'.[21] Perhaps the empire itself was indeed the greater marvel in the eyes of contemporaries – after all, Alexander the Great had conquered only barbarians, whereas the Romans ruled the people of the civilised world. From our perspective, however, it is the size of Rome that is remarkable, to be explained by the possession of such an empire.

The pre-industrial metropolis

Even from a comparative perspective, Rome was an exceptionally large city. The reasons for the rarity of such 'megalopoleis' in history are to be found in the nature of the economies of the societies that had to support them. In a pre-industrial, primarily agrarian economy there are strict limits on the extent to which productivity may be increased, and there-fore on the amount of surplus available; the maintenance of a huge

[16] Strabo 5.3.7; Cicero, *Rep.* 2.4–5.   [17] Garnsey (1988a), 191.
[18] Loane (1938); D'Arms and Kopff (1980).   [19] D. G. N. Barker (1993).
[20] Talmud, *Kiddushin* 49b.   [21] *Or.* 26.9.

population of non-producers in a metropolis requires the labour of many millions of agricultural workers and the surplus production of a vast area. Moreover, the concentration of these non-producers in a single large city creates further problems. Transport in a pre-industrial economy is expensive; the cost of transporting a bulky staple like grain long distances overland might be prohibitively expensive. It is no coincidence that most large pre-industrial cities were located on navigable rivers or on the sea.

Even if these logistical problems could be surmounted, there is the problem of how such giant cities paid for their keep. Given the low level of demand and high cost of transport in a pre-industrial economy, what goods or services could a metropolis provide that could not be offered more cheaply by smaller centres at a more local level? The simple answer is that the metropolis is invariably a 'political' city; the services it provides are those of a centralised administrative system and a concrete manifestation of the glory of the state. The population of the metropolis is fed from the taxes paid by the rest of the country; the high costs of transport are subsidised from state revenues. The political capitals of the ancient world, medieval China and early modern Europe are in fact prime examples of what Werner Sombart called the 'consumption city': 'By a consumption city I mean one which pays for its maintenance ... not with its own products, because it does not need to. It derives its maintenance rather on the basis of a legal claim, such as taxes or rents, without having to deliver return values.'[22] Not all of the urban population were literally 'consumers', of course; all such cities contained large numbers of petty craftsmen and shopkeepers, but they were a dependent element, 'whose existence was determined by the share of the consumption fund allowed to them by the consumption class'.[23]

Finley described ancient Rome as the quintessential consumer city, and certainly it fits the model very neatly.[24] A sizeable proportion of the grain required to feed its population was collected as tax from provinces like Sicily, Africa and Egypt, transported to the city at the state's expense, and distributed to 200,000 or more members of the *plebs*; by the Principate this distribution was free of charge.[25] The idea that the urban masses were a pampered mob, maintained in idleness with 'bread and circuses', has long been abandoned by historians; the populace needed money with which to pay for milling and baking the grain and to buy wine, oil and other foodstuffs.[26] However, they did not earn their keep in the manufacture of goods for export. The opportunities for employment in Rome were considerable, but they lay in the great state building

[22] Sombart (1916), I, 142–3.   [23] *Ibid.*.   [24] Finley (1985a), 194.
[25] Garnsey (1988a), 198–243.   [26] Whittaker (1993c).

projects, in servicing the needs of the land-owning elite whose political activities centred on the capital, and in the docks and *tabernae*, helping to supply the rest of the population.[27] The description of Babylon's desolation in Revelation announces that 'the voice of harpers and minstrels and flute-players and trumpeters shall be heard no more at all in thee; and no craftsmen, of whatsoever craft, shall be found any more in thee; and the voice of a millstone shall be heard no more at all in thee', while Ammianus records that in the fourth century the city contained 3,000 dancing girls and the same number of dancing masters.[28] Inscriptions provide evidence of more prosaic trades, but they all seem to relate to what Finley termed 'petty commodity production' for local consumption.[29]

There is no evidence for any large-scale exports from Rome; the city consumed almost everything produced there and still demanded more. The wages of its craftsmen, shopkeepers, porters and labourers were paid ultimately by the people of the empire, whose surplus was collected as taxes and rent, taken to the city of Rome and spent there by the state and by the land-owning elite. The size and wealth of the city were entirely due to its role as a political centre, head of the empire and therefore one of the chief beneficiaries of the spoils of empire. It offered nothing more tangible in return for its keep. For most contemporaries, or those of them whose thoughts on the subject are preserved, the city of Rome embodied the greatness of its empire, which brought peace and prosperity to the world. From a modern perspective, the views of Victor Hugo – 'the Roman sewer engulfed the world, sapping town and country alike' – or the vision of Revelation of Babylon the Great, the Mother of Harlots and Abominations, drunk with the blood of the saints, may seem more apt.

This characterisation of Rome as a consumer city is, however, only the first step in understanding its place in the economy and society of the empire. The fact that its supplies were paid for by taxes rather than the profits from commerce or industry does not detract from the scale and importance of those supplies. A sizeable portion of surplus production was expended in moving goods to the city from all parts of the empire; this supported an infrastructure of ship owners, merchants and dock workers – as the author of Revelation observed. Large profits could be made by those involved in supplying Rome: the real-life counterparts of Trimalchio, who lost one fortune in shipping wine to the city and made another with a cargo of wine, bacon, beans, perfume and slaves.[30]

Study of Rome's food supply has moved on considerably from the

27 Brunt (1980); Pleket (1993b), 19–20.   28 Revelation 18.22–3; Amm. Marc. 14.6.19.
29 Finley (1985a), 194.   30 Petronius, *Sat.* 76; cf. K. Hopkins (1983b), 101–2.

compilation of lists of imports known from literary sources.[31] The shipment of grain to the city has received particular attention, partly because of the obvious importance of this staple and partly because of the volume of surviving evidence relating to the *annona*, the system by which tax grain was supplied to the populace.[32] Study of the movement of other commodities has been transformed in the last twenty years by the evidence provided by archaeology, with increasing knowledge of the amphorae in which oil, wine and *garum* were brought to Rome from Italy, Gaul, Spain, Africa and other parts of the empire.[33] Excavations at Ostia and Rome have revealed not only the different areas from which the city drew its supplies but also the changing patterns of this trade; excavated shipwrecks also offer evidence for the organisation of the city's food supply.[34] Debate continues on many aspects of this trade – for example, on whether the Roman elite were directly involved – and the amphorae alone cannot answer many of these questions, but as direct evidence for the movement of goods around the Mediterranean they provide an essential starting-point for such discussions.[35]

The effects of the city's demands on the regions that supplied it have received far less attention. The economic impact of Rome on different parts of its empire, unlike its political, social and cultural impact, has not yet received a full-length study; its likely parameters have so far been discussed only in very general terms.[36] The reasons for this curious neglect are doubtless various; they include the prevalence of a view of 'economic development' that privileges trade and manufacture over agriculture, and the fact that evidence for changes in the countryside, other than scattered literary references, has become widely available only in the last twenty-odd years with the proliferation of archaeological survey projects. The main aim of this book is to help to fill this gap by offering a detailed study of the influence of the metropolis on one part of its empire.

It may seem extremely improbable that a city the size of Rome could have failed to have a significant impact on many parts of its hinterland – certainly this is the lesson to be drawn from comparison with other pre-industrial metropoleis, as will be seen in the next chapter – and therefore it can be argued that a study of this kind is long overdue, requiring little

---

[31] As in Loane (1938).
[32] Rickman (1971) and (1980); Casson (1980); Garnsey (1983) and (1988a), 198–243; Sirks (1991).
[33] Panella (1970) and (1981); Hesnard (1980); Rodriguez-Almeida (1984); Tchernia (1986); *Amphores.*
[34] Peacock and Williams (1986); Parker (1992); generally, Greene (1986), 17–44.
[35] Paterson (1982); Tchernia (1989); Whittaker (1985) and (1989).
[36] E.g. Garnsey and Saller (1987), 58–62; Pleket (1993b).

further justification. However, although the perspective offered here is new, the questions involved are somewhat well worn. This book lies under the shadow of two long-running debates in ancient history: on the one hand, that concerning the nature of the ancient economy, the economic role of cities and the possibility of growth and development; on the other, the much-disputed economic history of Italy in the late Republic and early Principate. I hope that I can offer a new perspective on the latter question, and a test case for certain ideas in the former.

Let us begin with the theoretical side, the historiography of which is convoluted but fascinating.[37] For the question of the impact of Rome on its hinterland, two lines of argument are of particular importance.

The first is that of the 'primitivist'/'substantivist' school associated with Moses Finley, which plays down the possibility of any economic growth or development in antiquity and emphasises the pre-modern, 'embedded' nature of the ancient economy and ancient economic thought.[38] According to this model, the city of Rome (as the archetypal consumer city) was a parasite, creaming off the surplus production of the rest of the empire and consuming it unproductively. It may be considered a stagnating influence on the economy of the empire; at best it simply replaced a class of local exploiters with more distant masters. If the city had paid for what it took through goods and services, it might have had a more positive impact – but the limitations of the ancient economic mentality and the dominance of agriculture and landed wealth made this more or less inconceivable. Finley did note in passing that Rome had a considerable impact on parts of the countryside which supplied it with wine and pork, but the point is not elaborated; there was no effect on urban production for export, which he sees as the key to economic development.[39] In general, the size of the city of Rome is explained by its political role and the consumption habits of the land-owning elite; it may be said to embody all the tendencies that kept the ancient economy undeveloped.

An alternative theory is that put forward by Keith Hopkins; namely, that the collection and expenditure of taxes by the Roman state were an important stimulus to trade.[40] Taxes were for the most part collected in the rich inner provinces of the empire (Italy was exempt) and spent in Rome and in frontier provinces; to raise cash to pay them, he argues, the inner provinces had to sell produce to the city and the army, supporting a massive expansion of trade in the late Republic and early Principate.

---

[37] For an introduction, see K. Hopkins (1983c); Garnsey and Saller (1987), 43–63; Jongman (1988a), 15–55.

[38] E.g. Finley (1985a); discussed by Frederiksen (1975).   [39] (1985a), 150.

[40] K. Hopkins (1978b), (1980), (1983b) and (1983c).

Hopkins mentions in passing that the need to pay taxes might inspire an increase in the volume of agricultural production.[41] He does not elaborate, but in an earlier article he links the expansion of Italian towns, among them the city of Rome, to the development of slave agriculture in Italy in the second century B.C.[42] The clear implication of the 'taxes and trade' model is that the demands of the city of Rome would have a twofold influence on its hinterland; farmers had to give up a portion of their surplus (possibly no more than they had been paying before the Romans arrived), but they could also benefit from the profits to be made in supplying those who benefited from the proceeds of empire.

Both these theories are formulated at the 'macro' level, dealing with the ancient economy as a whole, or at least with the entire Roman empire over six hundred years. Their very scope and importance makes them extraordinarily difficult to falsify or otherwise disprove – as Hopkins openly admits. For example, there is no consensus on the nature of the economy even of a city as well-documented as Pompeii; if one point of view were to win widespread acceptance, the town could then be dismissed as an exception, tangential to the wider debate.[43] It would appear that ancient economic history will continue to be a matter of choosing between different sets of basic premises (the two summarised above are by no means the only theories on offer) on the basis of personal inclination.

That is not to say that case studies, starting from one of these general theories, have no value; it is certainly a step forward to be able to argue that, in one particular instance at least, the evidence appears to support one view rather than another. The present study inclines to the Hopkins view of the Roman empire; within the limits of a pre-industrial economy, some economic growth was possible, and the growth of the city of Rome was an important stimulus to such growth. In the next chapter this argument will be presented in more detail from two complementary perspectives; a theoretical and historiographical critique of the primitivist/substantivist view of ancient cities and economic growth, and a comparative study of the place of the metropolis in the economies of medieval China and early modern Europe.

The remainder of the book examines the influence of the city of Rome on the economy of a particular region, Italy between 200 B.C. and A.D. 200. The first date marks the beginning of the period when Rome may be considered a true metropolis; the latter is largely a matter of convenience, since the question of the fates of Rome and Italy under the later Empire demands a full-length study of its own. Four hundred years seems to be a

[41] (1980), 101–2.   [42] (1978a), 11–15.
[43] E.g. Jongman (1988a); Purcell (1990); Laurence (1994), 8–10, 51–69.

suitable period for the study of long-term economic and demographic movements, especially since the evidence of archaeological survey is based on pottery chronologies which may span several centuries. The restriction of the study to Italy is also a matter of convenience, but there is no doubt that it makes a particularly interesting subject. As Rome's immediate hinterland Italy was likely to be affected earliest by the city's demands for goods and people, and arguably affected to a greater extent than other regions. The addition to the empire of provinces like Sicily, Africa and Egypt relieved it of the need to provide all of Rome's grain supply; land could be used for the production of different (and more market-oriented) crops without fear of food crisis. Moreover, after 89 B.C. all Italians became Roman citizens, and Roman citizens had not been taxed directly since 167. The Italian farmer therefore had a larger surplus at his disposal; he was not forced into the market (that part of Hopkins' model is inapplicable), but he was in a better position to choose to respond to the incentives offered there.

Given these twin factors of tax exemption and proximity to the market, it is somewhat surprising that the subject of 'Rome and Italy' has, at least in its economic aspects, been so neglected. In studies of Rome's food supply, most attention is paid to imports from the provinces, whether grain from Africa and Egypt or wine and oil from Spain and Gaul; Italy's contribution is less visible, and is therefore played down or ignored altogether. Conversely, studies of the development of Italy tend to deny any significant role to the Roman market, and this has led to some remarkably negative views of the state of the Italian economy through most of the period in question. Provincial economies are seen as dynamic, developing rapidly under the stimulus of 'Romanisation'; Italian agriculture limps from stagnation to crisis, embarking on a terminal decline from the late first century A.D.[44]

The evidence for widespread crisis in this period, rather than a crisis limited to certain regions and to a particular form of agricultural organisation, is unconvincing.[45] The nature of these changes will be discussed in more detail in Chapter 5. For the moment, we may note that a significant feature of the prophecies of doom is their obsession with exports as the determinant of an economy's health; the spread of villas in Italy is linked to the growth of a Gallic market for wine, and so the loss of this market under the Principate must spell disaster for Italian producers. Clearly this is an excessively modernising, formalist perspective – 'balance of payments' problems were not a major feature of the ancient economy – but it also ignores entirely the fact that the Roman

---

[44] Rostovtzeff (1957), 192–206; Carandini (1989).   [45] Patterson (1987).

market was as large and profitable as ever.[46] If the city of Rome is restored to the picture, the crisis of the villas is seen to be a far more complicated phenomenon than the traditional thesis of Italian decline would suggest, requiring a more sophisticated explanation.

The city plays a similarly subsidiary role in many accounts of the other great crisis in Italian agriculture, that of the post-Hannibalic period. For Rostovtzeff and Carandini, the establishment of the villa system is tied to the market for wine in Gaul, Spain and the Danube region; Rome is barely mentioned, and other crops (particularly grain) are more or less ignored.[47] Other work has redressed the balance somewhat: Toynbee and Hopkins place much more emphasis on the growth of the urban market in Italy, including the capital; Purcell and Tchernia have offered more sophisticated accounts of the spread of viticulture (in the latter case, backed by a careful study of the archaeological evidence), while Spurr has restored cereal cultivation to its rightful position in Italian agriculture.[48] A short piece by de Neeve proposes a model for the changes of the second century B.C. centred on the demands of the city of Rome, making use of von Thünen's model of agricultural location.[49]

Despite the quantity and quality of this work, I believe that this study still has something to contribute to the question of Italy's development during the late Republic. The general theories of agricultural change have not been properly tested against the evidence provided by archaeological survey; this is particularly important in the case of de Neeve's work, whose use of geographical models (especially the choice of von Thünen) is very similar to my own. Furthermore, previous historians have seriously underestimated the demographic impact of Rome on Italy; its demands for migrants were a significant factor in the economic transformations of this period.

After the discussion of the place of the metropolis in a pre-industrial economy, therefore, I turn to the question of demography; the population of Rome and its dynamics, the demand for migrants and the effects of this demand on the rest of Italy. Evidence from early modern Europe suggests that pre-industrial urban populations were incapable of maintaining their own numbers, let alone of expanding, without regular and large-scale immigration from the countryside. Post-Hannibalic Rome was an attractive destination for many people; the redistribution of population between city and country, and between agriculture and non-agricultural employment, has important economic and social implica-

---

[46] Cf. Frank (1927), 424–31.   [47] Rostovtzeff (1957), 1–36; Carandini (1989).
[48] Toynbee (1965), 155–89, 332–40; K. Hopkins (1978a), 1–98; Purcell (1985); Tchernia (1986); Spurr (1986).
[49] (1984a).

tions, while the development of a huge urban market is central to the model of metropolitan influence.

The third chapter offers a model of agricultural change in response to the demands of the expanding city, drawing on geographical theories and taking into consideration the slowness and cost of transport, variations in climate and soil and the economic mentality of Roman landowners. The central chapters of the book then test this model against three areas of Italy in turn, using evidence from literary sources and archaeological survey: the immediate hinterland of the city, the *suburbium*, whose economy and society were inextricably linked to the fortunes of the capital from a very early date; the central Italian heartland, home of the market-oriented villa system; finally, more distant regions like Apulia, the Po Valley and the Apennine highlands. The final chapter examines the development of systems of marketing and trade and the changing patterns of urbanisation in Italy under the influence of the metropolis, touching upon the wider question of the role of the city of Rome in the process of social and cultural change generally characterised as 'Romanisation'. Whether or not the development is to be labelled 'progressive', it is clear that the effort required to support this 'quintessential consumer city' affected the economy and society of almost every part of Roman Italy.

1 The metropolitan city in a pre-industrial economy

In one sense, all cities are consumers. The existence of urban centres depends on the ability of farmers to produce a regular agricultural surplus, and on the efficiency of economic, social and political institutions in mobilising this surplus for the use of a population which is not involved in primary production. Of course, this broad statement covers a wide variety of possibilities; in the modern industrialised world only a tiny proportion of the population is involved in agriculture, whereas in a pre-industrial, agrarian economy the figure may be 90 per cent or more. Chemical fertilisers and a mineral-based energy economy have transformed modern agriculture, and coal, oil and electricity have revolutionised the distribution of foodstuffs. In a pre-industrial society, surpluses are small and precarious, and transport is slow and expensive; cities are therefore wholly dependent on the performance of agriculture and the vagaries of the climate, and endemically vulnerable to food crisis.

However, the notion of the 'consumer city' implies much more than this basic dependence on agriculture.[1] In part, it and its sibling concept (the 'producer city') are concerned with the economic aspects of the relationship between city and countryside: the means by which the agricultural surplus is mobilised for the use of the urban population. The producer city pays for its keep through trade, manufacture and providing services to the countryside; the consumer city takes what it needs in the form of taxes and rents, offering little in return besides indifferently administered justice and government. No real city conforms entirely to either one of these models, but the use of ideal types like these permits the isolation of the essential nature of the city's economy for the purposes of classification, analysis and comparison.[2]

In this strict sense, ancient Rome was undoubtedly a consumer city; it exported little and consumed a great deal, paid for directly or indirectly by the taxes and rents of the empire. However, the implications of the label are far wider than this. It is a model of a type of city, not merely of

---

[1] Weber (1958), 65–89; Finley (1981b).   [2] Weber (1958), 70; Finley (1985b), 60–1.

a type of city economy; it seeks to encompass not only the economic but also the social and political aspects of the town–country relationship, not to mention the nature of urban institutions, power structures and ideologies. If you accept the model, it covers almost everything you might wish to know about the ancient city. This can, however, make it rather difficult to pin down.[3]

Above all, it is difficult to separate the concept of the consumer city from certain ideas about the role of towns in economic development and the emergence of modern industrial capitalism. Because of these assumptions, often left unspoken, 'consumer' all too easily becomes 'parasite': a statement about the way in which the city fed itself is taken to imply that the city had a particular, and thoroughly negative, effect on the countryside that supported it. The contention of this study is precisely the opposite, that a consumer city like Rome may nevertheless have had a stimulating effect on the economy of its hinterland.

The reasons for this confusion over the nature of the consumer city must be sought in the intellectual biography of the concept, placing it in its historical context. The dominance of the theory over all discussion of the city in the ancient world stems directly from the influential article by M. I. Finley, which examined nineteenth- and early twentieth-century work on the nature of the ancient city.[4] The article is more than a summary of previous work; indeed, it might be said that Finley discusses earlier writers in detail only in so far as they contribute to or prefigure his own theory.[5] Finley is concerned with the relevance of earlier theories for modern historical studies, and only indirectly with their historiographical context. He traces the origins of the consumer city model back to the works of Bücher and Sombart, observing that their studies are devoted not to the ancient city but to the rise of modern capitalism – apparently without considering that this might affect their use of the model. It may seem unnecessary to retread this ground, but an examination of the views of the three writers used by Finley, replacing their comments in their original context, reveals a great deal about the way in which the consumer city model has acquired so much ideological baggage in its relatively short life.

The origins of the consumer city

The idea that great cities are parasites, consuming the wealth of the countryside and giving nothing in return, has a long history, but before the middle of the nineteenth century the economic implications of this

---

[3]   E.g. Jongman (1988a), 191.   [4] Finley (1981b).
[5]   Meyer is treated with particular disdain: (1981b), 7, 13.

observation were not generally regarded.[6] Adam Smith had noted the peculiar nature of the metropolitan economy: 'Paris itself is the principal market of all the manufactures established at Paris, and its own consumption is the principal object of all the trade which it carries on.'[7] He also believed that the idleness induced by the flow of tax revenues would make it difficult to promote industry and the profitable employment of capital in such cities. However, the idea that the metropolis could have a damaging effect on the economy of its hinterland was first developed in the succeeding century in the work of Bücher.

Along with Karl Marx, Karl Bücher can be considered the founding father of the substantivist school of economic anthropology and the primitivist view of the ancient economy. Marx emphasises the primitive, non-capitalist elements of pre-modern economies so as to stress the contingent nature of the capitalist mode of production – it had not always existed, it would not continue for ever – leading to considerable tension between his yearning for the unrecoverable past and his belief in the necessity of social development.[8] Bücher, too, rejects the idea that rational profit-motivation is a natural characteristic of all human beings: 'civilised man has always had a great inclination to read his conceptions and feelings into the mind of primitive man; but he has only a limited capacity for understanding the latter's undeveloped mental life and for interpreting, as it were, his nature.'[9] 'An historically constructive view, such as we will here present, must from the start shake off the idea that any particular form in any department of economic activity can be the norm for all times and people.'[10] It was this attitude, and his adoption of Rodbertus' theory of the *oikos* economy, that led to the great debate with Meyer and other modernising ancient historians.[11]

Bücher occasionally shows some admiration for the unalienated life and 'perpetual cheerfulness' of the savage,[12] but in general he takes an optimistic view of the course of human development:

The comforting result of every serious consideration of history is, that no single element of culture which has once entered into the life of men is lost; that even after the hour of its predominance has expired, it continues in some more modest position to co-operate in the realisation of the great end in which we all believe, the helping of mankind towards more and more perfect forms of existence.[13]

'In the course of history mankind sets before itself ever higher economic aims and finds the means of attaining these in a division of labour, which

---

[6] See generally Williams (1973) and Holton (1986).   [7] A. Smith (1908), 158–9.
[8] See e.g. Marx (1973), 110–11 and (1976), 997–9; cf. Müller (1972).
[9] Bücher (1968), 3.   [10] *Ibid.*, 152.
[11] Discussed in Pearson (1957); relevant texts collected in Finley ed. (1979).
[12] E.g. (1968), 20, 82.   [13] *Ibid.*, 184.

constantly extends until finally it embraces the whole people and requires the services of all for all.'[14] The evident suffering caused by the alienation of workers from the means of production is simply the sign that a new social and economic order is being born, in which men will attain more perfect happiness, not in Marx's communist society but in the community of the *Volk*.[15]

It is within the context of this theory of the development of *Volks-wirtschaft* (the title of the American translation of the work, *Industrial Evolution*, is spectacularly misleading) that Bücher's comments on the consumer city must be situated. The main aim of his argument is to chart the stages of economic development, in which the separation of producer and consumer becomes ever more pronounced: from the independent domestic economy to the town economy and finally the national economy.[16] The driving principle, as already mentioned, is the need to satisfy ever-increasing wants, and old forms of economic organisation are abandoned when they fail to do this.[17]

In a subsidiary chapter, however, he turns to the subject of migration and urbanisation.[18] The movement of rural populations into urban centres in the nineteenth century is seen to have assisted in breaking down old forms of social organisation and leading mankind towards a higher order of existence; Bücher therefore asks himself whether earlier migrations should be regarded in the same way. He examines the two great periods of urbanisation, antiquity and the middle ages, and contrasts the different types of towns:

> The large cities of antiquity are essentially communities for consumption. They owe their size to the political centralisation which collected the surplus products of the extensive areas cultivated by individual husbandry at one point where the governing class was domiciled. They are imperial, or at least provincial, capitals ... These placed the productive labour of half a world at the service of the capital city and left open to the private activity of its inhabitants nothing but the sphere of personal services.[19]

This pampering by the state, and the fact that all important factory and agricultural work was done by slaves, meant that the free inhabitants had no need to change the social and economic order to satisfy their wants; hence, stagnation. The medieval town, in contrast, separated from the countryside by walls, became economically separate as well, and this division of labour led to the birth of a new order in Europe.[20] We may note in passing that Bücher has little to say about the vast majority of ancient cities which were not imperial capitals, other than his comments on the ubiquity of slave labour. More significant for our

[14]   *Ibid.*, 141.   [15] *Ibid.*, 313–14, 384–5.   [16] *Ibid.*, 83–149.
[17]   *Ibid.*, 108, 114.   [18] *Ibid.*, 345–85.   [19] *Ibid.*, 371.   [20] *Ibid.*, 373–83.

purpose is the fact that he is concerned specifically to contrast the ancient city with the medieval and modern varieties, and to explain the failure of the ancient world to develop as the later middle ages had. Undoubtedly the prevalence of slave labour was in Bücher's eyes the more important explanation of the stagnation of antiquity, but the contrast between the 'progressive' medieval city and the ancient 'community for consumption' was already clearly drawn.

The biography of Werner Sombart, our second key scholar, neatly encapsulates certain tendencies in the intellectual life of Germany at the turn of the century; above all, the equivocal reaction of the liberal intelligentsia to modernity.[21] His early career was marked – and to some degree hampered – by a close association with Marxist ideas. He accepted that capitalism would complete the conquest of the old patriarchal order and would lead inevitably towards socialism, and he positively welcomed the destruction of old forms of organisation like cottage industry: 'All moral impulses, all feelings of justice will necessarily have to come to terms with the foundation of an economically progressive order of society.'[22]

Gradually, however, he lost faith in the progressive nature of industrial civilisation, seeing only its numbing effect on the human spirit – and, so Mitzman argues, on his own *Sturm und Drang* personality.[23] National-ism, which had always been a significant strand in his work, was now brought to the fore. He turned increasingly to 'kitsch-Nietzschean' models of national heroism, idealising the unalienated medieval man and the Renaissance entrepreneur and denouncing the *bürger*, identified with the Jews, who thrived in the unheroic modern age.[24] As far as his reputation is concerned, Sombart was unfortunate to live long enough to hail Nazism as the force that would realise his ideas, restore the heroic age and put an end to the notion that even the most inconsequential nations had an equal right to existence and freedom of action.[25]

Sombart's classic work *Der moderne Kapitalismus* is a product of the earlier phase of his thought. He expressly sets out to establish the facts in the development of capitalism, and to provide an explanation without imposing his own values as to whether this development is 'progres-sive'.[26] Sombart's theory of historical change is essentially idealist; the moving force is the capitalist *Geist*, which may be manifested either in groups or (most significantly) in individuals.[27] This spirit may be found in any era, but only in the 'economic age' are the conditions right for its

---

[21] Mitzman (1973).   [22] Address to the 1899 meeting of the *Verein für Sozialpolitik*.
[23] Mitzman (1973), 193–208.   [24] Mitzman (1987); A. L. Harris (1992).
[25] Sombart (1937); A. L. Harris (1992), 44–52.   [26] Sombart (1902), II, 425.
[27] *Ibid.*, I, x–xxviii.

full development.[28] This for Sombart is the importance of the town in the late middle ages: its separation from the countryside both politically and economically permits the development of independent crafts and trade, and offers full scope for action to the heroic entrepreneur. The division of labour between town and country (Sombart is the first to insist on this economic definition of urbanisation) is an essential precondition if the *Geist* is to fulfil its potential.[29]

The idea of the consumer city appears in full only in the second edition of the work, and is essentially a polemical attack on the medievalist Henri Pirenne, who had argued that towns in the early middle ages were centres of trade and of a capitalism that differed from modern capitalism only in its intensity.[30] Sombart had located the birth of capitalism in the late middle ages and Renaissance; he argued that the towns of earlier periods did not offer an hospitable environment to the capitalist *Geist*, since they were not founded on a division of labour, and suggested an alternative model for them. 'By a consumption city I mean one which pays for its maintenance ... not with its own products, because it does not need to. It derives its maintenance rather on the basis of a legal claim, such as taxes or rents, without having to deliver return values.'[31] This extends his theory of town formation: the original city creators were consumers, who supported a dependent group of producers; only when the latter group increased its wealth and power and established some autonomy was the town capable of supporting the development of the capitalist *Geist* and hence of modern capitalist society.

The third architect of the consumer city model, Max Weber, resembled Sombart in many important respects. Both men came from the Berlin upper middle class, both began their careers by taking a reformist position against the old order and ended them in a state of utter pessimism about the alienating effects of capitalist society.[32] They were close colleagues for many years, and so the resemblances between their ideas are hardly surprising.[33] Weber's analysis of the emergence of the modern world is more sophisticated than Sombart's; as well as the development of the capitalist spirit (that is, modern economic rationality and the Protestant ethic), he considers the rise of the modern state and the legal institutions that made industrial capitalism possible.[34] However, the medieval town is still allotted a vital role in these developments; its political and economic separation from the feudal institutions of the countryside, he argues, permitted the emergence of Protestant religion,

---

[28]   *Ibid.*, I, 25.   [29]   On *Städtebildung*, see *ibid.*, I, 191–4; cf. Finley (1981b), 11.
[30]   Finley (1981b), 12–13; Bruhns (1985), 259–61.   [31]   Sombart (1916), I, 142–3.
[32]   Mitzman (1970) and (1987).   [33]   Finley (1981b), 13, 252 n.4.
[34]   Käsler (1988), 36–42, 74–94; Scaff (1989), 26–39.

rationalism and the social and legal structures necessary to support trade and industry.[35] 'Neither modern capitalism nor the state as we know it developed on the basis of the ancient city, whereas the Medieval city, though not the only significant antecedent developmental state and certainly not itself the carrier of these developments, is inseparably linked as one of the crucial factors with the rise of both phenomena.'[36]

The main difference between Sombart and Weber is that the latter was interested in the ancient world for its own sake, and produced a sizeable body of work on antiquity.[37] His primary concern, however, always remained the nature and origins of capitalism as he understood it, the principal manifestation of the peculiar rationalism of modern Western civilisation.[38] The world of Greece and Rome was interesting precisely because it had failed to develop in the same direction as medieval Europe. Weber's doctoral dissertation of 1899 set out to establish that the legal framework necessary to sustain capitalist trade and industry was not available in Roman law.[39] At the end of his 1909 work *Agrarverhältnisse in Altertum* he wrote:

A genuinely analytic study comparing the stages of development of the ancient polis with those of the medieval city would be welcome and productive ... Of course I say this on the assumption that such a comparative study would not aim at finding 'analogies' and 'parallels' ... The aim should, rather, be precisely the opposite: to identify and define the individuality of each development, the characteristics which made the one conclude in a manner so different from the other. This done, one can then determine the causes which led to these differences.[40]

Weber did believe that a form of capitalism existed in antiquity; the reasons for the failure of the ancient world must be sought in the social and political institutions within which ancient capitalism had to operate.[41] A number of explanations is put forward: the problems of an economy based on slave labour, and the consequences for wage labour; the limitations of Roman law; a low level of demand, due to the unequal distribution of wealth; the limited profit motivation of the ancient town-dweller.[42] Above all, however, there is the nature of the ancient *polis*, which differed in so many ways from the medieval town. The *polis* was dominated by the land-owning political elite, whose wealth derived from rents rather than trade or industry; there was no political separation of town and country, and so no chance for a class of entrepreneurs to

[35] Käsler (1988), 42–8.   [36] Weber (1978), 1323; cf. (1958), 181.
[37] Love (1991), 9–55.   [38] Bottomore (1985), 22–34.
[39] Käsler (1988), 24–32; Nippel (1991), 20.   [40] Weber (1976), 385.
[41] Weber (1976), 48–51; Capogrossi Colognesi (1990), 262–88 and (1995), 28–9; Love (1991), 20–1.
[42] Weber (1976), e.g. 53–8, 208, 347.

emerge; the city was a centre of consumption, not of production, and capitalism was always subordinated to political considerations.[43] In *Die Stadt*, published posthumously, Weber presented the ideal types of Consumer and Producer cities without linking them specifically to his ancient and medieval models; as ever, he is interested above all in the uniqueness of the medieval city, and for most of the work he ignores the producer/consumer dichotomy in favour of the contrast between the occidental and oriental city types.[44]

Finally, we may return to Moses Finley, who revived and popularised the idea of the consumer city – perhaps one might more accurately say, his own version of the idea – in ancient history. Finley's concern was with the ancient city itself, not with the development of capitalism, but the contrasts between antiquity and the modern world are an important theme in all his work on the ancient economy. Following a similar path to Karl Polanyi, once his colleague at Columbia, he asserts the 'otherness' of the ancient world: the absence of economic rationalism and interdependent markets, the degree to which the economy was 'embedded' in social values and subordinated to political concerns, and the irrelevance of neo-classical economic theory to pre-modern economies.[45] The influence of Weber is particularly important in this respect, leading Finley to adopt a sociological view of the ancient economy that stresses value systems; so too is the example of the Bücher–Meyer controversy, and Finley often cites Meyer as an example of the ludicrous modernising view of the ancient world against which he is arguing.[46]

As Jongman observes, the theme of the fundamental distinction between antiquity and later periods is most apparent in Finley's discussion of the ancient city.[47] The chapter in *The Ancient Economy* on town and country begins by defining the city and discussing its economic relationship with the countryside (consumer or parasite), and proceeds to assert the minimal role of trade and manufacture in the ancient economy, the limits to the division of labour, disincentives to technical innovation and the dominance of an acquisitive, rather than productive, mentality.[48] All the different strands of Finley's vision of the ancient world are brought together in the consumer city, united by opposition to the ideal type of the producer city and its archetype, the economically progressive medieval city. The apparently simple question of how the city mobilised

---

[43]   *Ibid.*, 337–52, 364; cf. Wood (1995), 158–67.

[44]   Weber (1958); Nippel (1991), 25; Bruhns (1987–9); Capogrossi Colognesi (1995), 30–2.

[45]   Finley (1985a), 22; Polanyi (1944) and (1968); Jongman (1988a), 28–39; cf. Cook (1966) and Engels (1990), 131–42.

[46]   E.g. Finley (1985a), 192; Nippel (1987–9).   [47]   Jongman (1988a), 29.

[48]   Finley (1985a), 123–49.

the surplus production of the countryside goes to the heart of the debate on the nature of the ancient economy.

Urbanisation and development

The ideal types of producer and consumer cities were developed to explain the rise of capitalism in the later middle ages and its absence (or at least its undeveloped state) in earlier periods. The consumer city lacked all the features which made the producer city so important in fostering economic rationality and exchange; it was therefore at best powerless to effect change and at worst a stagnating influence on the economy. This theory is accepted both by Finley and his partisans, and by those who argue that the ancient economy was more dynamic; the latter simply dispute the applicability of the model to the ancient city, taking its supposed implications for economic development (and the positive influence of a producer city) entirely for granted.[49]

It can be argued that this position is an improvement on the arguments of those who saw *all* urbanism as a force for economic development, arguing along the same lines as Braudel that 'a town is a town wherever it is' and that towns were 'so many electric transformers', 'accelerators of all historical time'.[50] The difficulty of producing an adequate cross-cultural definition of a 'city', and the existence of numerous examples of cities that were not obviously like electrical transformers, led to the adoption of more complicated systems of classification: producer and consumer, industrial and pre-industrial, occidental and oriental, generative and parasitic.[51] Only *some* cities were characterised as progressive; others lacked the necessary economic, social or political institutions.[52] In discussions of pre-industrial cities, it is clear that the medieval town remains the standard against which others must be judged; the archetypal generative, economically progressive city. Only the explanations offered for its progressive character seem to change.

Three main objections can be made to this picture. Firstly, the special qualities of the medieval town, which gave it such a prominent role in accounts of the emergence of capitalism, have been increasingly questioned in the last twenty years.[53] There was no clear division of labour between town and country; rural industry was of immense importance until the nineteenth century.[54] Discussions of economic growth in late

---

[49]   Leveau (1983); Goudineau (1983); Engels (1990); Whittaker (1990), 110–12.
[50]   Braudel (1973), 373; Davis and Golden (1954–5).
[51]   Hoselitz (1954–5); Weber (1958); Sjoberg (1960).
[52]   Compare the debate about urbanisation in the modern Third World: Timberlake (1985).
[53]   Holton (1986), 63–104.   [54]   Bolton (1980), 246–53.

medieval and early modern England now place at least as much emphasis on the development of agriculture, rather than the old obsession with manufacture and the export trade.[55] There was no clear political or social divide between town and countryside, and the degree of urban autonomy was limited. 'We cannot think of [feudal towns] as non-feudal islands within a feudal sea. Nor can we envisage the social and economic interests of the medieval burgesses as being in fundamental and developing antagonism to the interests of the feudal state and its land-owning ruling class.'[56]

Instead of the dynamic town acting on the inert and passive country, the transition from feudalism to capitalism is seen increasingly in terms of changes in society as a whole: the urbanisation of the town and the ruralisation of the countryside (that is, a geographical division of labour) are effects, not causes, of this process.[57] The second objection to the traditional picture is precisely that it reifies the town, treating it as an independent, cross-cultural variable. 'The town as a physical object is turned into a taken-for-granted social object and a captivating focus of analysis in its own right.'[58] Abrams suggests that urban history and sociology might now abandon the concept of the town altogether, 'to be replaced by a concern to understand towns as sites in which the history of larger systems – states, societies, modes of production, world economies – is partially, but crucially, worked out'.[59] The idea that a town, or a particular type of the town like the producer city, will always be economically progressive in any cultural or historical context is an example of the 'fallacy of misplaced concreteness'. In ancient history, Whittaker recently came to a similar conclusion, noting that 'the study of cities is only an imperfect way of studying the operations of power in society'.[60]

The third objection is the overtly ideological nature of many of the ideas involved in these discussions: above all, the assumption that Europe provides the blueprint for all 'economic development', and the idealisation of the medieval town for its role in this development. Discussing twentieth-century theories of the city, Castells bluntly stated: 'Urbanism is not a concept. It is a myth in the strictest sense since it recounts, ideologically, the history of mankind. An urban sociology founded on urbanism is an ideology of modernity ethnocentrically identified with the crystallization of the social forms of liberal capitalism.'[61] 'The unequivocal view of cities and the Western bourgeoisie as

[55]   John (1967); cf. O'Brien (1985); Brenner (1985a) and (1985b).
[56]   Hilton (1985), 186.   [57] Merrington (1975), 92; Abrams (1978b), 13.
[58]   Abrams (1978b), 9.   [59] (1978b), 10; (1978a), 3.   [60] Whittaker (1993b), 15.
[61]   Castells (1976), 70.

centres of economic progress as well as political virtue and social emancipation from tyranny is very much a product of the nineteenth-century industrial capitalist transformation of Europe.'[62]

In the literature of this period, a dualism is established between town and countryside: cities are closely identified with modernisation and progress, while the country is seen as being mired in the past, primitive and conservative.[63] The Romantic tendency to reverse the value judgements by praising rural simplicity and rejecting the city simply reinforces the dualism and the association between urbanisation and modernity. Historical and Third World societies are evaluated by the degree to which they conform to the European norm. In ancient history this discussion is, on the whole, safe, affecting only the ways in which the ancient world is used to construct our own cultural identities.[64] In the modern world, the practice of 'development economics' has had much more serious consequences for non-Western societies.[65]

It remains an interesting question why Western Europe developed in a particular way, but it is clear that the answer will not be found simply by examining the distinctive characteristics of its towns. It is less clear that the failure of the ancient economy to 'take off' demands an explanation, least of all one which measures that failure exclusively in terms of how far the ancient world conformed to the blueprint offered by parts of late medieval Europe. The obsession with finding or refuting examples of large manufacturing concerns or elite traders, with both sides in the dispute regarding agriculture as stagnant and unimportant, is another legacy of nineteenth-century theories of economic progress. It is clear that any explanation of Rome's failure to have an industrial revolution must be sought in the social and economic structures of ancient society as a whole, not in the peculiar character of its cities. The explanatory power of the consumer city model is inevitably lessened. It offers a neat encapsulation of the means by which cities such as Rome were supported, but the implications of the model for the economic effects of such cities can no longer be accepted without further argument.

Abrams argued that the study of urban centres should be replaced by concern with the division of labour in society as a whole; *where* those not involved in primary agricultural production happened to live is not really significant. In the case of a city as large as Rome, in a pre-industrial society, this is not the case. The centralisation (or 'crystallization') of

---

[62] Holton (1986), 9.   [63] *Ibid.*, 1–18; Williams (1973).

[64] Engels (1990), 131–42, offers not only a discussion of this process but a clear example of it in his own work. On the uses of 'classicism', see e.g. Taplin (1989) and Cartledge (1993), 1–7, 175–82.

[65] Hill (1986).

social and political functions in a defined space, the capital, promoted and permitted the massive growth of the urban population.[66] The concentration of so many people in one place has economic consequences that go beyond the effects of the division of labour that it represents: not only must that number of people be fed by the surplus production of the rest, but a proportion of the surplus (and, given the cost of transport in a pre-industrial society, a fairly large proportion) must be expended in moving the goods to the city from its hinterland. This portion of the surplus supports the infrastructure of merchants and shipowners, an infrastructure which would have been unnecessary if the non-producing population had been evenly distributed across the territory. The effort required to support the city is greater, and the effects may therefore be more noticeable. For this reason, 'the city of Rome', albeit loosely defined and certainly not considered as separate from its society, must remain the object of investigation.

Rome is not the only large city which has been regarded as a malign influence on its hinterland, a parasite draining the life-blood of the countryside. London and other European capital cities in the early modern period have been described in precisely those terms; in this case, however, the negative estimations of the economic influence of such cities have already undergone some revision.[67] Another example is the case of medieval China. On the one hand, Chinese cities are definitely not of the 'producer city' type (and were specifically contrasted with the European city by Weber); on the other, they are given an important role by many historians in the economic and social changes that took place in China under the Sung dynasty between the tenth and thirteenth centuries. A brief examination of work on both these periods offers some indication of how the influence of the city of Rome might be reappraised. It is not suggested that a new ideal type, the 'metropolitan' or 'capital' city, should be devised; the European example makes it clear that such cities do not affect their hinterlands in the same way. Nevertheless, a comparison of how different societies have overcome the basic constraints of a pre-industrial economy and maintained huge capital cities, and the effects that this effort had on society in its turn, is instructive.

The city in medieval China

By the eleventh century K'ai-feng, capital city of the Northern Sung, contained over 200,000 registered households, making its total popula-

---

[66] Cf. Eisenstadt and Shachar (1987), 68–74.
[67] In a session of the Tenth International Economic History Conference, collected in Aerts and Clark (1990).

tion around a million.[68] The later capitals, Hang-chou and Peking, may have reached even greater sizes. When the capital was moved to Hang-chou in the twelfth century, it involved the migration of 20,000 salaried officials with their families, tens of thousands of clerks and over 400,000 soldiers from the north of the country into the city and the surrounding region.[69] The imperial capitals of medieval China are the only serious rivals to Rome's status as the greatest pre-industrial city.

The capital was the seat of the emperor, the royal family (which ran into the hundreds) and a vast household, with a thousand people employed in the kitchens alone.[70] The old land-owning elite followed the court, bringing with them their own retinues and a generally luxurious and extravagant lifestyle. The city was also the centre of the bureaucratic hierarchy that ruled the empire, so that tens of thousands of mandarins and other officials, along with their families, resided there. Another facet of the centralisation of power under the Sung was direct control over the army, to prevent the re-emergence of powerful warlords; large numbers of troops were therefore stationed in and around the capital.[71] A huge population of merchants, craftsmen and shopkeepers, not to mention artists, musicians, beggars and aspiring office-holders, gathered in the city to enjoy their share of its prosperity and to provide services for the wealthy elite.[72]

This population was supported by the tribute of the empire, collected by the cities further down the hierarchy, who kept a portion of it to support local officials and channelled the rest upwards.[73] Eighty per cent of K'ai-feng's demands for official rice (which fed the imperial household, the bureaucracy and the army) were met by taxes in kind, the transport of which to the city was heavily subsidised by the state.[74] Rice for the rest of the population, along with other foodstuffs and fuel (the latter particularly important in northern latitudes) came through the free market, paid for ultimately from taxes and rents.[75] The need to ensure the supply of its officials and soldiers, and the importance of information in controlling the empire, led the state to spend large sums in improving communications to the city, especially by extending the canal network, which assisted the transport of other supplies to the rest of the people.[76]

Weber proposed a separate ideal type for the Oriental city (meaning above all the Chinese city), in part because he saw that markets and trade were under tight political control and deeply embedded in traditional

[68] Kracke (1975), 65–6.   [69] Shiba (1975), 19; Hartwell (1982), 386; Chao (1986), 56.
[70] Ma (1971), 113.   [71] Ma (1971), 106–13; Kracke (1975), 49–51.
[72] Shiba (1970), 140; Kracke (1975), 51–2.   [73] Skinner (1977a); Corradini (1987).
[74] Shiba (1970), 67.   [75] Hartwell (1967), 124–34.   [76] Elvin (1973), 131–45.

cultural values.[77] As far as an imperial capital like K'ai-feng is concerned, however, the label 'consumer city' fits it as well as it does Rome: the size of the city is explicable only by reference to its political, social and symbolic importance, and urban crafts and services were dependent on the purchasing power of the elite. Nevertheless, the medieval Chinese city is not generally regarded as a parasite, draining resources from its hinterland and promoting economic stagnation. On the contrary, the growth of the imperial capitals is seen as a vital factor in the 'medieval economic revolution' of the Sung period.

The extent of this 'revolution' may be questioned: the evidence is simply not available from which to calculate changes in real incomes, for example, and Elvin's pioneering work on the subject tends to neglect the considerable variations in the way different areas responded to the changes he describes.[78] While their significance may be in doubt, however, there is no disputing the extent and number of changes in the Chinese economy between the tenth and thirteenth centuries. New strains of seed and new techniques for preparing the soil appeared; wet-field rice cultivation spread through the south, made possible by new technology; there was a growing academic interest in farming, as educated officials wrote, printed and disseminated treatises on the subject.[79] The canal network was improved, so that most major waterways were linked to one another.[80] A growing volume of inter-regional trade led to the expansion of markets, increasingly freed from political control, to the spread of monetisation (including paper money) and to the development of credit institutions.[81] The character of cities further down the urban hierarchy changed, with the emergence of more complicated structures of exchange; peasants became more involved in the market, and the old separation of town and country (the word *Ch'eng* denotes both 'city' and 'walls') became less important.[82] By the thirteenth century, China may have achieved a level of urbanisation of nearly 20 per cent.[83]

Taxes and other levies, which touched the entire empire, were the precursors of the deeper commercialization of later times. Political pressure acted as a pumping mechanism to create a circulation of goods of which economic demand by itself was incapable. The expenditure of wealth derived from taxation created new industries and new trade in the service of the upper classes, but generating skills that were in course of time to be of wider use.[84]

The imperial capitals represented a huge market for all kinds of goods, and the profits to be made in supplying this market acted as an incentive

[77]   Weber (1958), 91–120.   [78] Elvin (1973); cf. the review by Myers (1974).
[79]   Elvin (1973), 113–30.   [80] *Ibid.*, 131–45.   [81] *Ibid.*, 146–78.
[82]   Skinner (1977b); Chaudhuri (1985), 177–9 and (1990), 354–60.
[83]   Chao (1986), 56.   [84] Elvin (1973), 165.

to peasants and the owners of 'manors' alike to increase production and to improve farming techniques.[85] State expenditure on the transport network, prompted in part by the need to ensure the supply of the capital, benefited private suppliers and allowed increasing regional specialisation; the flow of goods to the centre supported the development of markets and financial institutions. The growth of K'ai-feng is offered as the main explanation of the eleventh-century revolution in the iron industry of north-east China.[86] Eventually, so it is argued, the profits to be made in this trade allowed the peasantry to increase their consumption of manufactured items and other luxuries (spices and condiments, for example), permitting the autonomous development of local markets and urban crafts.[87]

K'ai-feng did not support the emergence of a new class or a set of values separate from traditional Chinese culture; the main beneficiaries of the economic revolution were the old land-owning elite, who had the resources to respond to the incentives offered by the market, while the merchants remained wholeheartedly attached to the old social system (and often invested their profits in getting themselves or their descendants into an improved position in the hierarchy). The imperial capital did not support itself by trade or industry; rather, it was its political role, and the politically managed flow of goods into the city, that gave it such economic importance.

The European metropolis

In an article about the role of the town in a pre-industrial economy, Wrigley questions the notion of the 'parasitic' town:

> The danger of any parasite is that it weakens the host and in extreme cases kills it. Describing a town as parasitic implies that it represents a drain on the resources of the society and that the host would be better off without the parasite. Paradoxically, the first proposition may be true in a limited sense without the second necessarily following. If the surplus creamed off for consumption in towns would otherwise either have been used to sustain a larger population in the countryside or have been used for conspicuous consumption by the community or individuals within it, it is not clear that the countryside would have been better off without a 'parasitic' town except in the short term.[88]

To consume the surplus in the countryside, rather than surrender it for consumption in cities to meet the needs of a ruling urban elite, is no doubt gratifying to those whose bellies are filled as a result, but it is reasonable to view it as a small matter where the surplus is consumed, and a much more serious matter that it is

[85] Perkins (1969), 139–68.   [86] Hartwell (1967), 124–45.
[87] Shiba (1970), 202–13.   [88] Wrigley (1978), 307–8.

disposed of, whether in town or country, in a way which makes it improbable that the next generation will be any better clad, housed or fed.[89]

As in the Chinese example, the movement of goods to cities as taxes or rents could nevertheless 'liberate' economic forces that might otherwise have remained dormant. Part of the surplus is spent on transporting the goods to the city, thereby supporting an infrastructure of merchants, shipowners, carriers and porters; another part is returned to the country in exchange for other goods, which may then serve as an incentive to producers to change their farming strategies. The clearest example of this process is to be found in the influence of London on its hinterland between the sixteenth and eighteenth centuries, the subject of a classic article by Wrigley.[90] The massive growth of the English capital over this period, which had dramatic effects on the economy and society of the rest of the country, is directly attributable to its political importance and the taxes and rents that supported most of its population.[91]

Wrigley begins with a simple model of the demographic effect of the city's growth between 1650 and 1750. The population rose at an average rate of about 2,750 per year, but high urban death rates meant that the actual number of migrants was more like 5,000, the equivalent of the natural increase of half the population of England. An increasing number of people therefore experienced metropolitan life at some stage in their lives, which contributed to a gradual dissolution of 'traditional' forms of social life and to the spread of new habits of consumption. The movement of people from farming to urban professions implies that there was a significant increase in agricultural productivity – perhaps of the order of 10 per cent per head, since exports were rising during the same period. The concentration of consumers in the capital inspired specialisation and intensification in the regions that supplied it, while the movement of goods to the city promoted increased integration of the nation's markets and supported the development of credit institutions, banks and improved transport facilities. As Wrigley notes, 'it is always well to be chary of accepting explanations that explain too much', and the changes in the English economy over this period (a vital foundation of the Industrial Revolution) cannot be attributed to the capital's influence alone.[92] However, it is equally clear that these changes cannot be understood without reference to the demands of London.

London was an exceptionally large and successful city during this period; by 1750 it contained over 10 per cent of the English population, a level of urbanisation equalled only by the Netherlands and attributable

---

[89]   *Ibid.*, 298.   [90] Wrigley (1967).
[91]   Fisher (1934–5); Patten (1978), 85–9; Clay (1984), 197–213.
[92]   Wrigley (1967), 63.

to special qualities of the English rural economy dating from at least the sixteenth century.[93] It was by no means the only large city in Europe: the emergence of unified nation states in many areas of Europe went hand in hand with the establishment of national capitals, which grew rapidly in size, wealth and importance.[94] Political power was centralised: the court became sedentary, and gathered round itself the institutions of law, administration and (in some countries) representation; the great land-owners took up residence close to the source of privilege and pa-tronage.[95] A vast population assembled to cater for the needs of those magnates – over 30 per cent of workers in eighteenth-century Madrid were employed as servants – whose luxurious urban lifestyles were paid for from the rents and taxes collected by an increasingly efficient state bureaucracy.[96] Even in London, which had been an important commer-cial centre since the early middle ages, less than a fifth of the population in 1700 were being supported by the proceeds of trade; profits from commerce amounted to less than the king's allocation from the civil list.[97]

At the same time, the capital was itself used to magnify the central power; as one seventeenth-century writer proposed: 'In great monar-chies it is necessary to establish a capital or capitals ... the grand metropolis as the centre of administration and public display of the glory of the state.'[98] This tended to involve grandiose building projects, set in motion by the monarch and imitated by the aristocracy and church hierarchy. Cities like St Petersburg were created as capitals more or less from scratch, and so could be carefully laid out in accordance with the latest architectural fashions. London retained its confused medieval street plan even after the Great Fire, but was endowed with magnificent buildings scattered throughout the city.[99] In both cases, the demand for palaces, churches and elite residences created more oppor-tunities for employment.

The European metropolis is a classic example of the consumer city, its huge population supported from the surplus production of the rest of the country, extracted in the form of rents and taxes. The ways in which such cities could affect the economy and society of their hinterlands are conveniently summarised in Wrigley's article; not only the economic effects of their demands for migrants and food, but their cultural influence. As Clark puts it: 'Metropolitan cities became megawatt

93   Cf. Wrigley (1987), 157–93.
94   Braudel (1972), 344–52; de Vries (1984), 141–2; P. Clark (1990).
95   Ringrose (1990), 22–3.   96   Ringrose (1983), 66–87.
97   Braudel (1981), 528–9.   98   Quoted in P. Clark (1990), 4.
99   Braudel (1981), 534–40, 547–56.

transmitters of new ideas, manners, fashions, leisure activities, patterns of consumption, and new forms of social interaction' – not to mention political dissent.[100] However, 'it would be difficult to argue that there was a single model of metropolitan influence in early modern Europe'.[101] The presence of a large capital city may have different effects on different societies, as well as on different classes and regions within that society; something which must be taken into account when comparing the city of Rome with the European situation.

In the first place, different regions may respond to the same city in different ways; one might better speak of 'hinterlands' than of a single hinterland. 'Metropolitan influence occupied a range of spatial parameters. Of fundamental importance was the immediate adjoining area ... Merging into this was the regional hinterland, often a quite extensive area, delineated by migration and trade patterns. But by the eighteenth century one also has to think increasingly of a national and even an international zone of influence.'[102] The high costs of transport dictated the extent to which a region might respond to the incentives offered by the urban market; in the case of land-locked Madrid, logistics dictated that the city's immediate hinterland must be forced to grow grain to feed the urban population, since carrying bulk staples overland was prohibitively expensive.[103] Variations in climate and geography also have an effect on developments in different parts of the hinterland.

The influence of the city was restricted not only by material constraints like environment and transport. For its demands to stimulate changes in agricultural production, for example, it was necessary that producers should *wish* to increase their incomes by growing for the market, and that they should be free to change their practices if they wished. In Castile, the land-owning elite worked to ensure continued political control of the peasantry by forcing them to grow grain, and by taking their rents in kind rather than in cash.[104] The political importance of the capital city meant that the state sought to avoid unrest there at all costs, and therefore took on the responsibility of protecting its food supply; in some cases this led to close supervision of the grain market by the authorities, restricting the activities of merchants, as was the case in Paris in the seventeenth and eighteenth centuries.[105] The existence of a metropolis required the production and mobilisation of a regular agricultural surplus, but this might be obtained through increased burdens on the peasantry rather than increased productivity. In the same way, the use of the surplus in maintaining a modern state structure (a metropolis

---

[100] P. Clark (1990), 8; Ringrose (1990), 35.   [101] P. Clark (1990), 9.
[102] *Ibid.*, 4.   [103] Ringrose (1970); Wrigley (1990), 18.
[104] Ringrose (1983), 143–92; Wrigley (1990), 15.   [105] Kaplan (1984).

being partly a by-product of this phenomenon) might have both positive and negative consequences for the economy; internal stability, law and the spread of coinage versus heavy impositions and regulation.

What is clear is that the effort needed to maintain a huge metropolis could hardly fail to leave its mark on the society that chose to invest part of its surplus in such a city. To label this effect 'parasitic' or 'progressive' may be to make the same mistake as those who exalt the medieval city, of accepting the eventual course of development in Europe as being somehow natural, and praising anything that seems to contribute towards that end. It is true that the changes in English society set in motion by the demands of London were a vital prerequisite for, though not a sufficient cause of, the Industrial Revolution: the developments in agriculture, the formation of a market for manufactured goods, the apparent rise in real incomes.[106] In contrast, Madrid may be seen as having a malign influence on its immediate hinterland, since the city's demands led directly to the stagnation of agriculture in the region. Nevertheless, rather than retaining the old dichotomy of parasite and stimulus (with all its overtones of reification of the city), it makes more sense to concentrate on the striking similarities in the situations of these two cities, and of other metropolitan capitals. They were consumer cities, their populations supported from taxes or rents; they faced the same problems of feeding a large number of people, concentrated in one place, under the conditions of a pre-industrial economy. The fact that their societies responded to the problem in different ways is hardly surprising, and is probably more interesting (pointing to important differences in social and economic structures) than a more uniform response might have been.

Summary

This lesson applies still more strongly to the comparison of the European metropoleis and the city of Rome: the problem of how to feed their populations is the same, but the social and cultural context is very different. The comparative examples discussed above serve to illustrate possibilities, ways in which the city of Rome might have influenced the economy of Italy and other parts of its empire; in other words, likely areas of investigation. Above all, they combine with the earlier theoretical discussion to refute the idea that a certain type of city will always affect its hinterland in the same way; the consumer city can thus be relieved of its doom-laden reputation.

[106] Wrigley (1967) and (1987); on the Industrial Revolution see e.g. Cannadine (1984) and Hudson (1992).

The Roman empire did not witness the emergence of a class of entrepreneurs with a distinctive value system, threatening the old land-owning elite; nor did it experience a massive rise in real incomes per head, or a dramatic expansion of manufacturing. Agriculture remained dominant, involving well over two-thirds of the population even in highly urbanised regions like Italy; agricultural wealth, and the values of a land-owning elite, dominated political and social life. None of this excludes the possibility of limited economic change, of an expansion in the volume of trade and of changes in the way in which the land is cultivated. Certain basic constraints on the possibility of raising productivity operate with a pre-industrial, agrarian economy, but within those limitations a great degree of variation is possible. The fact that a metropolis the size of Rome could be maintained successfully is one indication that the capabilities of the ancient economy were greater than the labels 'primitive' or 'underdeveloped' might suggest.

Political considerations were central to Rome's expansion; indeed, it is difficult to imagine that such a city could have existed otherwise. What is important is that this centre of demand was created, and for all its dependence on taxes and rents it represented an incentive to producers and merchants. The fact that entrepreneurial forces remained subordinate to politics and the value system of the landowners is far less significant than the existence of a large and wealthy market for all kinds of goods. Before considering the influence of this market on agricultural production in Italy, however, it is necessary to examine more closely the process by which the population of the city grew in the last two centuries of the Roman Republic, and the effects of its insatiable consumption of people on the demography of the peninsula.

2   The demographic burden

The urban population

The city of Rome was, by pre-modern standards, an exceptionally large city. The views of contemporaries, the sheer scale of its buildings and a large quantity of incidental anecdotal evidence make this plain; as Hermansen notes: 'A city which absorbs 3,000 foreign chorus girls has a considerable population.'[1] However, it is difficult to move beyond such vague impressions to make more detailed statements about the city's size or the dynamics of its growth.[2] Upon close examination, the concept of 'the population of Rome' becomes increasingly elusive. The city's inhabitants were always changing; at any one time they could include tourists, merchants on a regular visit, farmers in for market, immigrants who were likely to die there and natives who still hoped to get out. 'Rome' itself was ill-defined enough. According to the *Digest*, '*Urbis* relates to the area within the walls; *Romae*, however, also includes the adjoining buildings, which is a larger area'; and Dionysius of Halicarnassus observed how difficult it was to decide where the buildings ended and the countryside began.[3]

For many purposes it is unnecessary to offer a more precise definition or quantification of the urban population; it is enough that Rome was the greatest city of the ancient Mediterranean. This is insufficient for the present argument. The impact of large cities on their hinterlands depends to a very great extent on the growth of their populations and hence their demands for resources. It is clearly essential to obtain a rough order of magnitude for these demands, and that requires a reconstruction of the demographic history of the city. It is certainly true that previous attempts at such a reconstruction have come to widely differing conclusions.[4] However, if the (admittedly rather meagre) evidence is treated with sufficient caution it is possible to obtain a plausible estimate of the population of Rome.

[1]   Hermansen (1978), 168.   [2]   *Ibid.*, 129; Purcell (1994), 648–50.
[3]   *Dig.* 50.16.2 *pr.*; Dion. Hal. 4.13.4.   [4]   Salmon (1974), 11–12.

No ancient writer offers an opinion on the size of the city, sparing us the problem of deciding whether such a figure could conceivably be relied upon. Instead, hypotheses must be constructed on the basis of evidence that is not directly concerned with population; the built-up area of the city, the city's food supply and the numbers receiving the corn dole. In each case it is necessary to choose figures for the unknown quantities in the calculation, such as the average level of wheat consumption or the likely population density. The assessment of these three approaches rests at least as much on how far the unknowns can plausibly be replaced as on the reliability of the sources themselves.

The first source of evidence is the city itself, its total area and the number of buildings within it, listed in the fourth-century Regionary Catalogues.[5] As Hermansen has shown, there are many problems with this approach. The figures in the Regionaries are internally inconsistent and frequently implausible – suggesting, for example, that there were nearly three and a half thousand *insulae* in *Regio VIII*, the Forum Romanum. It is impossible to decide how many people lived in each *insula*, since the totals from the Regionaries cannot be reconciled either with *insulae* known from archaeological remains or with the legal definition.[6] The catalogues are simply not intended to give an accurate account of the city's buildings; they are a form of tourist guide, designed to impress visitors, a panegyric expressed in statistics.[7]

The area within the third-century wall has been calculated at 1,373 hectares; the fourteen Augustan regions covered about 1,783 ha.[8] Parts of the city were uninhabited, occupied by public buildings, gardens and the like; von Gerkan argues for half of the total area, Calza for only 467 ha.[9] At any event, the real problem lies in deciding how tightly packed the ancient inhabitants were prepared to live, and that depends on preconceived notions of what the city was like. As Hermansen notes, 'von Gerkan sees Rome as a serene group of upper-middle-class residences, very remote from medieval conditions, while Calza and Lugli believe in a slummy metropolis'.[10]

An assortment of comparative evidence can be deployed. The population density in the poorest districts of nineteenth-century Rome was over 800 persons per hectare, and even higher figures are recorded for some areas of modern Hong Kong, Bombay and Calcutta.[11] On the other hand, the average density for Bombay as a whole (including

---

[5] von Gerkan (1940); Hermansen (1978).
[6] Cf. Packer (1971), 74–9.   [7] Hermansen (1978), 157–65.
[8] Friedländer (1928), 22–4; Maier (1953–4), 329; Homo (1971), 99.
[9] Hermansen (1978), 146–8.   [10] *Ibid.*, 167.
[11] Beloch (1886), 409; K. Hopkins (1978a), 97; Stambaugh (1988), 337.

uninhabited areas) was 452 persons/ha., which would imply a population for Augustan Rome of just over 800,000. Evidence from other cities
is equally varied; the most crowded district of Paris in 1821 had over
900 people to every hectare, while Berlin in 1890 had densities of 326
and 540 persons/ha. in different areas.[12] Clearly these figures can offer
only a rough check on other hypotheses, excluding the highest estimates
on the grounds of probability (a population of two million, which has
been suggested in the past, implies a quite incredible density of over
1,100 persons/ha. throughout the entire city), but leaving a very broad
range of possibilities.

Several ancient sources include references to the size of Rome's
imports of grain or its total consumption.[13] The figures are not compatible with one another, and scholars have tended either to combine the
Epitome with Josephus, or to favour the *Historia Augusta* supplemented
by the scholiast on Lucan.[14] Each side might fairly accuse the other of
combining texts that were written at very different times and refer to
different periods of the city's history. We may question whether any
ancient writer is likely to have had accurate knowledge of Rome's food
consumption; at best, the state may have kept records of its own imports
of tax grain, but hardly of private imports.[15]

Even if one of these totals is accepted, it is not entirely correct that 'the
one thing which is constant, which does *not* vary, is the average food
consumption of a human individual'.[16] In fact, only the broadest limits
can be established from modern nutritional studies; calorific intake can
vary widely according to age, sex, activity and individual metabolism.[17]
Oates' figure of 4 modii of grain per month per head is certainly too high;
a more plausible estimate is 2.5 modii per month, with grain providing 75
per cent of calorific requirements.[18] In that case, annual imports of 60
million modii (the figure obtained by combining the Epitome and
Josephus) suggest a population of two million; imports of 27 million
modii (the S.H.A. and the scholiast), a population of 900,000. The first,
based on the dubious method of combining the two sources, is basically
implausible.[19] The latter figure might conceivably represent the state's
own imports (one interpretation of the phrase *canon frumentarius* in the
S.H.A.) and can serve as a minimum, bearing in mind that many
recipients of state grain like soldiers or officials would have received more

[12] Friedländer (1928), 24; Duncan-Jones (1982), 276–7.
[13] Epit. *Caes.* 1.6; Joseph. *Bell. Iud.* 2.383–6; S.H.A. *Sev.* 3.2; schol. Lucan, ad *Pharsalia*
      1.319.
[14] Oates (1934), 103–7; Beloch (1886), 411–12.
[15] Oates (1934), 108–14; Garnsey (1983), 119.   [16] Oates (1934), 103–4.
[17] Foxhall and Forbes (1982), 47.   [18] Garnsey (1983), 118.
[19] Garnsey (1988a), 232; see above for the population density implied by such a figure.

than the basic ration. Clearly the size of the food supply is not on its own a trustworthy base for calculation of the urban population.

Finally, there are the figures for the numbers receiving the corn dole or other imperial donatives. Under Clodius these had swelled to some 320,000, which Caesar reduced to 150,000; they rose again during the civil war, perhaps as high as the 320,000 who received a cash handout in 5 B.C.[20] Augustus considered abolishing the dole altogether, but contented himself with reducing the list of those eligible to 200,000; at other times during his reign he distributed money or grain to members of the *plebs*, sometimes specifically defined as 'those in receipt of public grain', groups of 200,000 and 250,000 benefiting at different times.[21] A further reduction of the list at a later date may be implied by the fact that only 150,000 benefited under Augustus' will.[22]

Eligibility for the corn dole was based on citizenship rather than poverty; it represented the right of all Romans to share in the spoils of empire.[23] Since numbers were restricted by both Caesar and Augustus to an arbitrary level, it is clear that not all citizens were entitled to the dole; after the reforms, if not before, the *plebs frumentaria* was a privileged group within the *plebs* as a whole.[24] The recipients were free, adult males, living in or near the city (certainly the majority must have lived within easy walking distance). Once the lists had been closed, vacancies were probably filled by lot amongst those eligible, but clearly there was some additional criterion which determined who was excluded by the reforms of Augustus.

There are several objections to van Berchem's suggestion that it was necessary to have Roman *origo* to qualify.[25] The concept of *origo* was comparatively new, developing only after the Social War, and may not have been properly codified until the second century A.D.; the idea that non-Romans should be excluded goes against the image of Augustus as promoting Italian unity, and the likely popular outcry against such a measure would surely have been noted by our sources; finally, the theory assumes the existence of quite a large core group of original Romans within the city population, which does not fit with evidence that migrants (who would retain the *origo* of their native towns) played a vital role in the growth of the city.[26]

Virlouvet argues instead that it was necessary to be free-born, *ingenuus*,

[20] Garnsey (1988a), 211–14.
[21] Sue., *Aug.* 42.3; Dio Cassius 55.10; *Res Gestae* 15.
[22] Suet. *Aug.* 101; Tac. *Ann.* 1.8.5; Virlouvet (1991), 45 n.4.
[23] Rowland (1976); Garnsey (1988a), 212.
[24] van Berchem (1939), 60; cf. Fronto 210N.
[25] van Berchem (1939), 34–45.
[26] Virlouvet (1991), 49; Purcell (1994), 657; for migrants, see below, pp. 44–6.

to qualify, and that *all* freedmen were removed from the lists by Augustus, rather than just informally manumitted ones.[27] The evidence that all those manumitted *optime iure* were admitted to the corn dole is late, provincial and uncertain; Pompey and Caesar, on the other hand, were concerned to remove all recently enfranchised slaves from the list of grain recipients. An anecdote in Suetonius records Augustus' concern with the presence of freedmen at one of his distributions of money.[28]

This theory suggests therefore that Rome (the city and its immediate surroundings) contained 200,000-odd adult freeborn male citizens at the time of Augustus' reform of the corn dole. The age of eligibility appears to have remained at ten until later in the century, having been reduced (presumably from fourteen) by Clodius.[29] This implies a total freeborn male population of about 260,000 and a total freeborn population of 520,000.[30]

This is to assume a stable age structure and a balanced sex ratio in the population, assumptions which may be considered problematic. Comparative evidence supports the idea that the proportion of women and children in large cities may be lower than in the population at large.[31] The importance of migrants and imported slaves (including those who were later manumitted) in ancient Rome will certainly have affected the age structure, the sex ratio and the patterns of nuptiality of the urban population. However, the 200,000 dole recipients were a privileged group within the city. They were sufficiently well established to have gained access to the restricted group of the *plebs frumentaria*, and receipt of the dole presumably increased to a significant extent their ability to support a family. Certain patterns of behaviour, especially with regard to marriage and fertility, could be affected, with important demographic consequences. This group may indeed be considered as a 'core' population, having an age structure and sex ratio very different from the 'envelope' of more recent migrants.[32] On this basis the estimate of their total numbers, based on the assumption that adult males over ten years would constitute about 37 per cent of the population, remains plausible.

We still have to take account of other groups in the city; freedmen excluded from the dole, recent migrants, slaves, soldiers, foreigners and the elite. The first group comprised at least 120,000 men when Augustus decided to remove them from the lists of dole recipients; it can be argued that freedmen were less likely to marry or have children, and therefore it

---

[27] Virlouvet (1991), 49–55.   [28] Suet. *Aug.* 42.2.

[29] Cf. Suet. *Aug.* 41; Garnsey (1988a), 213, 236.

[30] $e_0 = 25$ (i.e. average life expectancy at birth is twenty-five years); introductions to demography in Willigan and Lynch (1982), Newell (1988) and Parkin (1992).

[31] Ringrose (1983), 34–5; de Vries (1984), 178; Desai (1961), 159.

[32] As in Madrid in 1850: Ringrose (1983), 35, esp. fig. 3.1.

is probably sufficient to double this figure to reach a total for the rest of the *plebs urbana*.[33] Soldiers, senators and *equites* numbered perhaps 20,000 all told; Friedländer's argument for 60,000 resident foreigners ('assumed, for the purposes of comparison, to be twice that of the foreign population of Paris at the time of its greatest splendour under Napoleon I') is hardly overwhelming, but the evidence does not exist on which to base a better estimate.[34] The numbers are small enough that their omission from the calculation is scarcely significant. The *plebs urbana* therefore numbered about 750,000, not including what may have been a large population of migrants (either temporary, or not yet sufficiently settled in the city to receive largesse from the emperor). The number of slaves is a matter of guesswork. Beloch's figure of 300,000 was based on a single comment in Galen that there were two free men to every slave in second-century Pergamum.[35] Clearly many people had no slaves, and some of the elite had only a few; the paranoia of elite writers about the numerical superiority of slaves need have no basis in fact.[36] An estimate of 100–200,000 seems as plausible as any.[37]

The total population of what we might call Greater Rome at the time of Augustus was therefore somewhere between 850,000 and a million. Taking only the 1,783 ha. built-up area, the population density (477–561 persons/ha.) is high, but not impossibly so. More plausibly, we may imagine that the population was divided between the urban core and a less densely settled penumbra, stretching 5 km or so (convenient walking distance) from the city. A total of a million or so is also compatible with the figure from the S.H.A. relating to the city's grain imports, and for the sake of convenience it will be used in calculations here.

It is still more difficult to offer convincing estimates of the population of Rome either before or after Augustus. The number of *vici* in the city increased at some point between the reign of Hadrian and the fourth century, which may reflect an increase in the built-up area, while the third-century wall marked a contraction in area from the original fourteen Augustan regions.[38] According to Frontinus, Claudius built his aqueducts in response to increases in both public needs and private luxury; Trajan too built an aqueduct, and issued an edict to restrict the height of buildings in the city, perhaps a response to the visible effects of a rising demand for housing.[39] It is dangerous to draw a direct line between an emperor's perception of a problem (and his perception of the

---

[33]   Brunt (1971), 382–3.   [34]   Friedländer (1928), 17–18.
[35]   Galen 5.49K; Beloch (1886), 403–4.
[36]   E.g. Tac. *Ann.* 4.27; Friedländer (1928), 19.
[37]   Brunt (1971), 383.   [38]   Homo (1971), 98–9.
[39]   Frontinus, *Aq.* 13, 65–73; Epit. *Caes.* 13.13.

correct response of an emperor) on the one hand and the reality of the situation on the other; aqueducts were built for prestige as much as anything, and even the most public-spirited emperor can have had only the vaguest idea of whether the existing water supply was sufficient for the city's needs.[40] The city may have continued to grow over the first two centuries A.D., but it is difficult to believe that it could have greatly exceeded a million, even if the adjacent suburbs are taken into account.

Estimates of the republican population are based entirely on the development of the city's water supply. The construction of aqueducts under Augustus meant that the volume of water supplied in 2 B.C. was roughly double that of 125 B.C.; Brunt argues that this was a response to a perceived shortage, resulting from a doubling of the urban population over that period.[41] This is problematic, but no other index of the city's growth is available. On this basis, the population in 130 B.C. was half a million (375,000 according to Brunt, who starts from a lower figure under Augustus), and this must be at least double that of c.270 B.C. Two hundred thousand seems too high for the latter date, given the size of Roman territory at the time.[42] Simply as a working figure, the population at the beginning of the second century B.C. will be taken as 200,000, comprising 150,000 free and 50,000 slaves.[43]

Mortality in the city

In the last two centuries B.C., therefore, the population of Rome grew from about 200,000 to about a million; an average of 4,000 every year, or a rate of natural increase (the surplus of births over deaths) of 0.8 per cent per annum. The body of freeborn citizens grew from roughly 150,000 to 550,000, a rate of increase of 0.67 per cent per annum. Of course, cities do not tend to grow at a steady, reliable pace. For example, between 1550 and 1800 London grew from 120,000 to 950,000 people, an average of 3,300 per year. Within this period, however, there was considerable variation; between 1550 and 1600 the population rose by 1,600 people per year, while over the next fifty years this figure was more like 3,550, and by the end of the period it was well over 5,000 p.a.[44] It is easy to imagine that Rome experienced similar periods of acceleration and deceleration in the course of its expansion.

More importantly, there is a considerable quantity of comparative

[40]   On aqueducts, cf. Duncan-Jones (1977).
[41]   Brunt (1971), 383–4.
[42]   Cornell (1989), 408; estimates for earlier periods in Ampolo (1988) and Coarelli (1988).
[43]   Cf. K. Hopkins (1978a), 68–9.
[44]   Wrigley (1967), 133–4; Finlay and Shearer (1986), 39.

evidence to suggest that pre-industrial cities – even, indeed, small towns of a few thousand inhabitants – almost invariably experienced negative rates of natural increase.[45] The number of deaths consistently exceeded the number of births; simply to maintain a certain level of population, let alone to expand, cities depended on large-scale migration.[46] The nature of this 'urban natural decrease' has been much disputed by historians; above all, the orthodox position that the deficit is due entirely to higher levels of urban mortality has been questioned. Sharlin has argued that the main cause is a lower level of fertility among migrants, while permanent residents were capable of reproducing themselves. Migration can indeed be seen as causing the problem of the urban deficit rather than solving it.[47]

Clearly, urban populations were not homogeneous; different groups had different levels of nuptiality and hence fertility. However, it is difficult to distinguish between these groups on the evidence available; further, it is hard to determine whether it is immigrant status rather than socio-economic position that determines the observed differences in the net reproduction rates of citizens and non-citizens.[48] Certainly many immigrants did marry, though often at a later age than the rest of the population. Sharlin's argument can be accepted in part, recognising the equal importance of fertility in any discussion of population dynamics, without abandoning the idea that higher levels of mortality in the pre-industrial city were more significant for the phenomenon of urban natural decrease.

Between 1550 and 1824, the number of baptisms in London compared with all English baptisms follows faithfully the percentage of the population resident in the capital; the number of burials is out of all proportion.[49] Even given the high level of celibacy or late marriage among certain sectors of the urban population, it is hard to account for the consistent surplus of deaths over births except by the hypothesis that mortality was noticeably higher in London than elsewhere.[50] This seems to be confirmed by a detailed examination of the London Bills of Mortality and of two Quaker registers from the eighteenth century, which found exceptionally high infant mortality (28–40 per cent of all deaths recorded); this is far higher than in the rest of England, and suggests a high level of mortality in the urban population as a whole.[51]

Although a high level of mortality is still considered the most

[45] Wrigley (1967), 134–5; de Vries (1984), 179–97.
[46] Schiavoni and Sonnino (1982), 107–9; de Vries (1984), 199–212.
[47] Sharlin (1978) and (1981).   [48] Finlay (1981b); de Vries (1984), 184.
[49] Wrigley and Schofield (1981), 166–70.   [50] Finlay (1981a), 83–110.
[51] Landers (1987), 63–8, and (1993), 129–95.

significant factor in the demography of pre-industrial cities, Sharlin's work has had the effect of promoting a more thorough examination of the causes of this level of mortality.[52] The subject had previously been discussed vaguely in terms of the masses of people and their insanitary living conditions, often with an overtone of moral condemnation; much along the lines of the eighteenth-century commentator who considered the London Bills of Mortality proof of 'the manifest differences between a clear, open, free thin air and a close, sultry, smoky Atmosphere, not ventilated, but loaded with excrementitious and animal Effluvia; and between a moderate discreet use of the Necessaries of Life with due Exercise and an effeminate, slothful, luxurious spending of our days'.[53] Similar notions can be found in certain studies of the city of Rome – albeit with considerable justification, as Scobie's study of urban sanitation has shown.[54]

The unhealthfulness of cities has two main causes, both connected to the incidence of disease. The first is the extent to which urban living conditions aid the spread of infection.[55] Diseases that are transmitted on the breath or through the skin will spread more rapidly in situations where people live in close proximity to one another and are in regular contact with strangers. Parasites that are transmitted by ingestion can spread easily if the population is dependent upon a communal water supply (the most famous example of this is the outbreak of cholera in Soho in 1854), and poor sanitation increases the chances of contamination of food or drink.[56]

The relevance of this for ancient Rome is clear. The suggested population figure of a million implies a fairly high density throughout the city; in areas of lower-class housing it will have been much higher, and the impression gained from literary and archaeological sources is that the mass of the *plebs* lived in very crowded circumstances.[57] Scobie's assessment of Roman sanitation is still more pessimistic: the majority of houses were not connected to the sewers, having instead a cesspit, often in or adjacent to the kitchen. The public fountains, since they were served by a constant stream of water, may have been safer, although inscriptions were set up specifically to prohibit the pollution of public basins. The public baths, far from promoting cleanliness, may have aided the spread of disease; it is not clear how often the water was changed, while the sick were encouraged to visit them regularly. The Tiber received both the Cloaca Maxima and (presumably) a large amount of other excrement; it

---

[52]   Cf. Sharlin (1978), 127, 138.   [53]   Short (1973), 57; cf. Williams (1973), 215–32.
[54]   Scobie (1986); Hermansen (1978), 167; Frier (1982), 250; Yavetz (1958).
[55]   Manchester (1992), 8–9.   [56]   Cholera in London: Snow (1965).
[57]   Scobie (1986), 401–11; Packer (1971), 74–9.

is likely that river water continued to be used for drinking and washing, and certainly fish from the river were eaten.[58] Scobie lists the many diseases, especially gastric infections, that would have thrived in such conditions; poor sanitation was a major contributor to high levels of urban mortality in Europe well into the nineteenth century, and it remains a problem in the modern Third World.

At least as significant as urban living conditions, however, are the urban diseases: pathogens that are not normally found (or not found in the same form) in rural contexts. Tuberculosis is a good example.[59] In its original form the infection passes from cattle to humans by ingestion of contaminated food or water, and causes gastrointestinal disease; with an increase in urbanisation, the bacillus adapts to a more advantageous mode of transmission, via water droplets in the breath, and causes chronic lung disease. In this form, tuberculosis is largely confined to urban contexts, since it is density dependent; that is, the disease can become endemic only if the population is large enough, the critical point being determined by the number of births per week.[60] Smallpox, mumps, whooping cough and measles are similarly found only in large, concentrated populations. Urban populations in which these diseases were endemic were therefore exposed to a set of pathogens which their rural compatriots encountered only in sporadic epidemics; the result was a much higher – but more stable – level of mortality.[61]

The history of disease in Europe is to a great extent the history of the migration of pathogens from India and other parts of Asia across very sparsely populated areas.[62] The 'epidemiological barriers' of steppes and desert were sufficient to prevent many diseases from colonising Europe until after the Roman period; bubonic plague may have first arrived in the sixth century, typhus in the fifteenth and the virulent strain of Indian cholera in the nineteenth. It is more difficult to assess the incidence of other diseases, for the same reason that it is difficult to match ancient descriptions of illness with a modern diagnosis: the different views of ancient and modern doctors on the proper recording of symptoms.[63] For Rome, there is the additional problem that most ancient doctors and medical writers were of Greek origin, and both they and later historians have tended to study diseases in that context.

Thus, discussions of smallpox have concentrated on the fact that no city in ancient Greece was large enough for the disease to become

[58]   Lanciani (1888), 49–73, 233.   [59]   Manchester (1992), 10–11.
[60]   Cockburn (1971), 50–1; McNeill (1980), 29–32; D. R. Hopkins (1983), 8; Sallares (1991), 243.
[61]   Landers (1993), 242–300.   [62]   McNeill (1977), 106–7.
[63]   Grmek (1989), 1–2, 17–46; Sallares (1991), 225.

endemic; at most, smallpox may have been the cause of epidemics like the plague at Athens or the one that struck the Carthaginians at Syracuse in 396 B.C.[64] Of the density-dependent diseases, measles requires a population of about half a million to become endemic, and the others probably less; in other words, while no city in Greece could support smallpox, it could certainly have become established in Rome.

On the one hand, there is no mention of anything resembling smallpox in the standard Greek medical textbooks (Roman descriptions of the plagues their city suffered are insufficiently detailed for any identification).[65] On the other hand, markings on the skin of some Egyptian mummies have been identified as traces of the ravages of smallpox.[66] The Nile Valley was very densely settled, an hospitable environment for all kinds of diseases, with a characteristic demographic regime of very high fertility and mortality.[67] Egypt's regular commerce with Rome is well known; if smallpox was endemic there, it is likely to have colonised the metropolis also, while spreading into other, less densely populated regions of the empire only occasionally (the Antonine plague has been attributed to smallpox, although measles is another possibility).[68]

Tuberculosis is well attested in the ancient medical corpus.[69] It is worth noting Sallares' observation that the standard Coale and Demeny life tables do not cover populations which suffer from TB because of its distorting effect on age structures, tending to affect young adults above all, especially women. Rome escaped the ravages of plague, typhus and cholera; however, the ancient Mediterranean had the additional scourge of malaria, something which the cities of temperate Europe escaped.[70]

The fact that certain diseases were absent from ancient Rome does not mean that mortality was necessarily lower than in early modern London. Certainly the conditions of urban life and the incidence of at least some density-dependent, 'urban' diseases support the idea that mortality in the city was noticeably greater than in the countryside; assuming that fertility was no higher, Rome must have experienced the same 'urban natural decrease' as other pre-industrial cities.

The difference between the crude death rate and the crude birth rate in London between 1650 and 1750 has been estimated at 10 per thousand per annum or more; the Bills of Mortality record surpluses of burials over baptisms of between 10 and 18 per thousand p.a., although this

[64] Sallares (1991), 244–62; Patrick (1967), 239.
[65] Jackson (1988), 23; Grmek (1989), 89; Sallares (1991), 243.
[66] D. R. Hopkins (1983), 14–16; Grmek (1989), 86; Sallares (1991), 465 n.359.
[67] Bagnall and Frier (1994), 173–4, 177–8.
[68] Sallares (1991), 255; McNeill (1977), 115–86.
[69] Grmek (1989), 177–97; Sallares (1991), 237.   [70] Grmek (1989), 277–82.

takes no account of under-registration of deaths.[71] These raw figures suggest that a city of a million people would have required at least 10,000 immigrants every year simply to maintain its numbers; since not all groups in the urban population had the same rates of nuptiality and fertility, the actual numbers of migrants must have been much higher. To shed light on this question it is necessary to construct a rough model of the city's demographic structure.

It was suggested above that the recipients of the corn dole were freeborn adult male citizens, who were sufficiently settled in the city to have gained access to the lists of those eligible. It was also suggested that receipt of the corn dole increased their ability to marry and reproduce; hence the total numbers of the *plebs frumentaria* were reconstructed on the basis of a stable age structure and sex ratio. This implies that the average age of marriage and net reproduction rate in this core population were broadly similar to those found in areas outside Rome; hence, that the crude birth rate was also similar. On these assumptions, and given the higher level of mortality suggested for the city, the deficit of 10 per thousand per annum can be taken as a working estimate. Comparative evidence suggests that some urban populations had higher levels of fertility than their rural counterparts; on the other hand, the estimate for mortality is fairly conservative.

This core population grew from roughly 150,000 to about 550,000 in the last two centuries of the Republic; given a deficit of 10 per thousand per annum, this growth involved a net immigration of 6,000 people every year (the actual numbers involved must have been greater, to replace those who left the city). 'Migration' in this case means a change of status rather than of residence; migrants into the *plebs frumentaria* were drawn from the rest of the urban *plebs*, who gained access (via *sortitio* or some other method) to the corn dole. The group from which these 'migrants' were drawn consisted of the sons of freedmen, recent migrants to the city and more established residents who had not yet succeeded in getting on the lists. The remainder of the *plebs*, the freedmen, along with the slaves, were not eligible. The demography of all these different groups is something of a problem.

Recent migrants to the city, and those of the urban *plebs* who did not have access to the corn dole, were, arguably, less likely to marry; certainly they were likely to marry later, and therefore to have fewer children. On top of this, migrants to the city were more susceptible to urban diseases than natives. In eighteenth-century London this is particularly obvious in the case of smallpox, whose existence in Rome is not

[71]   Wrigley (1967), 46; Landers (1987), 63, Table 1.

established, but other diseases would contribute to a higher level of mortality among recent immigrants than among the settled population, who had had time to build up some immunity. Migrants tend to be young adults; a high level of mortality in this group, before its members have had a chance to reproduce, clearly affects the reproduction rate of the whole population.

The sons of freedmen and their dependants may not have been very numerous at all. Certainly, given the number of inscriptions set up by freedmen in the city of Rome, there are few traces of their freeborn children.[72] Many freedmen were probably quite old when manumitted; many may have remained celibate.[73] Epigraphic evidence tends to favour the more prosperous; the majority of freedmen may not have been in a position to support a family. Brunt has suggested that the bulk of manumissions simply filled the gaps left as freedmen died without having reproduced themselves, rather than swelling the ranks of citizens.[74]

There is evidence that offspring was expected from slave women, and epigraphy attests to the fact that slaves did marry and reproduce; it cannot, of course, show how common this was in practice.[75] Slave relationships are more likely in urban than rural contexts; however, it does appear that there were always more male than female slaves. The slave population in Rome was heavily dependent on regular imports; such involuntary migrants would, like those who moved to the city willingly, be more susceptible to urban diseases, and would therefore suffer a higher level of mortality.

Since we are concerned here with the scale of Rome's demographic demands on the rest of Italy, it is not necessary to consider the complex structure of the slave and freedman populations in any more detail, except to estimate the number of their descendants who may have gained access to the corn dole. There is no evidence on which to base this figure, except for the argument from silence that there seems to be surprisingly little trace of the descendants of freedmen in the city; as a working hypothesis, it is assumed that they supplied 1,000 of the 6,000 annual migrants into the *plebs frumentaria*. The remaining 5,000 were drawn from a shadowy population, made up predominantly of migrants from outside the city, both newly arrived and more settled. As suggested above, this group is likely to have exhibited a still greater surplus of deaths over births, at a rate of perhaps 20 per thousand p.a. or higher. Supposing that this group numbered about 100,000 (a guess, erring on the low side), total migration into this group from outside Rome over the

[72] Duncan-Jones (1980), 72–3; cf. Purcell (1994), 656.
[73] Treggiari (1969), 35; Brunt (1971), 143–6.
[74] Brunt (1971), 145–6.   [75] Bradley (1984), 47–80.

two centuries up to the reign of Augustus must have averaged over 7,000 people per year to fill the deficit left both from natural urban decrease and from the migration of 5,000 people every year into the *plebs frumentaria*. We may note in passing that if slaves and freedmen exhibited a similar rate of natural decrease (based on a crude death rate that is 10 per cent higher, and a crude birth rate that is only 10 per cent lower, than those of the core population), another 7,000–odd migrants would be required to maintain their numbers.

Rome's consumption of bodies was large and regular. The urban mortality regime means that the city's growth cannot be attributed to a single event, like the sudden influx of slaves after the Hannibalic War or the supposed crisis of the peasantry at the same time. Such events would produce a brief acceleration in the process of expansion, which would soon slow or even briefly slip back. The achievement of a population of a million was based on the steady annual import of slaves and migrants; the former from newly conquered territories and the fringes of the empire; the latter, it is argued, predominantly from Italy.

There is no way of proving this latter assertion. Few migrants (indeed, few free-born people of any description) have left any epigraphic record of their origins. However, a number of factors make it likely that Italians formed the great majority of migrants to Rome during the last two centuries of the Republic, if not thereafter. The first is proximity, aided by the Romans' work in improving lines of communication across the peninsula. The second is the acquisition of citizenship rights which could be exercised in Rome, at first by selected groups of allies and then, after the Social War, by all Italians outside Cisalpina, which followed them in the middle of the first century. Italians were in a better position than anyone else to respond to the opportunities offered by the city, and so it is assumed here that the 7,000 annual migrants were indeed drawn from Italy. The reasons that large numbers of people chose to move to the city will be considered later in this chapter. It is first necessary to turn to the wider context within which the demands of Rome must be set; the demographic history of Italy.

The population of Italy

In 225 B.C., in the face of a Gallic invasion, the Romans ordered their allies to make returns of all men of military age. The resultant figures, recorded by Polybius, form the basis of estimates of the total free population of Italy in this period.[76] The totals do not include Bruttians

[76]   Polybius 2.23; Brunt (1971), 44–60.

or Greeks, for whom a rough estimate must be made; they do appear to count 210,000 men twice over. The corrected figures must then be multiplied by a certain amount to account for under-registration, especially by the allies, and then further multiplied to account for women and children. The whole calculation is extremely approximate, with high margins of error, but there is no other evidence on which to base an estimate of the Italian population. The resulting total is nearly three million, to which must be added a further estimate for the population of Cisalpine Gaul. The figure of 4.5 million is generally accepted as a working total by most historians.[77]

Population totals for the next two centuries are drawn from the Roman census, which counted citizens alone; it is only after the Social War and the enfranchisement of the allies that these figures include all Italians outside Cisalpina. The accuracy of the two censuses following this enfranchisement has been strongly disputed. Brunt, following Beloch, argues that the second (in 70–69 B.C.) at least was fairly accurate; this gives a total of about 900,000 male citizens, possibly not including some 70,000 soldiers overseas, implying a total free population (excluding Cisalpina, as before) of around 3–3.5 million.[78] Frank rejected this census as more or less useless, since it was entirely incompatible with his interpretation of the census of 28 B.C.[79] His position receives some support from Wiseman's study of the administration of the first-century censuses; he casts doubt on the idea that the new citizens could register in their home towns rather than at Rome, and also suggests that certain politicians had a vested interest in keeping the numbers of registered citizens as low as possible.[80]

The argument hinges on the interpretation of the figure of 4,063,000 citizens recorded in the Augustan census of 28 B.C. Two positions have developed; that of Beloch and Brunt has been dominant over the last twenty years, with only the *Oxford Classical Dictionary* registering obvious dissent.[81] The main difficulty lies in the fact that neither position is entirely convincing, but no middle course is possible. Brunt and Beloch interpret the figure of 4,063,000 as referring to all citizens, including women and children; only in this way can the total be reconciled with earlier censuses.[82] A figure of 2 million is suggested for the number of slaves, giving a total population of 6 million. Support for this view comes from a passage of Pliny, where the author appears to believe that

---

[77] Beloch (1886), 388–443; Frank (1933), 56–9; Bernardi (1977); K. Hopkins (1978a), 68–9.
[78] Brunt (1971), 91–9.   [79] Frank (1933), 217.
[80] Wiseman (1969), esp. 71.
[81] *OCD* 2nd edn (1970), 863; cf. the critique of Beloch by Lo Cascio (1994a).
[82] Brunt (1971), 113–20.

censuses always included everyone; moreover, the aims of the census may have changed, being no longer concerned with military strength but with marriage and fertility, as were other pieces of Augustan legislation.[83] If this version is accepted, it would appear that, despite the enfranchisement of the Transpadani and the manumission of large numbers of slaves, the free citizen population had actually declined since 225 B.C. Brunt links this to the effects of war and expropriation on the free peasantry, reflected in the sources relating to the Gracchan crisis of the late second century.[84]

Frank, in contrast, takes the Augustan figure as referring to adult male citizens alone, as in previous censuses: the total free population is therefore about 10 million, with another 4 million slaves, this massive increase being accounted for by manumissions, by the enfranchisement of the Transpadani (he argues that the region was more densely settled than Beloch allowed) and by the natural increase of the population.[85] There is, on this reading, little trace of a second-century crisis; the history of Italy in the late Republic is one of a steady increase in the size of the population and the density of settlement.

The relationship between population and resources is a central part of the economic history of a society; the size of the population is therefore a matter of critical importance. Beloch and Brunt's hypothesis of decline or stagnation in the free population has been linked to the comments of various sources about the state of the Italian peasantry, the effects of war and the spread of slave estates in the post-Hannibalic period.[86] If Frank's estimate were by some means to be proven, the history of this period would have to be entirely rewritten, abandoning the literary sources altogether and examining archaeological evidence for changing patterns of settlement in a very different light.

It is impossible to decide between these two accounts on philological grounds alone; it is therefore necessary to examine their plausibility with respect to economic and demographic considerations.[87] One approach to the problem is to consider the question of resources: how the different estimates relate to what is known of agricultural productivity. The difficulty is that little is known of agricultural productivity, and if Frank's theory could be proved it would serve as evidence that Roman agriculture was more productive than has previously been thought. It is worth noting Brunt's comment that a population of 14 million would make Italy more densely inhabited than it was in the nineteenth century,

---

[83] Pliny, *HN* 33.16; cf. Den Boer (1973), 31, 42.
[84] Brunt (1971), 121–30.   [85] Frank (1933), 315.
[86] See e.g. Toynbee (1965); K. Hopkins (1978a), 1–98.
[87] The plausibility of *both* accounts, not just Beloch's; *pace* Lo Cascio (1994a), 40.

by which time large areas of fertile land (especially in the Po Valley) had been brought into cultivation.[88]

Jongman suggests a figure of 100,000 km^2 for the total area of agricultural land in Roman Italy.[89] If 75 per cent of this was under cereals on a two field system, yielding on average 400 kg/ha. on top of seed, Italy could feed 7.5 million people with 200 kg of grain per head per year. In other words, the Italy of Beloch and Brunt appears to be slightly under-populated, especially considering the contribution made to the feeding of the city of Rome by imports from other parts of the Mediterranean. Frank's Italy, however, is far too crowded; such a population is conceivable only if fallow was suppressed throughout the countryside, or if average yields were much higher than we might expect from the available evidence.

An alternative approach is to consider the problem from the demographic angle.[90] At first it would appear that neither theory can be ruled out on this basis. Beloch and Brunt see the free population as declining from 4.5 to 4 million; since a portion of the Augustan population was presumably made up of freedmen, the decline among the original Italian stock was still greater. As Hopkins observes, very small changes in the factors affecting fertility have significant consequences.[91] Given the military burden on the peasantry during this period, and the anecdotal evidence for their economic difficulties, the idea of such a decline cannot be ruled out – although the argument runs the risk of circularity, as population decline proves second-century crisis and the crisis of the peasantry supports the idea of demographic decline.

In contrast, a rise in the population from 4.5 to 10 million requires a rate of natural increase of about 5 per thousand per annum, a figure which Wrigley considers optimistic, but not impossible, for early modern England.[92] At this point, it is helpful to reintroduce into the argument the city of Rome and its demands on the population of Italy. As noted above, Rome required at least 7,000 migrants every year to support its growth during this period. Comparative evidence suggests that migrants tend to be young adults, between fifteen and thirty.[93] Mortality, especially infant mortality, tends to be very high in a pre-industrial society; young adults are the survivors from a much larger number of births. In a population with an average life expectancy at birth of twenty-five years ($e_0 = 25$), 7,000 people at the age of twenty are the survivors of a birth

[88] Brunt (1971), 130.
[89] Jongman (1988a), 67, and (1990), 52–3.
[90] Cf. Lo Cascio (1994a), 33–40; (1994b), 94–111.
[91] K. Hopkins (1974), 77.   [92] Wrigley (1967), 47.
[93] Cf. Bagnall and Frier (1994), 160–9, on migration in Egypt.

cohort at least twice as large; say 15,000 births.[94] In a population of 4.5 million increasing at a rate of 0.5 per cent p.a., 15,000 births represent two-thirds of the total natural increase, siphoned off to maintain the city of Rome instead of swelling the Italian population. A population whose rate of increase was less than 0.33 per cent p.a. would start to decline under the pressure of this emigration.

If this constant drain is taken into account, a rise in population from 4.5 million to 10 million (or rather 9.4 million, excluding the free population of Rome) in two centuries required a rate of natural increase of over 6 per thousand per annum. This may be considered implausibly high, especially given the demands on manpower of Rome's wars. Moreover, it is necessary to include also the effects of urbanisation in the rest of Italy as an additional burden on the reproductive powers of the Italian peasantry. Many towns were small enough to escape the worst aspects of urban life, and therefore presumably suffered less from natural decrease, but by the time of Augustus there were already a number of cities whose demands for replacement migration must have been considerable.[95] Frank's interpretation of the Augustan census figures may therefore be rejected on the grounds of demographic implausibility. Taking into account the demands of Rome, a rate of increase among the rural free population of 3 per thousand per annum would have resulted in a slight decline over two centuries, from 4.5 to 4 million. This is close to the Augustan census of 48 B.C., although it undoubtedly masks considerable variation in the rates of both mortality and fertility among the Italian population over this period.

Rome and Italy

Consideration of the place of the city of Rome in the demography of Italy supports the reconstruction of the history of the Italian population proposed by Beloch and Brunt. It is less supportive of their interpretation of the decline of the free population. Rome's demands for migrants may be a sufficient explanation of that decline, without need for recourse to theories of the expropriation of the peasantry by slave labour and grasping landowners; at any rate, it tends to mute the severity of that crisis. There is no need for anyone to be forced off the land; the city merely creams off the surplus population that might otherwise have put pressure on local resources.

Studies of migration have often been concerned with the reasons behind it, and in particular the balance of 'push' and 'pull' factors.[96] The

[94]   Cf. Parkin (1992), 147–8.   [95]   Cf. Jongman (1990), 48; see Chapter 7 below.
[96]   Oberai (1983), 25–49; Jongman (1990), 49.

standard model of the economic changes in second-century Italy emphasises the 'push' element: peasants are displaced by slave villas and so
forced to migrate, to colonies overseas, to Rome and to other Italian
cities. De Neeve has offered an alternative theory: low grain prices in
this period made small-scale farming uneconomical, so that peasants
migrated to the cities and their place was taken by slaves.[97] Either
picture can be questioned on the basis of archaeological evidence for the
survival of smaller sites in many areas, and the fact that slave villas
depended on being able to hire free labour locally at certain seasons.[98]
Migration was only one of the options open to a dispossessed peasant;
there were other ways of existing on the land besides being a free
smallholder.[99] Evidence for grain prices is more or less non-existent,
besides which it is generally supposed that peasant involvement in the
market was strictly limited.[100]

Above all, there is the fact that the growth of the city of Rome
depended on a consistent stream of migrants over two centuries. Undoubtedly this stream was much larger in some years than in others,
swollen by local harvest failures or other problems, but the city's rise
cannot be attributed to a single crisis, however protracted. If disposses-
sions in the second century had raised the free population of Rome to
half a million by 100 B.C., the city would then have required an average
of 5,000 migrants per year over the next century to maintain this level.
There must still have been a free population in the countryside whose
surplus could be siphoned off. In other words, it is necessary to
emphasise the 'pull' factors in migration to Rome, the positive reasons
for choosing this option.

As an imperial capital, Rome became increasingly wealthy. The
governing elite supported a large population through their expenditure
on luxury goods; their building projects and those of the state demanded
a large amount of labour, and a further group of people could find
employment in providing services for these workers. Rome offered the
prospect of wage labour, quite possibly at rates higher than could be
obtained in the countryside (although of course prices were also higher).
The institution of the corn dole must have served as an additional
inducement, and of course we cannot know how far the 'bright lights, big
city' side of metropolitan life may have attracted people. In his description of the adherents of Catiline, Sallust talks of 'the young men who had
maintained a wretched existence by manual labour in the country,
tempted by public and private doles had come to prefer idleness in the

[97] (1984b), 106–8.   [98] Rathbone (1981).
[99] Garnsey (1980b).   [100] de Ligt (1990), 33–43 and (1991a), 68.

city to their hateful toil'.[101] Another impression of the migrants is offered by Seneca, writing from the perspective of his own exile:

> Some have been drawn here by ambition, others by the obligations of an official position or mission; still others are tempted by luxurious self-indulgence, or by the lavish opportunities for vice. Some come to Rome for education, others to see the games. Some come to visit friends, others come as workers, because Rome gives them greater scope for displaying their skills. They have brought something to sell, a beautiful body or an attractive eloquence; every type of human swarms into the city, which offers high rewards for both vice and virtue.[102]

The most important consequence of this movement of people was the formation of a large and wealthy market for all kinds of commodities, especially foodstuffs, fuel and building materials. This promoted changes in agricultural practices in many parts of Italy – which in turn promoted further urbanisation in Rome and other towns, as landowners spent the profits they had made in supplying the metropolis. The rest of this book considers different aspects of this process, especially the impact of the city on farming practices in different parts of the peninsula. First, however, we may consider some of the other possible effects that migration to Rome may have had on the countryside.

In his model of London's influence, Wrigley observed that the capital's share of the total English population grew from 7% in 1650 to 11% in 1750, and that this implies a rise in productivity per head.[103] Rome contained 15% of the Italian population under Augustus, compared with barely 4% two centuries earlier. However, since much of this population growth was supported by increasing volumes of imports from the provinces, it is difficult to argue that this rise tells us anything about productivity; there is little scope here for Boserup's theory that population pressure can stimulate economic development.[104] Rome's political clout, which allowed it to ensure its food supply by calling on the resources of the empire, instead reduced pressure on Italian agriculture, allowing it to develop or stagnate as it wished. Until Domitian's edict on viticulture (the significance of which is still disputed), there was no attempt by the state to dictate what farmers should grow.

The suggestion that urbanisation elsewhere in Italy may have increased from 9% to 20% would imply a rise in productivity, or at least a rise in the volume of production entering the market rather than being consumed by its producers.[105] Roughly the same number of farmers were supporting twice as many non-producers in the first century A.D. as they were two hundred years before, a rise in productivity of over 10%.

---

[101] Sallust, *Cat.* 37.7.   [102] Seneca, *ad Helviam* 6.
[103] Wrigley (1967), 56.   [104] Boserup (1965) and (1981); cf. Grigg (1980).
[105] K. Hopkins (1978a), 68–9.

However, evidence for the level of urbanisation at any period is extremely thin.[106] I will argue in Chapter 7 that urbanisation outside Rome (in the sense of non-agricultural employment rather than simply urban residence) was more of the order of 10–15%, still a significant level by premodern standards. This increase may imply a rise in productivity; more likely, however, is an increase in the rate of exploitation, especially of slave labour.

Part of Wrigley's model for London which does seem to be applicable to Rome is the role of the metropolis as an agent of change in the social and cultural life of its hinterland.[107] This follows directly from the demography of its growth. If we take the crude birth rate of the Italian population as a whole as 43 per thousand per year (at $e_0 = 25$ and a rate of natural increase of about 0.3% p.a.) and the free population of Italy excluding Rome as 4 million, then the total number of births in one year would be 172,000. Of these births, 15,000 were, so to speak, earmarked for Rome; the survivors to adulthood of nearly one tenth of all births in Italy would end up in the city. This is a figure for net migration only; we can envisage considerable migration out of Rome into the countryside, so that the gross total for migration into the city must have been higher. If this is so, more than a tenth of the Italian population had, at some point in their lives, experience of life in the capital.

Speaking of London, Wrigley suggests that this level of migration 'must have acted as a powerful solvent of the customs, prejudices and modes of action of traditional rural England'.[108] The extent to which this is true for Rome depends on the extent to which urban (especially metropolitan) culture was differentiated from rural culture in the first place. Certainly we might see this movement of people, coupled with the expansion of exchange, as a significant force in promoting the monetisation of the countryside. The city can be seen as assisting the integration of the peninsula, as migration led to an increasing homogeneity of social and consumptive practices. For example, the diffusion of a taste for wine and the change from *puls* to bread in the diets of many Italians, which had significant economic consequences, may be linked to the spread of urban tastes.[109] Finally, assuming that migrants retained links with their place of origin (and possibly returned there eventually), an increasingly complicated social network, centring on the city of Rome, might come into being across Italy.

Finally, there is the effect of large-scale migration on structures of

---

[106] Duncan-Jones (1982), 259–87; see below, Chapter 7.
[107] Wrigley (1967), 50.   [108] *Ibid1., 51.*
[109] Tchernia (1982) and (1986), 58–60; Purcell (1985), 13–15; Pucci (1989).

land-holding and labour.[110] Carandini has described the replacement of peasant smallholders with slave villas as 'the most drastic separation of producers from their means of production and products that history has known before the modern expropriation of the yeoman'.[111] Even when the idea of a single crisis is abandoned in favour of a picture of steady, continual movement to the city, this point remains valid: large numbers of peasants chose, or were forced, to abandon the security of the land (where except in the most adverse circumstances the farmer might hope to be able to keep his family fed) in favour of a free labour market in the metropolis.

In her work on the origins and economic role of 'over-large' primate cities in the modern Third World, Smith offers a class-based analysis: the growth or decline of urban centres, and the nature of the urban system, rest ultimately on the economic interests of the politically dominant urban elite.[112] The advantages to the Roman elite of the migration of peasants from the land are obvious; they could be replaced with slaves, from whom a larger surplus could be extracted. Only in some circumstances – the problems caused by the disappearance of the old peasant-soldier class, or violent disturbances in the city of Rome – was the dissolution of the old order mourned by certain members of the elite. They might be equally happy with a free labour market in the city, informal, flexible and highly competitive (and therefore cheap), rather than relying exclusively on traditional structures of dependence. It should be remembered that this urban workforce also provided a market for the produce of their estates.

Smith's theory is primarily concerned with the causes of labour mobility and migration; it is certainly not incompatible with the ideas about the possible effects of that migration discussed above.[113] The city of Rome absorbed a large portion of the natural increase of the population of Italy over several hundred years, growing to an extraordinary size. The remainder of this study examines the effects of that growth on the Italian economy; in particular, the effect of its demands for food on agricultural production, the dominant sector of the economy.

[110] Standing (1980–1).   [111] Carandini (1981), 250.
[112] C. A. Smith (1985a) and (1985b).   [113] Cf. C. A. Smith (1985b), 166.

3   A model of agricultural change

Demand and supply

The dramatic growth of the population of Rome was impossible without an equally dramatic increase in the city's food supply. In part, this was achieved through state action. The political imperative to feed the urban *plebs* led magistrates and emperors to intervene in the grain supply, buying additional supplies in times of shortage and distributing grain collected as tax at a reduced price or without charge. The system of the *annona* became increasingly sophisticated, with the appointment of a *praefectus annonae* and incentives offered to shipowners to supply the city.[1] The state may also have attempted at times to manipulate the market, by releasing quantities of state grain or by withholding it to drive prices up, but it was not in the administration's interests to antagonise the private traders who made an equally important contribution to the city's food supply.[2]

State action alone was insufficient to keep the metropolis fed; a sizeable proportion of the city's demands for grain was met through the free market. Moreover, until the *annona* was expanded to include oil (at the turn of the second century A.D.) and wine and pork (in the 270s), Rome's supplies of all other foodstuffs were brought in through private channels.[3] The elite may have fed their households from the produce of their own estates; the majority of the urban population had no option but to rely on the vagaries of the market. It must be supposed that prices in the city were sufficiently high to attract merchants; to judge from the limited evidence, they were indeed higher than those obtainable in the countryside, at least in the west of the Mediterranean.[4] In general, taking into account the times when harvest failure, war, piracy or simple logistical problems led to shortages, the food supply of the city seems to

---

[1]   Casson (1980); Garnsey (1988a), 231–5.
[2]   Garnsey (1988a), 238–9; cf. Erdkamp (1995), 177, who seriously overestimates the role of the free market.
[3]   The extension of the *annona*: S.H.A. *Sev.* 18.3; *Aur.* 35.2, 48.1.
[4]   Duncan-Jones (1982), 345–7.

have kept pace with the growth in population. It was of course the ability of producers as well as traders to respond to this demand that allowed the city to continue to grow.

Such an increase in the food supply could be achieved in two ways. Firstly, the area from which supplies were drawn might be expanded; prices in the city might be sufficiently high to offset the cost of transporting goods from more distant regions. The effects of these demands on the regions in question would depend on the way in which the surplus was mobilised for consumption at Rome. If it was taken as tax in kind or as rent on a share-cropping basis, the effect on local agriculture is likely to have been minimal; the region as a whole might be impoverished, if a surplus previously consumed locally was now being taken to Rome, but individual producers would have no incentive to change their production strategies.[5] If, on the other hand, the surplus was exchanged for money, whether to pay rents and taxes in cash or to buy other goods, there might be significant changes in the local economy as a result.[6]

This brings us to the second way in which the supply of food might be increased: by increasing the amount obtained from existing areas of supply. Taxes and rents could simply be raised; in all likelihood with deleterious consequences for farmers, which might lead in the long term to a decrease in the revenue obtained. Alternatively, farmers might be persuaded to sell more of their produce (potentially risky, if it increased their reliance on the market for their own subsistence) or to sell it to the city rather than local markets. Finally, producers might attempt to increase their marketable surplus by changing their farming strategies. Dramatic changes in agricultural practice might thereby follow: greater specialisation in certain crops, larger inputs of labour and capital, the adoption of different techniques and changes in the organisation of production. In general, we might expect a greater orientation of agriculture towards the urban market, and closer integration of the region into wider economic (and consequently social and cultural) networks.

Study of the development of Rome's food supply has tended to concentrate on the demands it made on its expanding empire. At the end of the third century B.C., Sicily and Sardinia became regular suppliers of grain through tax; they were joined by the newly created province of Africa in 146 B.C., and by Egypt in the reign of Augustus.[7] As major grain-producing regions, these provinces must also have contributed a sizeable portion of the city's imports outside the *annona* scheme. The

---

[5]   de Neeve (1984b), 15–18; de Ligt (1990), 33–43.
[6]   K. Hopkins (1980); cf. Duncan-Jones (1990), 30–47; Howgego (1994), 10–11 and 17–20.
[7]   Rickman (1980), 94–119; Garnsey (1988a), 182–8, 231–2.

growth of the city goes hand in hand with the expansion of the empire, both through the increase in the size of the tax base and through the securing of areas of supply and supply routes. Changes in agricultural practice in the provinces can also be seen, with the development of vineyards in Gaul and Spain and oil production in Spain and Africa; a large proportion of this production was destined for the Roman market, and these changes must surely be linked to the demands of the city.

The role of Italy in supplying Rome has often been neglected. From 167 B.C., Roman citizens were not subject to the *tributum*, and after the Social War this privilege was extended to all Italians; they were therefore free from that pressure to increase productivity. However, much of the country was in a good position to respond to the incentives offered by the Roman market. It has been argued that the influx of provincial grain made cereal production unprofitable in Italy, just as provincial imports are said to have later ruined Italian viticulture.[8] It is hard to believe that a region like Campania was greatly disadvantaged in comparison with Africa or Egypt, either in fertility or in its access to the Roman market. At the most, Italian grain may have become proportionally less important to the metropolis as provincial imports grew, without the actual volume of production necessarily declining.

More significant, however, was Italy's response to the city's demands for wine, oil and other foods, not to mention textiles, wood and assorted luxuries. By the time of Augustus, a large portion of the urban population was being provided with a sizeable proportion of its subsistence needs by the state; it may be assumed that recipients of the corn dole had more income to spend on other goods, and the aggregate demand this implies is considerable. Until the middle of the first century A.D., Italy held a *de facto* monopoly on the supply of most food items apart from grain, due to its proximity to the market and to the undeveloped state of agriculture in many of the provinces of the empire. It is difficult to imagine how Italian agriculture could have remained unaffected by the demands of the city.

As was seen in the first chapter, the influence of a metropolitan city on its hinterland is pervasive, but it can take very different forms in different contexts. Madrid's influence on Castile was essentially negative, leading to the stagnation of the region's economy, while London's influence on England was in some sense 'progressive'. In both cases, costs and benefits were distributed very unevenly between different classes in society. In other words, the optimistic assessment of metropolitan influence is by no means the only model available. It is possible to construct a theory

---

[8]   Cf. Spurr (1986), 133–44.

whereby the growth of Rome may be reconciled with the decline of Italy; a return, in fact, to the image of Rome as parasite.

The argument here leads towards the opposite conclusion. Rome was not London, but there are clear resemblances; the demands of the city promoted changes in agriculture and other areas of economic life that may, with due caution, be termed 'progressive'. The picture does of course change over time, in response to the rhythm of the city's growth and to changes elsewhere in the empire; the idea that Italian agriculture suffered a crisis at the end of the first century A.D. must be considered in this context. The scope for economic development – another loaded term – was limited in the ancient world by a number of factors; Rome's relationship with Italy shows how far things might progress, but also offers the chance to consider why they progressed no further.

Patterns of land use

In classical economic theory, agricultural producers aim for optimum land use, in terms both of the type of crop (or mixture of crops) grown and of the intensity of cultivation (that is, the ratio of inputs to land area), based on the prices that can be obtained in the market.[9] If prices change, the optimum type of land use and level of intensity also change, and farmers should alter their production strategies accordingly. It may prove advantageous to change the type of land use, turning arable land over to pasture or specialising in particular crops. Alternatively, the level of inputs may be altered to match the new point of diminishing marginal returns. If prices rise, for example, marginal land may be brought into cultivation, additional labour may be hired (or the existing labour force made to work harder), and it may prove worthwhile to invest in new tools, machinery or animals. There might also be changes in farm management, to make certain operations more efficient.

Farmers do not of course respond instantaneously to every fluctuation in the market; they may follow longer- or shorter-term strategies, but in general they are planning at least a year ahead, working not only on current prices but on the likely vagaries of the weather.[10] There is therefore a tendency towards conservatism in decision-making, with the persistence of traditional strategies and methods; changes in market conditions must be significant and apparently sustainable to elicit much response. However, the growth of the city of Rome and the consequent rise in demand (and therefore prices) was sustained over at least two

[9] Found (1971), 12–32.   [10] *Ibid.*, 19–20, 106–23.

centuries. Such a change in market conditions would be large and reliable enough in the long term for the optimising farmer to respond to it, changing his cultivation strategy to a significant – and hence historically visible – extent.

Some responses to rising demand are likely to leave clearer traces in the literary or archaeological records than others. Thus, a decision by farmers to increase labour inputs by working more hours per week will hardly be visible to the historian, whereas a fundamental change in the organisation of labour might be more obvious. Furthermore, those changes which can be detected, in patterns of land use, agricultural technology or rural prosperity, cannot be classified automatically as responses to the growing demands of the city of Rome. It is necessary to consider alternative hypotheses, perhaps social or political rather than economic, even when alterations in the rural landscape correspond to the predictions of economic theory.

So far, discussion has focused on the possible responses of an ideal farmer at an unspecified location. It may at times be necessary, owing to the nature of some of the evidence, to talk in vague terms of changes in 'Italian agriculture', but ideally we should produce a more specific model. For this we may turn to the theory of land use patterns developed by J. H. von Thünen in *The Isolated State*, first published in 1826.[11] This deals with the spatial distribution of agricultural activities around a market; and, while the model is presented in the idealised world of economic theory, and was derived from von Thünen's experiences with his own estate in Germany, the principles set forth in the book can easily be adapted for consideration of the agricultural activities around a particular market, the city of Rome.

Von Thünen developed a concept of economic rent independently of Ricardo, the economist who is most frequently associated with the idea. This concept, which underlies all questions of competition for the use of land, may be defined as the net value of the returns on production on a given piece of land in a given time period, taking into account not only the cost of inputs but also the opportunity costs, the value that these inputs might have if put to alternative uses. On any piece of land, the enterprise that yields the highest economic rent will be conducted.

Von Thünen's chief contribution lies in his stress on the importance of location in calculating the costs of production, whereas Ricardo was concerned with the effects of differences in fertility. The cost of transporting goods to the market must be taken into account when calculating the net return from a particular land-use type; the costs of certain inputs

---

[11]   Hall (1966); Found (1971), 57–82; Chisholm (1968), 20–32.

may rise with distance from the market. Every land-use type has a characteristic rent-distance function – that is, the way in which the economic rent it yields varies with distance from the market. Thus, the economic rent on perishable goods like soft fruit declines sharply beyond a certain distance. The rent-distance function is affected also by the bulk of the goods relative to their value, and by the level of inputs required in their cultivation.

To demonstrate the effects of distance on land-use patterns, von Thünen described *Der isolierte Staat*:

Imagine a very large town, at the centre of a fertile plain which is crossed by no navigable river or canal. Throughout the plain the soil is capable of cultivation and of the same fertility. Far from the town, the plain turns into an uncultivated wilderness which cuts off all communication between this state and the outside world ... The problem we want to solve is this: What pattern of cultivation will take shape in these conditions?; and how will the farming system of the different districts be affected by their distance from the town? We assume throughout that farming is conducted absolutely rationally.[12]

Different crops have different rent-distance functions; thus at a certain distance from the market one crop yields the highest economic rent and hence is cultivated, while further away it is replaced by a different crop. This is shown in Figure 1. Figure 2 shows the pattern of land use that von Thünen envisaged for his Isolated State; a series of zones, concentric on the market, moving from horticulture and dairying closest to the town to forest, intensive arable, long-ley arable, three-field arable and finally ranching. Both the type of crop and the intensity of cultivation vary with distance.

The model as it stands is static, a description of the distribution of agricultural activities around the market at a given moment. It is not difficult to see how it might change over time. An increase in demand for all types of goods, based on a rise in the population of the town, would allow the zones of cultivation to spread outwards, as higher prices in the market offset higher costs of transport. As supply rises to meet demand, prices return towards their original levels, resulting in a contraction of the zones; in other words, there is a continual process of adjustment, especially at the boundaries of different zones. If demand continues to grow in the long term, the result is a permanent extension of cultivation over a wider area.

When the market in question is a metropolis like London or Rome, the zones of cultivation extend over whole countries or beyond.[13] In 1724, Defoe wrote of 'the general dependence of the whole country upon the

[12] Hall (1966), 7–8.   [13] Chisholm (1968), 68–100.

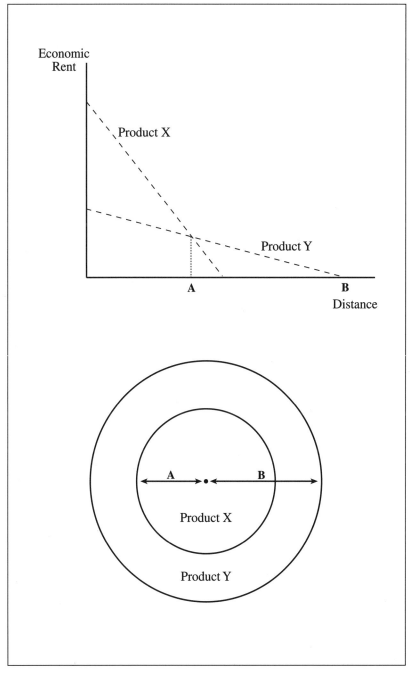

Figure 1   A simple model of agricultural location.

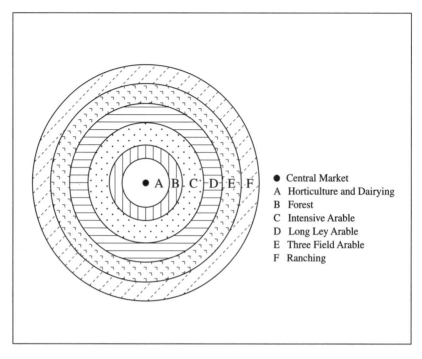

Figure 2   Von Thünen's *Isolated State*.

city of London for the consumption of its produce'.[14] From a very early date, London promoted changes in the agriculture of East Anglia and Kent; over the seventeenth and eighteenth centuries, the whole of England became increasingly oriented towards the demands of the capital, with the spread of local specialisation (the most obvious example being the development of fruit farming and market gardening in Kent) and the adoption of new techniques.[15]

Of course, with the exception of the band of intensive horticulture in the immediate vicinity of the city, English agriculture was not neatly arranged in concentric circles around the metropolis. Von Thünen's model is designed to isolate a particular set of economic relationships, and to this end it involves a number of clearly unrealistic assumptions; the uniform fertility of the plain and the uniform ease of access to the market are the most obvious. These assumptions, and the consequences for the model if they are relaxed, will be considered in detail below, The important point remains that, according to the model, different regions

[14]   Quoted in Fisher (1934–5), 51.   [15]   Fisher (1934–5); Wrigley (1967), 55–8.

of Italy, and indeed of the rest of the empire, would respond to the demands of Rome in different ways, ease of access to the city being one vital factor in determining both the form and the extent of their response.

Distance and transport costs

Von Thünen noted that one of the ways in which his Isolated State differed from reality was the assumption of equal ease of access to the urban market from all parts of the territory; most major cities, he observed, were sited on navigable rivers.[16] Transport costs for water travel were much lower than those for land – von Thünen thought they might be as low as one tenth of the overland rate. The existence of a navigable river therefore leads to the extension of the zones of cultivation along its length, as it alters the rent-distance function of each crop. The presence of a superior road, and above all easy access to the sea, would similarly increase the area from which the urban market could draw its supplies.

Comparative examples are not hard to find; the dependence of Paris on the network of French rivers, and the importance of the Thames and the North Sea for the development of London.[17] Various goods, especially bulky staples, could be transported over long distances by water, allowing such cities to grow dramatically and permitting their immediate hinterlands to specialise in non-staple crops. The plight of land-locked Madrid offers a still stronger instance of the importance of water transport; since it was prohibitively expensive to transport grain for any great distance overland, it proved necessary to compel the farmers of the city's immediate hinterland to specialise in cereals.[18] Madrid's geographical position, at least as much as social or political factors, explains the city's stagnating effect on Castilian agriculture.[19] Other great cities in this period could rely on grain from the Netherlands or the Baltic, imported via sea and river, and so had less reason to attempt to regulate farmers; the Parisian authorities, for all their concern about the city's grain supply, concentrated their efforts on the activities of merchants, millers and bakers.[20]

One source from early eighteenth-century England suggests that the cost ratios of different forms of transport were of the order of 1 for sea, 4.7 for river and 22.6 for land; in other words, a given good could be transported 5 miles overland, 25 miles by river and 115 miles by sea for the same price.[21] The figures for transport costs in Diocletian's Price

[16] Hall (1966), 171.   [17] Braudel (1981), 421, 548–9; Grigg (1982), 135–50.
[18] Ringrose (1970), v-xxii, 120–41.   [19] Ringrose (1983), 1–16.
[20] Kaplan (1984), 7–12, 23–40.
[21] Duncan-Jones (1982), 368; cf. Clark and Haswell (1970), 191–214.

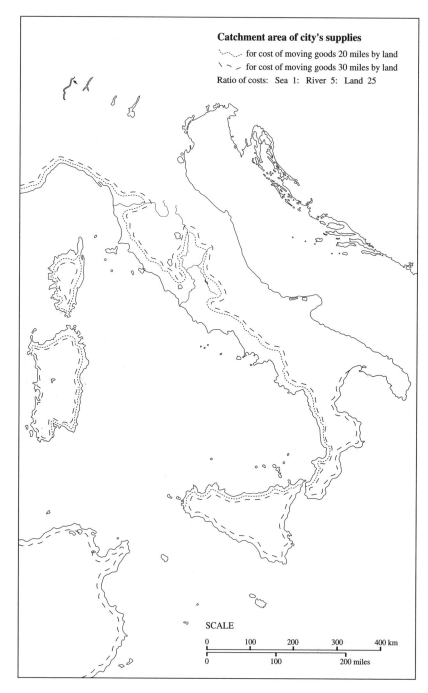

SCALE

| 0 | 100 | 200 | 300 | 400 km |

| 0 | 100 | 200 miles |

Map 1   The effect of transport costs.

Edict suggest that carrying grain overland would cost 55% of the load's value for every 100 miles, whereas sea transport cost only 1.3% per 100 miles; a first-century Egyptian papyrus gives a figure for river transport of 6.38%. The cost ratios in the Edict are 1 for sea transport, 4.9 for river and 42 for road (although carriage by camel was 20% cheaper).

A commonly cited example of the consequences of the cost of overland transport is the famine that struck Antioch in A.D. 362–3, despite the fact that grain was available fifty miles down the road.[22] The importance of Rome's location, on a navigable river with good access to the sea, was noted by ancient writers. Strabo describes merchandise being brought down the Tiber; Appian notes that, when Marius and Cinna were besieging Rome, they blockaded the river both above and below the city; Cicero observes that 'the city can not only bring in by sea but also obtain from the land, carried on its waters, whatever is most essential for its life and civilisation' – while noting also that Rome was far enough inland to escape the moral corruption common to most maritime cities.[23]

It is clear that Rome could grow so large because it had access to (and control over) the Mediterranean, and was therefore able to draw on the resources of a very wide area (above all the grain-producing regions). It is equally clear that the relative costs of different forms of transport would determine which areas of Italy were most strongly affected by the city's demands; not all parts of the peninsula enjoyed the same ease of access to the urban market. Map 1 offers some indication of this differential effect; using a ratio of 1: 5: 25 for sea, river and land transport, it shows the areas from which supplies could be drawn for the cost of moving goods 20 and 30 miles overland. A clear pattern emerges; long stretches of the Italian coast are as close to Rome in terms of the cost of transport as parts of inland Latium and Etruria. We might expect the zones of cultivation oriented towards the urban market to follow a similar pattern. However, it is necessary to consider the question of the cost of transport in the ancient world in more detail.

The first point is that the cost of sea transport in Diocletian's Edict seems suspiciously low. This might be explained in several ways. The cost is derived from the rate quoted for carriage between Alexandria and Rome. The importance of the capital's food supply might have persuaded the emperor or his advisers to keep this figure at an artificially low level (even at the risk of antagonising shipowners). Another possibility is that the route was so well-travelled that the price *was* relatively low. Alternatively, some but not all of the figures quoted in the Edict may have

---

[22] Finley (1985a), 126–7.   [23] Strabo 5.3.7; Appian, *BC* 1.67; Cicero, *Rep.* 2.3–5.

been affected by inflation; the price of wheat may be exceptionally high and quite out of line with the cost of transport.[24]

The figure quoted takes no account of the costs of loading and unloading vessels, a task that involved the hiring of large numbers of manual labourers at either end of the journey (although during the voyage fewer workers were required than would be necessary for over-land carriage).[25] Finally, the real costs of sea carriage must include the risk of shipwreck (and the cost of insurance) and vulnerability to the vagaries of climate – not only the restricted sailing season, but also the chances that a voyage could be delayed by contrary winds.[26] Never-theless, there is still no reason to doubt that sea transport was the cheapest way of transporting bulky staples over long distances.

The bulk of our evidence concerning river transport comes from Egypt, which was dominated by the Nile; it is of limited use for Italy.[27] Most Italian rivers were too small and too irregular – either floods or trickles, depending on the season – to be much use for transporting goods.[28] The importance of river transport on the Tiber has been noted; in the rest of Italy, only the Arno and the Po are large enough to have been used regularly for transport. There was also the canal which ran alongside the Via Appia through the Pomptine Marshes, which was regularly used by travellers and presumably also for merchandise.[29] Several emperors made plans for other canals, like Nero's project for linking Rome to Campania; Suetonius lists this scheme under the praiseworthy, or at least pardonable, acts of the reign, and the impor-tance of getting goods up-river to the city means that the idea should not be dismissed as just another ludicrous imperial folly.[30]

In most parts of Italy, therefore, the choice was between land and sea transport – or most likely a combination of the two. Varro describes the mule trains bringing oil, wine and grain down from the Apulian high-lands to the coast, and something similar must have occurred in other regions.[31] Such an arrangement is found in Egypt, with wagons and donkeys used to carry goods to the nearest river or canal.[32] The important question is how far goods could be carried overland to the sea before the cost became prohibitive. If land transport was as expensive as Diocletian's Edict suggests, Rome's influence, however far it extended along the coast of Italy, would be limited to a very narrow coastal strip. In many areas of the peninsula, of course, this coincides with the location

[24]   Duncan-Jones (1982), 368, 386.   [25]   Greene (1986), 42.
[26]   Casson (1971), 270–8.
[27]   Greene (1986), 30–5; on the Nile, D. J. Thompson (1983) and Bagnall (1993), 34–8.
[28]   Walker (1967), 270.   [29]   Cf. Horace, *Sat.* 1.5.
[30]   Suet. *Nero* 16; cf. Rickman (1991) on the over-crowded Tiber.
[31]   Varro, *RR* 2.6.5.   [32]   Bagnall (1985) and (1993), 38–40.

of the more fertile land. However, there is reason to suspect that the Edict gives a misleading impression of the cost of overland transport, just as it exaggerates the cheapness of sea travel.

Clearly it would matter what kinds of goods were being transported. It was prohibitively expensive to cart grain overland for any great distance because the charge for transport was levied in terms of weight, and grain has a low value per unit weight. Transport charges would not absorb so much of the value of more expensive and less bulky items, even staple goods like oil and wine (especially the more expensive wines). Various types of goods are better suited to land transport; sheep and other livestock will walk themselves to market, while carrying them by sea would be expensive and liable to reduce their value. Maps based on the transport costs of individual goods will vary significantly.

The transport of livestock would not involve hire charges for vehicles and draft animals; the only costs in monetary terms would be rent for the use of pasture on the journey, and the maintenance of the drovers. Hire charges would be equally irrelevant to a farmer or estate owner using his own means of transport, whether mule or ox-drawn wagon. If the cost was calculated at all, it would be in terms of time lost from other activities.[33] The farmer's trip into market could be multi-purpose, taking in the purchase of other items and various social activities as well as selling produce. The limit of Rome's penetration inland might therefore be set not by transport costs but by the distance farmers were prepared to travel in a day; goods could be drawn from a wider area than strict economic calculation would consider feasible. Richer estate owners might make use of their own ships as well as animals, and it is arguable how far the cost of this transport (let alone the notional 'opportunity cost' of the investment in a vessel) would be reflected in an inflated selling price. Finally, if cost is measured in time rather than money, it is worth noting that land transport could be both faster and more reliable than sea travel; when transporting perishable goods like fruit or lettuces, it is hardly profitable to risk having to wait for a favourable wind.

With regard to hired transport, comparative evidence suggests that a distinction may be drawn between long- and short-haul carriage.[34] In both early modern Spain and seventeenth-century England, the former, carried out by town-based professional carriers, was far more expensive than the service offered by local peasant carriers.[35] Roman laws dealing with land transport recognise different forms of hiring; one could hire the equipment alone, or pay the carriers a daily wage, or hire an outfit for a specific task.[36] The risks and legal responsibility were apportioned

[33] Cf. Rathbone (1991), 266–78.   [34] Ville (1990), 19–21.
[35] Ringrose (1970), 79–86; Clay (1984), 181–2.   [36] S. Martin (1990).

differently in each case, and we may suppose that the costs were also. Short-haul transport was, however, highly seasonal, based on the use of peasants' animals in slack agricultural seasons.

Finally, there is the question of the economic effect of Roman roads. The agronomists consider that proximity to a road is as important in locating a farm as access to the sea or a navigable river.[37] In the immediate vicinity of Rome, roads may have lowered transport costs by permitting the use of large wheeled wagons (over much of Italy, the terrain was more suitable for pack animals).[38] Other beneficiaries included those involved in bringing animals, especially sheep, down from the mountains.

Even if transport costs overland were halved, this would do little to offset the massive advantages – with all the caveats noted above – of sea transport. It should be noted that Map 1 was drawn using a ration of costs of sea to land of 1: 25, rather than the 1: 40 which is suggested by the figures in Diocletian's Edict. It is clear that Rome was not surrounded by neat concentric zones of production; its economic hinterland extended along the coast of Italy much further than it reached inland, even along the Tiber. The map serves to emphasise the enormous advantages which the coastal regions of central Italy had over the rest of the peninsular, not to mention other provinces of the empire, in their access to the Roman market. This is the area in which we may expect the most significant response to urban demands. Further afield, we can expect considerable differences in the development of the rural landscape between coastal areas and inland regions along much of the Tyrrhenian seaboard.

Nevertheless, some reconsideration of the map is necessary. The fact that land transport might be cheaper than is generally accepted, or that its cost might not be taken into account at all, means that the 'narrow coastal strip' may be less narrow than strict cost-accounting would indicate. Goods with a greater value per unit weight could be carried over longer distances, and many inland regions produced goods which walked themselves to market. In particular, there is the possibility that it might be economical to carry more expensive goods overland from the Adriatic coast rather than attempting the long sea journey: from Umbria and Picenum to the navigable stretches of the Tiber, and from the Po Valley across to the Ligurian coast. There is some evidence for contact between Genua, the port of Liguria, and the Po Valley.[39] Cisalpina may not have been as isolated as is generally assumed, or as the map of transport costs appears to indicate.

---

[37] Spurr (1986), 145.   [38] K. D. White (1984), 128–9; S. Martin (1990), 313–14.
[39] Garnsey (1976b), 16–17.

Climate and soil fertility

The idea of equal access to the market from all parts of the hinterland is not the only unrealistic assumption in the Isolated State. Variations in soil fertility and other environmental factors are of immense importance in determining the success and profitability of agriculture; Ricardo derived his theory of economic rent from study of the effects of differences in soil fertility.[40] The optimum land-use type and combination of inputs will differ for different types and qualities of land: at the same distance from the market, it will be profitable to grow a particular crop on some land and not on others. This may be true of adjacent farms, or even of different fields within the same farm. Thus it is unlikely that there will be complete homogeneity within a region, either of crop types or of intensity of cultivation, and particularly favourable conditions may permit the production of some crops at a greater distance from the market than von Thünen's theory would indicate.

Rising demand encourages the cultivation of more marginal lands when the supply of the best land is inelastic. For example, the area within which horticulture is profitable is strictly limited by the speed of transport; around a large city, all but the poorest land will be turned over to intensive cultivation. The growth of the market therefore tends to increase the homogeneity of land use types in particular zones, as well as leading to the extension of those zones. Further from the city, marginal land may be left unexploited – or, to be more exact, left for less intensive exploitation, like hunting or pig-keeping. In general, however, variations in fertility and in the availability of resources like water mean that we can expect to find a variety of farming systems in most regions of Italy.

The climate and terrain of Italy are often classified as 'Mediterranean', permitting generalisation about the types of farming systems appropriate to such an environment, both in the Mediterranean itself and in regions with a similar geography like California or Chile.[41] In very broad terms – in comparing 'the Mediterranean' with 'north-west Europe', for example – there is some truth in such a category, but it serves to conceal a great deal of variation; not only between Italy and other Mediterranean countries (and still more southern California) but also within Italy itself. The mirage of a uniform climatic regime and farming system is particularly unhelpful for a discussion of the effects of Rome's demands on different parts of the peninsula.[42]

One basic distinction is that between mountains, hills and plains.[43] Less than a quarter of Italy lies below 300m or can be described as

[40] Ricardo (1951).   [41] Semple (1932), 83–101; Grigg (1974), 123–51.
[42] Spurr (1986), 4, 18.   [43] Braudel (1972), 25–85; Delano Smith (1979), 159–60.

'plain', and most of it is in the Po Valley. Plains were often prone to drainage problems and malaria, and their alluvial soils were sometimes too heavy to be cultivated with animal-drawn ploughs. Meanwhile, large areas of the peninsula lie above the limit of cultivation of olives and vines, and are inhospitable to most forms of arable cultivation. The classic Mediterranean farming system is largely confined to a narrow strip of land, consisting for the most part of low hills, between the mountains and the sea.

The picture is still more complicated; climate and geology both show considerable variation, and interact with one another to affect farming conditions. Humidity in the peninsula is strongly affected by relief, due to its origin in complicated movements of air pressure in winter and summer; thus not only is the north wetter than the south, but the west receives more rain than the east.[44] Rainfall over the peninsula (the Po Valley and the Alps have very different climatic patterns) is very seasonal in character; in the south, most rain falls in the winter, while further north it tends to produce autumn and spring maxima.[45] Rain generally falls in short, heavy showers, punctuating long periods of sunshine and evaporation, a pattern which tends to accelerate the erosion of certain soils.

The geology of Italy is similarly complex, with the quality of soils in different regions deriving not only from the character of the parent rock but also from the effects of cultivation, the level of forestation and the degree of erosion.[46] On the basis of physical features and climate, Walker distinguishes six distinct regions in central Italy and five in the south, each with its own peculiar geography.[47] However, he also stresses the degree of variation within these regions; especially, but not solely, the distinction in terms of soil, climate and forms of cultivation between hills, mountains, and valleys or plains.

It is clear that some regions of Italy were in a better position to respond to the demands of Rome than others; further, that different regions would respond in different ways. The distinction between the predominantly arable lowlands and the predominantly pastoral highlands is most obvious; the latter might grow cereals for their own consumption, but in supplying the city both location and environment would encourage specialisation in animal products. In the lowland areas, some soils seem to be particularly favourable to cereal cultivation (Spurr highlights Etruria, Campania and Apulia), others to vines (for example, on the Alban hills today they amount to a virtual monoculture).[48]

[44] Walker (1967), 51–62.   [45] Spurr (1986), 18–22.
[46] Walker (1967), 70–92; Cornell and Matthews (1982), 16; Spurr (1986), 1–10.
[47] Walker (1967), 95–229.   [48] Spurr (1986), 8; Walker (1967), 176.

Other markets

The city of Rome was not the only market for agricultural produce in Italy. Italy experienced a notable increase in urbanisation from the first century B.C.; few of these towns could rely on imported grain, and their demands for other goods were also generally met locally. These demands will have affected patterns of land use in their territories in the same way, albeit on a much smaller scale, as those of the city of Rome; intensive cultivation immediately outside the town (or even within it, as at Pompeii), followed by arable farming, and grazing up in the hills.[49] Within the zones of cultivation centred on the capital, therefore, we may expect to find pockets of more intensive farming, oriented towards local markets. In some cases, local demand might be sufficient to absorb the entire agricultural surplus of the region. Most areas of Italy were not so highly urbanised, but in certain regions – Campania and the Po Valley, especially – the pull of the local market must be kept in mind when considering the changing patterns of land use and settlement.

There were also markets for Italian produce outside the peninsula. This export trade has at times been over-emphasised in the history of Italian agriculture, but it should not be ignored altogether. Wine from the Tyrrhenian coast was shipped in considerable quantities to Gaul, and wine from Apulia and the Adriatic exported to the eastern Mediterranean. In particular, there is the large and profitable market represented by the demands of the Roman legions for food, textiles and other goods; the vagaries of the climate meant that it could be dangerous to rely on local supplies even for staples like grain.[50] Campanian wine amphorae have been found on the northern frontiers of the empire, while the Po Valley was in a position to supply troops stationed on the Rhine and the Danube.

Economic rationality

Traditional economic theory relating to land use is based on very specific assumptions regarding the behaviour of the decision-maker and the conditions under which he operates. Man is assumed to have complete information related to a decision (all prices, pay-offs, etc.), to be able to compare all inputs and outcomes on some preference scale of values (e.g. price), to be capable of any calculations necessary to determine an optimum decision, to optimize some objective (e.g. maximize income), and to be capable of carrying out the decision.[51]

---

[49] On gardens in Pompeii, see Jashemski (1979).
[50] Whittaker (1994), 99–113; cf. Cornell (1995); Middleton (1983).
[51] Found (1971), 124.

It is perfectly possible to query the validity of any of these assumptions for the modern industrial-capitalist economy, let alone for the pre-industrial Roman empire. Economic theory, as has already been noted, makes unrealistic assumptions for the sake of isolating and studying particular economic relationships.[52] It is necessary to consider how far these assumptions are unrealistic for the ancient world: whether they are so inappropriate as to render the entire model worthless, or, if not, how far the model should be modified to take account of them.

The assumption of complete information is clearly unrealistic. In the modern world, farmers have to make decisions a year or more in advance, based on current prices and their estimates of future trends and the weather. Various theories of behaviour have been developed to consider decision-making in such conditions of uncertainty.[53] The main finding is that in most situations a number of strategies are not only possible but equally rational; a farmer may try to maximise possible gains, or minimise possible losses, or follow other strategies with differing degrees of risk. The greater the uncertainty, the greater the tendency towards a fairly conservative strategy, aiming at income maximisation in the long term even at the expense of missing out on short-term gains.

The diffusion of information through the ancient world was obviously limited by the speed of the transport which conveyed it; it was also highly selective. News of the death of an emperor, or imperial edicts, might be expected to spread fairly quickly along the main lines of communication; in fact, the evidence suggests that even here the journey times are long and irregular, and of course greatly affected by the sailing season.[54] Less important news, spread by rumour and gossip rather than official promulgation, would certainly take longer, and we might remember Cicero's comment about 'people who live in the territory of the Sallentini or Bruttii, where they can get news scarcely three times a year'.[55] In any case, the information received from passing merchants or other travellers was unlikely to be of great economic importance. News of a famine at Rome might encourage a grain merchant to buy up stocks and ship them to the city, but news that wine prices were high in Rome would more likely be spread by the arrival of a trader looking to buy up local produce (who clearly had an interest in concealing the state of the market).

Only if high prices were seen to be a regular occurrence, an impression perhaps confirmed by signing a contract with a wine dealer, was the farmer likely to alter his cultivation strategy. The obvious exception to this is the senator or other large estate owner who spent much of the year

---

[52] Schneider (1974), 10.   [53] Found (1971), 124–37.
[54] Duncan-Jones (1990), 7–29.
[55] Cicero, *Pro S. Roscio Amerino* 132; cf. *ad Fam.* 3.7.3, 4.4.1.

at Rome itself, and who could therefore determine production strategies on the basis of more complete (though hardly perfect) information about prices. The weather meanwhile remained entirely unpredictable. Even so, the lack of complete information is no more a bar to rational decision-making in the ancient world than it is today; at most, it encourages conservatism in production strategies.

The comparison of inputs and outcomes, and the determination of optimum solutions, are related problems. Ignorance of double-entry bookkeeping in the ancient world has often been blamed for the restricted development of Roman agriculture, and cited as an example of the lack of sophistication of Roman economic thought:

Lacking the techniques by which to calculate, and then to choose among, the various options, for example the relative economic merits of growing or buying the barley for slaves and the stakes for vines; lacking the techniques by which to calculate the relative profitability, under given conditions, of one crop and another, or of agriculture and pasturage; relishing independence from the market as buyers, from reliance on others for their own necessities, the land-owners of antiquity operated by tradition, habit and rule-of-thumb.[56]

According to this view, Columella's oft-cited calculation, designed to demonstrate the profitability of viticulture, is in fact clear evidence that the Romans lacked both the conceptual tools and the technical ability to carry out such a calculation.[57]

Finley's comments cover both the mentality of Roman farmers, which will be dealt with below, and the techniques at their disposal. It is certainly true that double-entry bookkeeping was not invented until the fourteenth century, and not widely adopted for a few centuries more. Furthermore, the Romans apparently lacked certain important economic concepts: Columella's calculation takes no account of depreciation or the amortisation of capital, which are often considered central to the calculation of the profitability of an investment in modern economic theory. Certain inputs are simply not conceptualised in monetary terms. It seems unlikely that the average farmer calculated the cost of his and his family's labour; Columella may have omitted the cost of maintaining the slaves in his vineyard because it was assumed that they would work to maintain themselves.[58]

Even the detailed accounts of the Appianus estate in Egypt do not contradict the assertion that Roman landowners were incapable of calculating the productivity of their estates and comparing it with the likely returns on other investments; however, such a calculation would be of little use in an economy which lacked other investment opportunities

---

[56] Finley (1985a), 110; cf. Mickwitz (1937) and de Ste Croix (1956).
[57] Finley (1985a), 117, on Col. 3.3.8–10.   [58] Carandini (1983), 184–6.

and which placed a high social premium on the ownership of land.[59] The fact that the Romans lacked certain techniques is certainly not evidence that they were incapable of making decisions about how to run their farms. The question is whether, given an investment in land, they had the knowledge and techniques to manage their estates in a rational manner, to compare different production strategies and to choose between them. To demand a higher level of 'rationality' of the ancients is, de Neeve suggests, anachronistic: 'What [Mickwitz and Finley] have done is to choose a model which does not even apply to present-day agriculture as a whole, measure the ancient economy by it, establish that the ancient economy does not answer to the model, and conclude that the ancient economy is primitive.'[60]

The model of land-use patterns proposed in this chapter assumes that the farmer is capable of choosing between possible production strategies. This does not require double-entry bookkeeping; medieval English estates were capable of organising production quite adequately on the basis of single-entry account books.[61] Especially under the constraints of a pre-industrial economy, decisions on whether to increase production of certain crops depend on factors which would simply not appear in the accounts, such as the suitability of the land and the availability of labour. The documents of the Heroninos archive do include information which might be used to calculate the productivity of different crops, although this does not appear to have been their main purpose.[62]

Even in modern farming, it is more or less impossible to locate the intensive margin – the point at which increasing inputs ceases to be productive – with any precision, especially as it varies with fluctuations in market prices. Instead, farmers operate within a 'zone of rational action', aiming for satisfactory results in the long run (just as conditions of uncertainty tend to favour longer-term strategies).[63] Reliance on rules of thumb, tradition and experience, regarded by Finley as signs of economic primitivism, are instead valid tools in determining production strategies; Macve concludes that 'if the farmer is closely involved with day-to-day management he may well get an adequate feel for how things are going without elaborate records'.[64] In such cases, failure to consider the cost of labour in monetary terms may also be unimportant. A smallholder can take his own labour and that of his family for granted, so that his problem is simply how these resources should be deployed. The impor-

---

[59] Kehoe (1993), 483; on the Appianus estate see Rathbone (1991).
[60] de Neeve (1985), 94; cf. Foxhall (1990), 100.
[61] Macve (1985), 240, 247–52; Pleket (1993a), 341.
[62] Rathbone (1991), 369–87.   [63] de Neeve (1985), 88.
[64] Macve (1985), 252; cf. Found (1971), 138–61.

tant decision for the owner of a larger estate could be how to employ his
slaves, not whether to employ them. Knowledge of the soil and the
climate, and a basic idea of likely prices, may therefore be enough to
allow him to develop a 'rational' strategy.

Motivation

If it is accepted that Roman farmers possessed the fairly rudimentary
tools necessary to choose between production strategies, within the limits
imposed by uncertainty and incomplete information, it remains to be
considered whether they would choose to deploy these in response to
market incentives. Economic theory assumes that its actors will in
general pursue a strategy of income maximisation, and that their
behaviour will be affected by significant changes in market prices. The
primitivist/substantivist model of the ancient economy regards this
assumption as anachronistic: ancient farmers (not only peasants but also
the elite) aimed for self-sufficiency on their estates, not for income
maximisation; they were not concerned with improving productivity so
long as they received a sufficient income to satisfy their needs.[65] Estates
were managed on the basis of keeping costs to a minimum – Cato's
maxim of 'sell, don't buy' – with no idea of raising productivity by
investing capital. The elite drew a steady income from their vast estates
to support their luxurious urban lifestyles; peasant farmers pursued the
same strategy from a far more precarious position.[66]

It should be noted that neither self-sufficiency nor the minimisation of
production costs are inherently irrational from an economic point of
view – provided that they are not taken to extremes, or made into the
overriding aim of the enterprise.[67] For a farm to be able to specialise in a
single crop, a reliable source of supply of all other goods must be
available, at a reasonable price. Even if these goods can be obtained from
outside, specialisation increases the danger that a single bad harvest may
be ruinous. Given the unpredictability of the climate and the limitations
of ancient transport (hence problems in obtaining goods through the
market), self-sufficiency may be seen as a rational strategy to minimise
risk. Certainly this is implied by the younger Pliny's use of an agricultural
metaphor in describing his rhetorical technique:

On my farms I cultivate my fruit trees and fields as carefully as my vineyards, and
in the fields I sow barley, beans and other legumes, as well as far and siligo; so
when I am making a speech I scatter various arguments around like seeds in
order to reap whatever crop comes up. There are as many unforeseen hazards

[65] Finley (1985a), 108–22.   [66] *Ibid.*, 104–8.   [67] Rathbone (1991), 395.

and uncertainties to surmount in working on the minds of judges as in dealing with the problems of weather and soil.[68]

Growing a mixture of crops could also serve to ensure that workers are employed throughout the year, especially if those workers are slaves. Finally, it is possible that some landowners might aim for self-sufficiency within a group of estates, so that one grew sufficient cereals to support another specialising in viticulture. Such a redistribution of resources is found on the Appianus estate in Egypt, and a line in Varro may well imply the existence of a similar system in parts of Italy: 'For many have among their holdings some into which grain or wine or the like must be brought, and on the other hand not a few have those from which a surplus must be sent away.'[69]

The minimisation of costs can also be seen as a response to the conditions of a pre-industrial economy, where the efficacy of increased inputs of labour and capital may be fairly limited. Once an estate has been purchased and properly equipped, a strategy of maximising returns by keeping outgoings to a minimum and carefully policing the labour force may be entirely rational, even if lacking in the 'entrepreneurial spirit'.[70] As Rathbone notes, ancient landowners would normally have had little room for manoeuvre; the area over which they had most control was the organisation of production, and through the careful allocation of resources and the close supervision of the workforce (aided, of course, by the keeping of accounts), landowners could maximise revenue by raising efficiency.[71]

The ideal of self-sufficiency and the drive to minimise costs, both often quoted as evidence for the economic primitivism of the Romans, are quite compatible with the pursuit of efficient farming for the sake of profit. It still remains to be shown that Roman landowners were indeed concerned with maximising income from their estates. The younger Pliny claims to have considered buying an estate in Umbria simply because it happened to be for sale at a bargain price and was adjacent to one he already owned; he does not mention its likely profitability, or talk at any length of the possible economies of scale.[72] Against this attitude we may set the works of the agronomists, and Columella in particular, advocating serious attention to farming with the aim of increasing efficiency and maximising profit.[73] It is hardly possible, simply by quoting different literary sources, to decide which approach was more 'typical' of the Roman landowner (or whether Pliny was indeed as lackadaisical as he

[68] Pliny, *Ep.* 1.20.   [69] Rathbone (1991), 265–78; Varro, *RR* 1.16.2.
[70] Cf. Finley (1985a), 113.   [71] Rathbone (1991), 385–7.
[72] Pliny, *Ep.* 3.19.   [73] Cf. Purcell (1995).

claims – too avid a concern with money-making would hardly fit with his self-presentation in the letters).

If landowners were largely uninterested in their estates, we may expect little change in land-use patterns around the city of Rome; if they were concerned with profits and efficiency, we can expect to find changes in crop types and the organisation of production in response to the demands of the market. This question must be reconsidered as the evidence for land use in the different parts of Rome's hinterland is examined in the following chapters. The ideal – or, in the case of peasants, the necessity – of self-sufficiency would clearly affect the degree to which farming practices changed. Specialisation in a single crop seems unlikely; instead, we may expect to find zones of agricultural systems – particular combinations of crops, different levels of intensity of cultivation – rather than zones of products.[74] For example, vines may be ubiquitous in lowland areas of Italy, but their relative importance within a system of mixed cultivation, and the intensity with which they are cultivated, may be expected to vary with distance from the market.

Market institutions

Another aspect of economic theory frequently criticised by substantivists is its assumption of the existence of the free market and associated institutions.[75] Although it can be argued that the major constraint on growth in a pre-industrial economy is technological – that is, its dependence on organic sources of energy – there is little doubt that institutional factors also play an important role.[76] The extent to which market exchange can develop in a society is determined not only by the costs of production and of transporting the goods to market, and by the level of demand, but also by transaction costs: the cost of measuring the valuable attributes of what is being exchanged, and the cost of protecting rights and enforcing agreements.[77]

Small-scale local exchange can take place without sophisticated institutions; in a face-to-face society, transaction costs are low because exchange is personalised, the parties involved share a set of values and enforcement is provided by informal social mechanisms within the social group.[78] As the size and scope of exchange increases, it becomes more difficult to personalise transactions in this way. If large-scale, long-distance exchange is to develop, transaction costs must be reduced through the development of impersonal exchange, based on institutions

[74] de Neeve (1984a), 13.
[75] See, above all, Polanyi, Arensberg and Pearson (1957).
[76] North (1981), esp. 33–44.   [77] North (1990), 27–35.   [78] *Ibid.*, 36–45.

such as enforceable property rights, contract law and the means for measuring the value of goods – and on the means for enforcing agreements.[79] In the latter case, especially, the state plays an important role in facilitating exchange by constraining the behaviour of individuals.[80]

The most obvious concrete example of this is the development of money and the diffusion of Roman coinage through the Italian peninsula. Money provides a means of measuring the exchange value of commodities, a vital prerequisite for most forms of exchange.[81] The adoption of Roman coinage throughout Italy by the middle of the second century facilitated exchange by providing a common measure of value.[82] The same is true of the provision of sets of weights and measures conforming to the Roman standard in the market-places of many Italian towns, donated by local magistrates.[83]

Coinage also had a practical role as the principal means of exchange; the ancient world did not develop any form of paper money, like the bills of exchange which became important for inter-regional trade in the middle ages.[84] The fact that Roman coins became accepted in all parts of Italy served to lower transaction costs and encourage exchange, although this economic function was to a great extent an accidental consequence of the existence of coinage, which the state issued for its own (for the most part non-economic) purposes.[85] Of course, trade with the city of Rome might promote the adoption of Roman coinage as much as the adoption of coinage facilitated exchange. Monetary unification meant that bills of exchange were not necessary for the transfer of money between different regions, and the inconvenience of transporting large quantities of coin was evidently insufficient to promote the use of more flexible means of moving wealth. One reason for the lack of sophistication of Roman financial institutions could be that they were not regularly used by the elite.[86] It is possible that many of the payments made by merchants to elite landowners took place in the city itself, in which case the bulk of the coinage would be less of a problem.

Finally, there is the question of contract law and its enforcement. One consequence of the extension of Roman citizenship to the rest of Italy was the spread of the privilege of *ius commercii*, the right to make contracts which were enforceable under Roman law.[87] Transactions between citizens and non-citizens were covered only by the *ius gentium*,

[79] *Ibid.*, 46–60.   [80] North (1981), 20–32.   [81] Hodges (1988), 96–9.
[82] Crawford (1985), 70–2; Greene (1986), 48–63.   [83] Frayn (1993), 108–11.
[84] de Ligt (1993a), 103–4; cf. Braudel (1982), 112–14; Finley (1985a), 141–2.
[85] Crawford (1970); cf. Lo Cascio (1981); Howgego (1992), 16–22.
[86] Howgego (1992), 29.
[87] Sherwin-White (1973), 33; Frayn (1993), 117–19.

the law common to all people.[88] Disputes in such cases might be handled by a sympathetic magistrate by the formulaic fiction of treating both parties as citizens, but the absence of full legal protection made large-scale transactions between citizens and non-citizens highly risky for one or even both of the parties involved.[89] It seems likely that enfranchisement would be accompanied by a significant increase in the volume of trade between the area in question and the city of Rome.

For citizens, the Roman state provided the means of enforcing contracts, extracting payment and compensation and determining liability in situations not covered by the contract; a necessary framework for the development of long-distance, impersonal exchange. It was only a very basic framework. Roman contract law was flawed in certain respects, and probably rather cumbersome to use.[90] The laws on partnership and banking were rudimentary, and changed little during this period.[91] We should particularly note the extent to which the legal system, both *de iure* and *de facto*, was biased in favour of the land-owning elite.[92] Of course, the same bias against litigants of lower status and wealth can be found in most legal systems, not least those of early modern Europe; it should not obscure the fact that the Roman state, whose economic policy was not so much *laissez-faire* as non-existent, nevertheless provided the basic institutional framework necessary to support the supply network of the city of Rome. It is significant that the area of law which did see considerable development during the Principate was that involving the sale of agricultural produce and land.[93]

Availability of capital

Finally, it is necessary for the model that farmers should have the resources with which to respond to market incentives if they should wish. Wealthy landowners were in a position to purchase labour, farm equipment or animals if they felt it necessary; they could also increase the amount of land at their disposal, through purchase, leasing or (until the late second century B.C.) the illegal occupation of *ager publicus*. Their ability to do this did ultimately depend on the availability of a supply of labour, both slave and free, and on the degree of activity in the land market, but in general the land-owning elite were not restricted by lack

[88] Justinian, *Institutiones* 1.2.2; Kunkel (1973), 75–80.
[89] *Formulae ficticiae*: Kunkel (1973), 88–9.   [90] Watson (1977), 12–22.
[91] E.g. Rougé (1966), 415–35; Garnsey and Saller (1987), 54–5.
[92] Crook (1967), 92–7; Kelly (1966), 6–68; Garnsey (1970), 181–218.
[93] This will be discussed further in Chapter 7.

of capital if they wished to increase production or move towards the optimum size of estate and mixture of crops.

Smaller farmers could increase labour inputs without undue difficulty, simply by working themselves and their families harder, but their access to land and capital was much more restricted. Moreover, such investment might not in fact have helped their position. An ox, for example, is not economically viable on a small farm, since its contribution to productivity does not offset the fact that it competes directly with people for resources.[94] This problem can be exaggerated: oxen could be shared between a group of farms, permitting a small increase in productivity on each.[95] In general, however, the best option for a small farmer would be to expand his holding through purchase or leasing and also to buy an animal to help work the additional land – and this degree of expansion might well be beyond the means of most smallholders.

It should not of course be assumed that all small farmers were 'peasants', struggling barely above subsistence level on 5–iugera plots. The inscription from Ligures Baebiani relating to the Trajanic alimentary scheme provides evidence for the existence of an intermediate class of landowners, with medium-sized plots of perhaps 50–80 iugera.[96] Such landowners would presumably be in a better position to respond to the market (whether Rome or the local town) than the genuine subsistence peasant, by leasing additional land, hiring labour or using animal power (farms of this size were large enough to support both family and animals). Some tenants are known to have leased not only land but also slaves, animals and other equipment; clearly they too are in a class above the peasant smallholders.[97]

We may therefore expect a considerable degree of variation in the response of farmers to the demands of the market. Broadly speaking, the larger the surplus (that is, the proportion of production not earmarked for consumption by the farmer and his dependants), the more likely that a farmer was able and might wish to change his farming practices. The peasant smallholder – in so far as this class survived the second century B.C. at all – was unlikely to respond to any great extent.[98] Tenants, meanwhile, came in a variety of forms. Some were essentially subsistence-oriented, though the need to pay the rent might inspire them to produce for the market; others seem to operate on a grander scale – although the prevalence of short-term leases might discourage such men

---

[94] Jongman (1988a), 152–4.   [95] Lirb (1993).

[96] Garnsey and Saller (1987), 75–6.

[97] de Neeve (1984b), 15–18, 81–2; Foxhall (1990), 104–11; Pliny, *Ep.* 10.8.5; Dig. 19.2.61 *pr.*

[98] de Ligt (1990), 33–43; see Chapter 7 below for further discussion of peasant involvement in the market.

from attempting any major improvements on the farm.[99] Wealthier landowners could choose among a variety of strategies for managing their holdings, including direct exploitation, leasing a sizeable estate to a single tenant or leasing large numbers of smaller farms. In most areas of Italy, we may expect to find the persistence of a variety of farming systems, as some owners oriented production towards the market and others continued their traditional strategies.[100]

However, it is possible that, in certain regions, such a variety of forms of production could not survive; certainly the disparity between small subsistence holdings and larger, more market-oriented farms may be expected to widen over time.[101] Peasants were placed at a disadvantage in selling their surplus, since larger farms benefited from economies of scale and could afford to store produce until the price improved. At the same time, the larger landowners became more prosperous and could augment their holdings to attain an optimum size. The position of peasants, precarious enough at the best of times, might be undermined by this competition; increased demand for their land, coupled with increasing problems of subsistence, may have persuaded many of them to seek employment in the towns or the army. Their place in the countryside was taken by more slaves, by colonial settlements and, increasingly from the late second century, by tenant farmers.[102]

The phenomenon of 'capitalist' villas, and hence of these particular problems of the peasantry, was limited in area, as de Neeve makes clear with his use of von Thünen's land-use model. The extent to which peasant farms disappeared from these regions will be considered when examining the evidence for land-use patterns in different parts of Italy in subsequent chapters. Two initial points can be made. Firstly, de Neeve makes no mention of any intermediate class of farmers between the slave-run villas and the subsistence peasants; such a class might have sufficient resources to withstand competition and respond to the market. Secondly, villas and peasants were not necessarily in direct competition in selling their produce; large estates clearly had an advantage in shipping in bulk to distant markets like the city of Rome, but they might actually be less able, or less inclined, to compete in local markets.

Nevertheless, in general it is clear that certain classes in the countryside would benefit more from the demands of the city of Rome than others. Economic theory suggest that these demands might persuade some farmers to acquire more land to reach the optimum size of farm, and so changes in the numbers and sites of farms might be expected – a process

[99] Foxhall (1990), 104–11; Finley (1976), 108–9.
[100] de Neeve (1984a), 13–15.   [101] *Ibid.*, 29–35.
[102] de Neeve (1984b), 31–62, 130–42.

which must clearly involve someone losing land. The success and increasing prosperity of a number of farmers may go alongside, or even directly or indirectly cause, the impoverishment of others, just as the development of English agriculture in the sixteenth century led to the creation of a landless lower class through the spread of enclosure.

Summary

For a number of reasons, we cannot expect a neat series of concentric circles of production zones around the city of Rome. The limitations of ancient transport served to channel the city's influence in particular directions, along the coast and up the Tiber. Within these zones, too, it is improbable that we will find a single crop being grown, or a single form of production system. Variations in fertility and climate, and local demand for produce, may be as important as distance from the metropolitan market in determining the profitability of different crops. Different groups within the countryside are more capable than others of responding to the demands of the market; we may expect most change on the larger estates of elite landowners and the wealthier tenant-farmers, while the market involvement of smallholders is limited to the sale of a small surplus. The ideal of self-sufficiency, which is at least in part a response to real limitations within a pre-industrial economy, means that in any case production for the market would tend to be only a part of total production on any farm. Rather than zones of specialised production, we may expect zones of farming systems, differing in the number of farms whose production is oriented towards the market, and in the intensity of cultivation. Most importantly, we must expect the picture to change over time, in response to the growth of the city and other factors.

4   The transformation of the Roman *suburbium*

It is within the immediate hinterland of the city, the region with the best access to the urban market, that we may expect to find the most significant and visible changes in agricultural practice; a greater degree of orientation towards the market, with specialisation in a particular set of crops and more intensive cultivation. An examination of the history of this region is therefore the obvious starting point for this study.

The definition of this 'immediate hinterland' is inevitably somewhat arbitrary, and depends above all on the particular questions that are being considered.[1] It could be defined as the area characterised by a particular set of activities – the intensive horticulture which von Thünen's model predicts for land close to the urban centre – so that its expansion or contraction over time can be charted. Alternatively, a region could be defined on the basis of territorial homogeneity. The advantages of this latter approach are that it emphasises the variety of activities that may take place within the same geographical area, interacting and competing for resources. Production is not considered in isolation from consumption or from social and demographic change.

The Roman lowlands, bounded by the Monti Sabatini, Sabini and Tiburtini, the Colli Albani and the sea, can conveniently be considered as a territorial unit (Map 2).[2] Most of this area lies within 30 km of Rome, extending a little further up the valley of the Tiber; it can fairly be described as the immediate hinterland of the city. Not all parts of the region enjoy the same ease of access to Rome: the Tiber and the Anio are both perennial and navigable in their lower reaches. The region's geology consists overwhelmingly of rough tufa; small streams, most of them seasonal, have over the centuries formed this landscape into a confusion of ridges and valleys, making cross-country travel difficult. To the north-west and south-east are ranges of hills formed by volcanic activity, often containing lakes within former craters; to the north-east are the foothills of the Apennines.

---

[1]   C. A. Smith (1976), 3–7.   [2]   Walker (1967), 171–9.

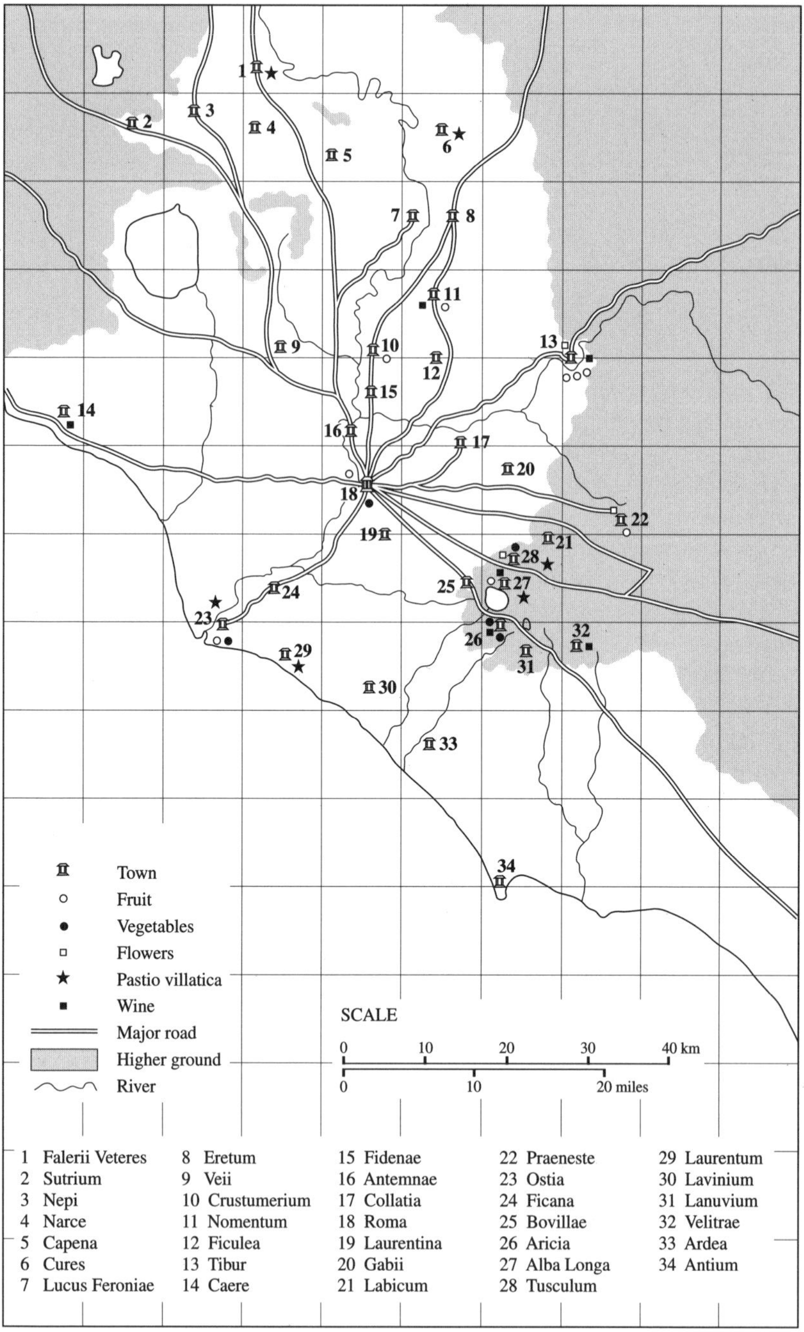
Town
Fruit
Vegetables
Flowers
Pastio villatica
Wine
Major road
Higher ground
River
SCALE
0 10 20 30 40 km
0 10 20 miles
1 Falerii Veteres
2 Sutrium
3 Nepi
4 Narce
5 Capena
6 Cures
7 Lucus Feroniae
8 Eretum
9 Veii
10 Crustumerium
11 Nomentum
12 Ficulea
13 Tibur
14 Caere
15 Fidenae
16 Antemnae
17 Collatia
18 Roma
19 Laurentina
20 Gabii
21 Labicum
22 Praeneste
23 Ostia
24 Ficana
25 Bovillae
26 Aricia
27 Alba Longa
28 Tusculum
29 Laurentum
30 Lavinium
31 Lanuvium
32 Velitrae
33 Ardea
34 Antium

Map 2 Production in the Roman *suburbium*. (For references to classical sources see Appendix on p. 107.)

Historically, the entire region was linked to Rome from a very early date. By the third century B.C. it was firmly under Roman political and military control, after the defeat of Veii (396), the dissolution of the Latin League (338) and the destruction of Falerii Veteres (241).[3] The economic effects of this domination, and above all of the drain on manpower resulting from Roman military demands, must be taken into account.[4]

The fact that Rome, with its Mediterranean empire, could draw supplies from beyond its immediate hinterland, coupled with the tradition relating to the decline of peasants in Latium and Etruria, has led some historians to regard the Roman Campagna in antiquity as neglected and deserted, analogous to the malaria-ridden wasteland of the nineteenth and early twentieth centuries.[5] Archaeological survey, and reappraisals of the literary sources, have done much to correct this picture, reviving Dionysius of Halicarnassus' portrait of a densely occupied region:

If anyone wishes to estimate the size of Rome by looking at these suburban regions he will necessarily be misled for want of a definite clue by which to determine up to what point it is still the city and where it ceases to be the city; so closely is the city connected with the country, giving the beholder the impression of a city stretching out indefinitely.[6]

The nature of the region's relationship with Rome must have been affected by the building of the Aurelian Wall in the third century, which decisively separated city from countryside, but it continued to be densely populated at least until the Gothic War.[7] The Campagna was finally abandoned only in the sixteenth century, when a combination of ravaging armies, bandits and landowners brought about a flight of peasants to the city and the spread of extensive pastoralism, which in turn led to the neglect of drainage works and the spread of malarial marshes.[8] This phenomenon was intimately related to the demands of the city for meat and of the land-owning elite for profit; the region's economy remained tied to the city, even though in this case the result was ecologically disastrous.

In earlier periods, too, the fortunes of this immediate hinterland were closely tied to the economy of Rome. Imports of foreign grain in no way reduced its economic importance for the city; instead, the *annona* freed

---

[3] W. V. Harris (1971); Clemente (1990).   [4] Brunt (1971), 345–53.
[5] Summary of earlier views in Quilici (1974b), 412–14.
[6] Dion. Hal. 4.13.4; works on the *suburbium* include Lugli (1924); Ashby (1927); Quilici (1974b) and (1979); Champlin (1982/5).
[7] Quilici (1991).
[8] Delumeau (1975), 128–56; Caroselli (1984) and (1987); Gross (1990), 153–74.

the region from the burden of having to supply Rome with staples, permitting the development of more diverse forms of agricultural production. Of course, in the vicinity of a metropolis there might be competition for land and other resources for uses other than production, but first let us consider the evidence for a particular style of cultivation in the region.

Production

According to von Thünen's model of agricultural location, high economic rents in the region near the city, based on high prices in the urban market and relatively low costs of transport, serve to promote intensive, market-oriented, specialised production of expensive perishables; fruit, certain vegetables, diary products.[9] The city is not only a market for this produce but also a source of manure, tools, labour and above all the grain and other staples that permit farmers in the suburbs to specialise in non-staple crops. Meanwhile, other forms of cultivation are pushed onto marginal land, if not forced out of the city's immediate hinterland altogether.

Evidence for land prices in the vicinity of Rome, as with Italy in general, is scanty, and somewhat contradictory.[10] That they were generally perceived as high is shown by two letters of Cicero, concerning his attempts to buy a plot of land for a grave, and by a passage in one of Seneca's letters.[11] The elder Pliny, however, remarks at one point that the price of land in all districts around the city, especially near Nomentum, was notoriously low; the only plausible explanation so far offered of this curious statement suggests that he may have been contrasting it with the price of land *within* the city.[12]

The Roman agronomists were aware of the importance of location in choosing an estate; this suggests that they would be prepared to pay more for land close to the city, and hence that the price of land in the *suburbium* would indeed be higher than elsewhere.[13] Cato's advice, that the farm should be near 'a flourishing town, or the sea, or a navigable stream, or a good and much-travelled road', is echoed by Varro and Columella.[14] If the estate is close to the city, its owner may be more inclined to visit it and keep an eye on its management.[15] Varro notes that 'farms which have nearby suitable means of transporting their products to market and convenient means of transporting thence those things

---

[9]   Cf. Carandini (1988b), 339–40.
[10]   Duncan-Jones (1982), 52 n.4; de Neeve (1985), 79.
[11]   Cicero, *Att.* 12.23.3, 13.31.4; Seneca, *Ep.* 87.7.   [12] Duncan-Jones (1982), 52 n.4.
[13]   de Neeve (1985).   [14] Cato, *Agr.* 1.3; Varro, *RR* 1.16.1–2; Col. 1.3.3.
[15]   Col. 1.1.18–20.

needed on the farm, are for that reason profitable'; Columella amplifies this by observing that access to the market increases the value of stored crops.[16] The town is a source of goods and services as well as a market; few farms can be wholly self-sufficient, and in some cases it is cheaper to rely on outside suppliers, especially in the case of specialist workers like physicians or fullers.[17]

Any farm, therefore, is likely to be profitable if it has good access to a market. The agronomists go further, recommending particular crops if the farm is close to a town:

It is especially desirable to have a plantation on a suburban farm, so that firewood and faggots may be sold, and also may be furnished for the master's use. On the same farm should be planted anything adapted to the soil, and several varieties of grapes ... Plant or graft all kinds of fruit – sparrow apples, Scantian and Quirinian quinces, also other varieties for preserving, must-apples and pomegranates.[18]

Near a town it is well to have a garden planted with all manner of vegetables, and all manner of flowers for garlands ... The suburban farm, and especially if it is the only one, should be laid out and planted as ingeniously as possible.[19]

It is profitable near a city to have gardens on a large scale; for instance, of violets and roses and many other products for which there is a demand in the city; while it would not be profitable to raise the same products on a distant farm where there is no market to which its products can be carried.[20]

This advice is remarkably close to the precepts of von Thünen; close to the market one should grow perishable goods, exploiting the land intensively. It is interesting to note that Cato recommends the production of wood; forest formed the second zone of cultivation in the original German model, but the adoption of mineral fuels during the nineteenth century made this activity unnecessary and unprofitable. The importance of wood in a pre-industrial economy, and the cost of transporting such a bulky commodity over long distances, would make it profitable to have land (probably land which could not otherwise be cultivated – Cato suggests that poplars should be planted in wet ground and on river banks) given over to plantations.[21]

As well as recommending the cultivation of certain crops, Columella suggests different marketing strategies for livestock and related products in the vicinity of a town. The farmer is advised to sell most young lambs, keeping only enough to replace his stock, and to profit from the mothers' milk; similarly, he should sell sucking-pigs and induce the sows to have more litters, whereas in more distant regions raising the stock is the only

---

[16]   *RR* 1.16.2; Col. 1.3.3.   [17]   *RR* 1.16.4; cf. *Agr.* 135.   [18]   *Agr.* 7.1.
[19]   *Agr.* 8.2.   [20]   *RR* 1.16.3.   [21]   *Agr.* 6.2 on poplars.

thing that pays.[22] Near towns, new-born chicks can be sold for high prices, or the farmer may get involved in fattening hens for market.[23] All kinds of activities, generally referred to under the heading of *pastio villatica*, such as the raising of thrushes or pigeons or the keeping of fish, were profitable only in the vicinity of Rome.[24] Varro makes this clear; having described the huge profits to be made from the sale of fieldfares, he continues: 'But to reach such a haul as that you will need a public banquet or somebody's triumph ... or the *collegia* dinners which are now so numerous that they make the price of provisions go soaring.'[25] This form of cultivation was very closely tied to the Roman market, and also, we may suppose, limited in geographical extent to the city's hinterland.

The recommendations of the agronomists for the cultivation of farms near the city can be supplemented from literary sources. In several poems, Martial gives an indication of what the ideal suburban estate was expected to produce. In *Epigrams* 3.47, Bassus is shown travelling out to his estate with a wagon full of cabbages, leeks, lettuces, beets, fieldfares, hare, sucking-pig and eggs – everything that his villa should have provided for him, but all bought from the market. In 7.31, Martial himself offers gifts of hens, eggs, figs, kids, olives and cabbages as if they came from his country place rather than from the market. Such poems contrast the ideal, productive villa with the 'elegant starvation' which was to be found on some farms, playing on the moral and ideological importance of self-sufficiency and *frugalitas* for the Roman elite.[26] Long lists of the products that a 'proper' farmer should be growing for himself can be compiled. The majority of the goods are perishables, most of them on the luxurious side; fruit, vegetables, poultry and assorted delicacies, as well as olives and wine. Grain is mentioned in two poems (3.58.51 and 12.72) as something that might be produced on the farm. However, in 6.80 Martial observes that, whereas once Egypt sent winter roses to Rome, now Rome produces roses and relies on Egypt for its grain. Not all of Rome's grain needs were met from abroad, of course, but very little was drawn from the city's immediate hinterland by this date.

Among the peculiar precepts of *Satire* 2.4, Horace notes that 'cabbage grown on dry lands is sweeter than that from suburban farms; nothing is more tasteless than a watered garden's produce'; later he suggests that 'apples from Tibur yield to the Picenian in flavour, but in look are finer'.[27] The point of the poem is obscure, but such remarks offer more evidence about the productive landscape of Rome's immediate hinterland. Crops are associated with particular places; Aricia is 'mother of

---

[22] 7.3.13, 7.9.4.   [23] 8.5.9, 8.7.   [24] Rinkewitz (1984), 13–20.
[25] *RR* 3.2.16.   [26] Cf. Martial 3.58; Goddard (1994), 88–94, 104–8.
[27] *Sat.* 2.4.15–16, 70–1.

leeks', pear varieties are named after Crustumerium and Signia and so forth.[28] Places are associated with crops – Tibur was famous for its fruit trees – and authors like Varro offer agricultural advice in the form of anecdotes which refer to actual locations in the *suburbium*. 'Doubtless you know my maternal aunt's place on the Via Salaria? Well, from the aviary alone which is in that villa, I happen to know that there were sold 5,000 fieldfares, for three denarii apiece ...'[29]

Map 2 is based on a list of such references, and from it a few observations can be made. The majority of places named in the literary sources fall within the Roman Campagna, as delineated in the first section; the main exceptions are Signia in southern Latium, just off the eastern side of the map, whence came apples; Tarquinii, further up the coast to the north-west, which was associated with various forms of *pastio villatica*; and a number of places producing vegetables like turnips and cabbages, which could survive being transported over long distances.[30] Otherwise, whenever the cultivation of fruit, vegetables and flowers and the practice of *pastio villatica* are given a concrete location, it lies within the immediate hinterland of Rome.

Of course, the fact that farmers are enjoined to plant Praenestine nuts is no guarantee that nuts were grown in any quantity at Praeneste at the time of writing; at best there is an argument from silence, since no writer bothers to remark that, despite the name, no nuts come from Praeneste itself any longer. The map is certainly not evidence for specialisation in different parts of the region. The advice of the agronomists is meant to apply to anywhere within the city's hinterland, and, while Martial's small estate happened to be at Nomentum, his presentation of the 'ideal villa' is more widely applicable. In other words, we might expect the distinctive patterns of cultivation depicted in the sources to be found in most parts of the Roman Campagna, and the paucity of references to, for example, places within South Etruria is not necessarily evidence that the region was farmed in a significantly different manner. Of course, inter-regional variation is certainly possible, as localities differed in their soils and their access to important resources.

For the moment, however, we may continue to consider production within the Roman Campagna as a whole. A clear picture emerges from the various sources; an emphasis on the profits to be made from supplying the city with specialised, perishable goods and luxury foodstuffs. The hinterland of the city is perceived as closely associated with particular patterns of land use; Livy, for example, describes a region of Greece as 'covered with many trees and gardens, as in suburban districts',

---

[28]   Col. 10.139, 5.10.11.   [29]   *RR* 3.2.15.
[30]   Col. 5.10.11 (Signia), 10.125–9 (turnips); Pliny, *HN* 8.211, 9.173 on Tarquinii.

while Pliny notes the many fruit trees in the district surrounding the city.[31]

It is more difficult to offer a chronology for this development from the literary sources, except through crude comparisons of different writers – for example, the small amount of space that Cato devotes to *pastio villatica* in the second century B.C. contrasted with the extensive account in Varro's work in the late first century.[32] Etruria and Latium cease to be mentioned as major suppliers of grain to Rome in the second century B.C., although this could easily imply a decline in their importance relative to the grain-exporting provinces rather than any absolute decline in production, displaced by more specialised cultivation.[33] The elder Pliny dates the arrival of various forms of *pastio villatica* (fishponds, enclosures for keeping snails, the fattening of peacocks for the table) to the first century B.C.; Varro considers that 'our generation' was responsible for the spread of luxurious manners of raising game and poultry.[34] Other authors date the onset of moral decline, including the development of this taste for exotic foods, to the second century; a fragment of Scipio Aemilianus' Fifth Oration suggests that in 140 B.C. the region was already intensively cultivated, with villas, game reserves and fishponds.[35]

Since the second and first centuries were the period of the great expansion of the population and wealth of Rome, these are plausible dates for the beginning of the extension of the zone supplying fruit, vegetables and luxury products to the city into the surrounding countryside. Gardens were much older than that – Pliny notes that the garden was once seen as 'a poor man's farm; the lower classes got their market supplies from a garden' – but previously, we may suppose, they had formed a halo of limited extent around the city, as seen for example in maps of papal Rome.[36] Their expansion into the countryside, and the development of increasingly luxurious and expensive products for urban consumption, were regarded as relatively novel (and somewhat dubious) phenomena.[37]

Consumption

The expansion of this zone of specialised production into the Roman *suburbium* was not a simple process. Firstly, the establishment of market-oriented gardens and estates dedicated to *pastio villatica* involved fierce competition for resources; above all for land, but also for water and for

[31] Livy 33.6.7; Pliny, *HN* 17.1.8.   [32] Rinkewitz (1984), 17–20.
[33] Grain: Garnsey (1988a), 188–91.   [34] *HN* 9.168–74, 10.45; *RR* 3.3.6–10.
[35] Edwards (1993), 176–8; Gellius, *Noct. Att.* 2.20.6; Purcell (1995), 161.
[36] Pliny, *HN* 19.52; Carandini (1988b), 346–8.   [37] *HN* 19.50–8.

access to the market. It was suggested in the last chapter that certain groups, the wealthy land-owning elite above all, had an advantage in responding to the incentives offered by the urban market, and this can indeed be seen in the development of the city's immediate hinterland. In addition, competition for resources took place not only between different groups in the countryside but also between town and country, and between different ways of exploiting those resources.

The immediate hinterland of the city was characterised by particular forms of production, but there was also a distinctive suburban form of consumption.[38] The *suburbium* was a place of *salubritas*, *otium* and *amoenitas*. It was a refuge from the heat, crowds and insanitary conditions of the city; a place of leisure, for writing, reading and conversing with one's cultivated neighbours; a place of delightful beauty.[39] From the second century B.C. onwards, the Roman elite built luxurious villas in the region, where they could enjoy these amenities. In succeeding centuries the presence of the imperial court, and Trajan's law forcing candidates for the senate to invest in Italian land, increased the number and splendour of these residences.[40]

As with production, what gave suburban forms of consumption their distinctive character was the proximity of the city. The life of leisure was a complement to political life, not an alternative; the suburban villa filled the 'very urban need' for a temporary refuge in which to restore one's energies before returning to the fray.[41] It was almost unthinkable that a member of the Roman elite should turn his back entirely on the life of the city.[42] Columella, wishing to persuade members of his class to take farming more seriously, praises the advice of the Carthaginian Mago that farmers should sell their town houses, and then continues: 'But as things are, since political ambition often calls most of us away, and even more often keeps us away when called, I consequently rate it as most advantageous to have a suburban estate, which even the busy man may easily visit every day after his business in the forum is done.'[43] The younger Pliny eulogises his villa at Laurentum because it was close enough to Rome that he could spend the night there without having to cut short his day's work.[44] When writers mention the location of properties described as suburban, they inevitably lie within easy reach of the city, especially in the east of the *suburbium* near towns like Tibur, Praeneste and Tusculum.[45]

The suburban villa was an adjunct to the political life of the capital; it

---

[38] Champlin (1982/5).   [39] *Ibid.*, 100.   [40] Pliny, *Ep.* 6.19.1; Coarelli (1986).
[41] Champlin (1982/5), 101; references include Pliny, *Ep.* 1.9, and Juvenal 3.190–231.
[42] Pliny, *Ep.* 7.3.   [43] Col. 1.1.18–20.   [44] *Ep.* 2.17.2.
[45] Champlin (1982/5), 98.

was not expected to be productive in the same way as the owner's properties elsewhere in Italy and the empire.[46] Seneca observed that someone buying an estate at Tusculum or Tibur for the sake of their health was not concerned with how long it would take to recoup the purchase price, and this might be compared with Pliny's recommendation of a piece of land that a friend of his should buy, 'sufficient land for him to enjoy without taking up too much of his time'.[47] After a particularly poor year, Pliny contrasts his unproductive estates in Tuscany and beyond the Po with his Laurentine villa, which had at least produced some writing – clearly a reversal of the usual division of productive and unproductive properties.[48]

In pursuit of the country life that they idealised, the Roman elite spent vast sums in creating a peculiarly sanitised version of the countryside.[49] The residences that they built there were at least as opulent as their town houses, with baths, gardens and fountains; they brought with them all the furniture, books, works of art and other luxuries of town life.[50] Large areas were enclosed as game parks, stocked with wild boar and deer that came to be fed at the sound of a horn; huge aviaries were constructed, 'larger buildings than whole villas once used to have'; at villas on the coast (especially those further south in Campania), expensive salt-water fishponds were constructed, costing far more than the fish in them could ever be worth.[51]

The countryside around the city of Rome became urbanised, not only in the density of settlement there and the lack of a clear boundary with the city, but in its economy. Like the city, it was a place in which the Roman elite spent the income derived from their productive estates elsewhere. This might support producers in the region – Pliny's villa at Laurentum was supplied from local farms – and gangs of builders and other artisans, but alongside the picture of specialised production outlined in the last section must be set another picture, of large areas of land turned over to residential use and park land.

Of course, the suburban villa was not necessarily utterly inimical to production. The opening chapters of the third book of Varro's agronomic treatise are devoted to a discussion of what constitutes a 'real' villa.[52] Axius argues that a true villa should be a working farm:

What has your villa [the Villa Publica, on the edge of the Campus Martius] that is like that villa which your grandfather and great-grandfather had? For it has

---

[46] Cf. Purcell (1995), 154, 162–6.   [47] Seneca, *Ben.* 4.12.3; Pliny, *Ep.* 1.24.
[48] *Ep.* 4.6.   [49] Purcell (1987b).
[50] Champlin (1982/5), 107–10; Edwards (1993), 137–49.
[51] Varro, *RR* 3.3.6–10, 3.17.2–3; cf. Horace, *Carm.* 2.15.1–5; Edwards (1993), 139–40.
[52] Discussed in Purcell (1995), 151–4.

never, as that one did, seen a cured hay harvest in the loft, or a vintage in the cellar, or a grain harvest in the bins. For the fact that a building is outside the city no more makes it a villa than the same fact makes villas of the houses of those who live outside the Porta Flumentana or in the Aemiliana.[53]

Appius, however, points to the villa of Seius near Ostia, which had neither expensive decoration nor wine presses and grain mills, and Merula tells Axius:

Why, if your place in the Rosea is to be commended for its pasturage and is rightly called a villa because cattle are fed and stabled there, for a like reason that also should have the name of villa in which a large revenue is derived from *pastio*. For if you get a revenue from flocks, what does it matter whether they are flocks of sheep or of birds?[54]

Pastio villatica is recognised as a reputable branch of farming, in which considerable profits might be made, and we may recall Varro's dictum that farming should be for profit and pleasure together.[55] A distinction may still be drawn between productive and unproductive villas:

There are two kinds of *ornithon*; one merely for pleasure, such as our friend Varro has built near Casinum, which has found many admirers, and the other for profit ... Lucullus claimed that the aviary which he built on his place near Tusculum, formed by a combination of these two, constituted a third class. Under the same roof he had an aviary and a dining-room, where he could dine luxuriously, and see some birds lying cooked on the dish and others fluttering around the windows of their prison.[56]

Having divided *pastio villatica* into three classes, the aviary, the hare warren and the fishpond, Merula observes that 'each of these classes has two stages: the earlier, which the frugality of the ancients observed, and the later, which modern luxury has now added'.[57] The contrast is at times between the properly productive and the decadently extravagant (which may nevertheless yield a profit).

The *suburbium* contained a wide variety of different types of villa. Varro's treatise covers both vast game reserves at Ostia and Tusculum and the tiny estate near Falerii that specialised in honey, as well as villas that were clearly dedicated to consumption alone.[58] Some of Martial's poems, discussed above, draw on the contrast between what a 'proper' suburban farm should produce and the reality of the owner buying his supplies in the market. Some owners chose to make their suburban properties pay, others kept them simply as places of relaxation; some took advantage of windfalls, selling birds or game if the market was good without changing the essentially consumptive nature of their estates. At

---

[53] Varro, *RR* 3.2.4–6.   [54] *RR* 3.2.10–11.   [55] *RR* 1.4.1.   [56] *RR* 3.4.3.
[57] *RR* 3.3.6.   [58] *RR* 3.13, 3.16.10–11.

times production and consumption were combined; at other times they were in fierce competition.

A further demand for land came from the city itself. As the population grew, so did the demand for living space; this might be met in part by expansion upwards, as *insulae* increased in height to accommodate more people, but it also involved expansion outwards. Open spaces like the Campus Martius were increasingly filled up with monumental buildings, and the city expanded far beyond the limits of the old Servian Wall (and even, it would appear, beyond the line later marked by the Aurelian Wall).[59] Another pressure came from the development of vast gardens, *horti*, on the immediate outskirts of the city; from the middle of the first century B.C. into the Julio-Claudian period, culminating in the building of Nero's Golden House, vast areas of the city were turned over to the landscape artists.[60] As Pliny commented: 'Nowadays indeed under the name of gardens people possess the luxury of regular farms and country houses actually within the city itself.'[61] It was once more the elite who could afford to use large tracts of expensive land in an entirely unproductive manner.

The city also had a considerable waste disposal problem; not so much with excrement, which could be flushed into the Tiber or sold to farmers – a plentiful supply of manure is essential for horticulture – but with the large numbers of dead bodies which a population of a million produced every year.[62] Under the Republic, the poor were probably cremated or disposed of anonymously in cemeteries or in burial pits like those found on the Esquiline.[63] From the first century B.C., however, 'standards of dying' were dramatically raised; whereas once commemoration with tomb or grave-marker was the prerogative of the rich, or at least comfortably-off, the practice now became diffused among the lower orders of society.[64] Naturally this added considerably to the demand for land in the vicinity of the city.

This land was expensive; only the very rich could afford to use it for entirely unproductive purposes like gardens or tombs. The elite could also indulge in benefaction, building the *columbaria*, collective tombs, in which freedmen, slaves and other dependants might hope to be interred.[65] Free citizens without links to elite *familiae* had to develop other strategies. They might obtain proper burial with the help of the *collegia*, the associations of craftsmen, tradesmen and other members of the lower

---

[59]   Stambaugh (1988), 16–75.   [60] Grimal (1943), 113–20; Purcell (1987b), 203.
[61]   *HN* 19.51.
[62]   On manure, Scobie (1986), 413–14, and Col. 10.80–7; on death, Patterson (1992).
[63]   Lanciani (1888), 65; K. Hopkins (1983a), 207–10.
[64]   Purcell (1987a), 32–5.   [65] *Ibid.*, 38–9.

orders.[66] Another solution was to use the tomb plot productively, cultivating it as a garden and making it pay for itself; the practice is well known from Alexandria, and several Roman inscriptions attest to it.[67] The streets leading out of Rome, as well as the banks of the Tiber and the Anio, were lined with tombs, each occupying a small, regular plot which was growing vegetables for the urban market. The names on the inscriptions are, according to Purcell, indistinguishable from the ordinary population of the city, who must have travelled out regularly to their tiny properties.

As with the suburban villa, production and consumption could therefore be combined; indeed, only those who owned large tracts of land elsewhere could avoid the need to exploit suburban property as intensively as possible. The Roman hinterland was occupied by a variety of properties, each heavily dependent on the presence of the city. Different groups competed for a limited amount of land and other resources, and inevitably some were unsuccessful. For a clearer picture of the changing patterns of settlement in the *suburbium*, it is necessary to turn to the evidence offered by the archaeological survey projects that have been conducted there in recent years.

Survey

Archaeological survey, with or without complementary excavation of certain sites, is the main source of evidence for settlement patterns in the ancient countryside. Surface remains, above all sherds of pottery, are collected by field-walkers; the distribution and density of these finds offer the possibility of mapping the location of human activity in the area over time. The method is particularly suited to an *Annaliste* approach to history, studying change and continuity in a region over periods of several centuries; the level of Braudelian *conjonctures*, rather than *l'histoire événementielle*.[68] The historian of the Roman *suburbium* is particularly well provided (at least in terms of quantity) with survey evidence. South Etruria was covered by the pioneering survey of the British School at Rome; the east of the region has been studied by Italian archaeologists and published in the *Forma Italiae* and *Latium Vetus* series; only the south and south-west are largely unknown territory, mainly due to the ground conditions in these areas. There is, therefore, a considerable volume of material, on the basis of which the changing

[66] *Ibid.*, 39–40; K. Hopkins (1983a), 212–14; Patterson (1992), 19–22.
[67] Purcell (1987a), 35–6; on Alexandrian tomb-gardens, see Fraser and Nicholas (1958) and Fraser (1972), I, 25–7.
[68] Bintliff (1991).

patterns of settlement and exploitation of the land in Rome's hinterland may be reconstructed. Before examining this material, however, it is necessary to consider a number of problems associated with the collection and interpretation of survey data.

Firstly, there are the problems common to all survey projects.[69] There is a growing awareness among archaeologists of the ways in which the surface remains are affected by climatic, ecological and human factors, and a continuing debate on the best sampling strategies and ideal intensity of coverage.[70] The interpretation of the surface record, the attempt to move from a map of pottery finds to a map of human activity, is equally problematic. Large, distinct concentrations of finds are identified as 'sites', but attempts then to distinguish between different sizes and types of site, or to identify them with particular kinds of rural settlement known from other sources, are fraught with difficulty.[71] Variations in the rate of pottery supply, for example, or the fact that all sites might not have equal access to the fine wares on which dating is generally based, would upset any simple reading of the data collected.[72] As Alcock notes: 'Difficulties in the interpretation of survey data must be kept in perspective: in truth, they are neither less nor more intractable than any other sources of evidence for the ancient world.'[73] There is clearly a need, however, for the careful application of what she terms 'archaeological source criticism'.

In addition, there are problems specific to the material from the Roman *suburbium*. The soil of most of the region is prone to heavy erosion; sites on top of hills and ridges are often identified by material found further down the slope, making it difficult or impossible to estimate the size of the original scatter, while sites at the bottom of valleys are too deeply buried to be visible to survey.[74] The region is now heavily cultivated, and some areas close to the city were covered by urban sprawl before they could be surveyed.[75]

Precisely because the South Etruria survey was a pioneering study, some of its practices and methodology seem primitive by modern standards. For example, understanding of the chronology of Campanian black glaze pottery has improved greatly since the survey, leading to an attempted reinterpretation of the finds which have been preserved.[76] The area was covered fairly thoroughly, and sometimes sites were revisited over several seasons, but there was no systematic strategy, and a full final

[69]   G. Barker (1991); Alcock (1993), 49–53.   [70]   Cherry (1983), 390–405.
[71]   Vallat (1991).   [72]   Millett (1991).   [73]   (1993), 53.
[74]   Potter (1979), 19–29.   [75]   E.g. Quilici and Quilici Gigli (1978), 13–21.
[76]   Liverani (1984); on the pottery, see Morel (1981).

report has yet to be published.[77] The Italian surveys are reticent about their methods of field-walking, and many of them record and date sites on the basis of remains of building material rather than pottery. Clearly there are considerable difficulties in comparing the findings of these different projects, as local variations may simply reflect differences in survey technique. The problem is compounded by the variety of definitions and classifications of 'sites', often involving the subjective decision of the archaeologist about the context of the finds.[78] Finally, several of the studies place excessive emphasis on fitting the archaeological record into the narrative framework offered by the Roman historians, so that an apparent depopulation of the countryside, datable to within one or two centuries, is immediately linked to a particular battle.[79]

For all these problems, however, survey offers a unique insight into the changing patterns of rural settlement in the immediate hinterland of the city of Rome, which can be set against the picture of production and consumption derived from the literary sources. Rather than attempt to summarise the whole of the archaeological record in this chapter, certain broad trends in the data from published surveys will be described, some of which are common to the whole region and some of which appear to be more limited in extent.[80]

By the early Principate, all areas of the *suburbium* were densely settled. There is, of course, no guarantee that all the 'sites' which include diagnostic material dating to this period were occupied simultaneously throughout these centuries, but a comparison with maps of pottery finds for earlier periods shows that this was the phase of maximum occupation of the land. Sites were dispersed throughout the region rather than concentrated around urban centres. In South Etruria there was an apparent decrease in the density of settlement with distance from the city, which fits neatly with von Thünen's model predicting decreasing intensity of exploitation of the land. Even in the north, however, the countryside was occupied to an unprecedented degree, with sites on the most marginal land and new territory being opened up in the area around Sutri.

During the Republic there was much wider variation between different

---

[77] Potter (1979), 10–14; Mattingly (1993), 359 n.3.   [78] Cf. Liverani (1984), 47–8.

[79] E.g. Quilici and Quilici Gigli (1980), 290–2; Muzzioli (1980), 38–9.

[80] The South Etruria survey is summarised in Potter (1979), 93–137, drawing on G. D. B. Jones (1962) and (1963), Ward-Perkins, Kahane and Murray-Threipland (1968), Kahane and Ward-Perkins (1972), Hemphill (1975) and Kahane (1977). For Collatia, Quilici (1974a), especially 33–55; Antemnae, Quilici and Quilici Gigli (1978), 153–68; Crustumerium, Quilici and Quilici Gigli (1980), 273–304; Fidenae, Quilici and Quilici Gigli (1986), 361–436; Cures, Muzzioli (1980), 37–46; Tibur, Mari (1983), 33–9 and (1991), 29–47; the eastern *suburbium*, Musco and Zaccagni (1985).

parts of the region. In the first place, different areas had different settlement patterns before the Roman expansion in the fourth century; the clearest example is the contrast between the dispersed settlement of the pre-Roman Ager Veientanus and the more nucleated pattern in the north of the region.[81] Two-thirds of the sites around Veii continued to be occupied into the third century; the north saw a large increase in rural settlement as urban populations were dispersed, and massive discontinuity around Falerii Veteres, destroyed by the Romans in 241 and refounded several miles to the west.

At Crustumerium, Fidenae and Collatia the number of rural sites declined dramatically over the fourth and third centuries; urban centres contracted during the same period. Collatia began to recover in the late third century; nucleated settlements continued to decline, but the number of rural sites increased noticeably, especially along the main roads leading to Rome, and this continued into the first century A.D. At Crustumerium and Fidenae the recovery was delayed until the late second and first centuries B.C.; again, large numbers of new sites appeared in the countryside while the old urban centres were more or less abandoned. Most of these new buildings occupied entirely virgin sites; the impression is given of a complete reconstruction of the countryside, involving an entirely new population.

At Cures, at Tibur and in the eastern *suburbium* the initial impression, and the interpretation offered by the archaeologists, is one of continuity, with a gradual intensification and dispersal of settlement from the fourth century onwards. This picture may be misleading. The chronology of these surveys is based on architectural features rather than pottery; they record only large sites which have building remains, which might be less susceptible to disruption than smaller properties; finally, they often assume that republican sites are concealed beneath the remains of imperial villas, without adducing direct evidence for this.

A similar degree of continuity of settlement was claimed for South Etruria in the original publications, but this was based on a limited knowledge of the chronology of Campanian black glaze pottery, the basic diagnostic material for the mid-late Republic. According to Liverani's re-examination of the material collected, only 20 per cent of the sherds date to the second or first centuries.[82] He argues that this represents an economic and demographic crisis; Potter suggests instead an extreme conservatism of taste.[83] An additional possibility may be suggested by Millett's comments about the importance of changes in the rate of supply of pottery in determining the visibility of sites.[84] Many of

[81]   Potter (1991).   [82]   (1984).   [83]   Potter (1979), 95–6.   [84]   Millett (1991).

the sites which vanish from the map in the second century reappear later, which may be an indication that poverty rather than complete abandonment explains this gap in the archaeological record. As Potter suggests, selective excavation may shed more light on the problem.[85]

Before examining possible explanations of these patterns of change and continuity, the changing sizes and natures of sites may be considered. As has already been suggested, the relationship between the size of a scatter of artefacts and the subsurface remains that gave rise to this scatter is not as simple as was once supposed. Another problem arises from the fact that, in all the surveys considered here, the results are presented already within a system of classification and interpretation. The evidence is rarely available with which to attempt a reclassification, especially since the identification of a site as a 'villa' often involves subjective and unspecified considerations of its context.[86] This makes comparison of different surveys on the basis of the numbers of 'villas' found in each area more or less pointless; the only productive approach is to compare processes, such as changes in the sizes or features of sites.

A further caveat in interpreting the results of even a single survey is suggested by Rathbone: 'Have we been railroaded by the tradition deriving from Gracchan propaganda into making our basic distinction between 'small' and 'large' sites which we can neatly identify with the peasant smallholdings and villa-estates which that tradition makes us want to find?'[87] Certainly this tendency is found in both the South Etruria survey – the smallest size category, interpreted as representing sheds or shepherds' huts, is ignored on the maps, which are used to demonstrate the continuing vitality of the peasant farm – and the attempted reinterpretation by Celuzza and Regoli.[88] The use of the word 'villa' for the largest category of site, while it may be convenient, nevertheless brings with it a great deal of baggage, implying the existence of a uniform 'mode of production' which is the same in the *suburbium* as it is on the coastal plain of Cosa. An absolute distinction between the *villa rustica* and the *villa urbana*, as found for example in the Tibur volumes of the *Forma Italiae*, is equally unhelpful – and entirely inaccurate, as Varro's discussion of the wide variety of types of suburban villa demonstrates.

'Surely what we should expect to find is a wide variety in size and type of farm, and this is precisely what emerges from the evidence of excavations.'[89] The sites known from the *suburbium* support this assertion. Within South Etruria they range from the simple building at Monte

---

[85] (1991), 199–200.   [86] Celuzza and Regoli (1982), 54–9; Liverani (1984), 47–8.
[87] (1993), 19.   [88] Potter (1979), 135; Celuzza and Regoli (1982), 59–60.
[89] Rathbone (1993), 19; see generally Rossiter (1978).

Forco, interpreted as a veteran settlement, to the luxurious villa of the Volusii near Lucus Feroniae, which still incorporated a working farm.[90] A similar degree of variation in size and luxuriousness is found elsewhere in the region.[91]

Site 11 on the Via Gabina, to the east of Rome, is probably the structure about which most is known.[92] This developed from a simple farm building in the third century B.C. to a substantial farmhouse with walled *hortus* and modestly elegant decoration at the end of the century. It continued in occupation into the early Principate, when it was converted into a proper *domus* with atrium, marble floors and a bath suite. Shortly after the Hadrianic period it reverted to a mixed residence and farm, now fitted with oil-pressing equipment. In other words, sites can change in character over time, an important lesson when the size of a site is often estimated from the extent of a scatter of pottery deriving from all periods of its existence. The villa at Crocicchie on the Via Clodia also changed in character over several centuries, with new buildings (including a bath house) added to a simple rectangular farmhouse of the early Principate.[93]

Bearing this in mind, we may turn again to the survey evidence, considering changes in each area in turn. In South Etruria, as noted above, many of the same sites were occupied in both Republic and Principate, whether this involves a break in the second century B.C., a decline in prosperity or changing tastes in pottery. From the first century B.C., and above all in the first century A.D., larger sites appeared, associated with the remains of bath houses, marble decoration and a general increase in the quality of finds. These 'villas' did not displace smaller sites; rather, their appearance is part of the intensification of settlement in the region. Their frequency declines with distance from Rome; they constitute a third of sites in the Ager Veientanus, about a fifth in the Ager Faliscus and just over a tenth in the region of Sutri. The sites are often associated with access roads, linking them to the main roads leading to the capital and presumably built at the owner's expense, as one bridge is known to have been.[94]

In both Crustumerium and Fidenae, larger and smaller sites appeared together from the end of the second century B.C. With a few exceptions, the large sites are interpreted as 'working farms' rather than residential villas, lacking lavish decoration but still featuring hydraulic works, bath houses and mosaic tesserae. Generally they occupied entirely new sites, with good access to the main roads, while the smaller sites tended to be

[90]   G. D. B. Jones (1963), 147–58; Potter (1980), 74.
[91]   Lugli (1930); Quilici (1976), 267–74.   [92]   Widrig (1980).
[93]   Potter and Dunbabin (1979).   [94]   Potter (1979), 108.

located further into the countryside. In Collatia and the eastern *sub-urbium* the 'villa' arrived in the second century, with the larger and better appointed sites occupying positions with the best access and views. In Tibur their numbers increased from the first century onwards; the fate of smaller sites is unknown, since the survey is based on surviving architectural remains alone. Even in this region, most of the sites may be described as *villae rusticae*, working farms; the great residential villas are found in a relatively small area close to Tibur itself.

Whether or not we regard this phenomenon as the arrival of the villa, there was a change in both the size and the features (building remains, decoration, quality of finds) of sites over the period between the second century B.C. and the first century A.D. The precise dating is uncertain: although the literary tradition dates the villa phenomenon to the second century, Settefinestre and other Cosan villas were found to date from the middle of the first century, and several suburban villas are also known to have been built around the Sullan period.[95]

Archaeology offers no evidence as to the identity of the owners of these villas or of the smaller sites, nor can it identify the status of the men who worked them; even on an excavated site, slaves look much the same as free but dependent labourers.[96] Thus the 'large farms' in South Etruria have been interpreted both as free smallholdings and as tenant farms dependent on the villas. We are left with scattered literary references, and the evidence of epigraphy. Cicero claimed that 'the whole district of Praeneste is owned by a few individuals', and observed that few of the great landowners of Tusculum were natives of the area.[97] Brunt takes this to mean that the region was occupied by great estates worked by slaves; against this there is the epigraphic evidence from Tibur, which attests to the presence of senators and equestrians but consists overwhelmingly of freedmen, members of the local elite and ordinary citizens.[98] A similar pattern is found in inscriptions from Collatia.[99]

There is no problem in reconciling these pieces of evidence if it is assumed that most occupiers of the land were tenants. In so far as members of the elite acquired large tracts of suburban land, tenancy would appear to be the most attractive way of exploiting their holdings.[100] The classic Catonian villa was hardly the most suitable way of exploiting land so close to the city; the demands of the market and high price of land would favour smaller, more intensive farms, while the

[95] Carandini, ed. (1985b); Arias (1939); Stefani (1944–5).   [96] Purcell (1988), 197.
[97] Cicero, *Leg. Ag.* 2.78; *Planc.* 21.   [98] Brunt (1971), 345–50; Mari (1991), 44–7.
[99] Quilici (1974a), 45–55.
[100] Cf. de Neeve (1984b), 92–3, 106–8, 127, who argues that tenancy was attractive only in extensive farming.

variety of tasks and skills involved in horticulture would make it less suited to the widespread use of slave labour.[101] Doubtless some farmers had slaves, working alongside them in the fields, but there seems limited scope in the *suburbium* for the chain-gangs of the wine-producing villa.

It is also difficult to draw much from the material remains about the type of farming undertaken at these sites. Fragments of grain mills are found in South Etruria; the remains of wine or oil presses in South Etruria, Tibur and the eastern *suburbium*; the traces of an irrigation system, which might be related to horticulture, in Crustumerium. Activities like horticulture and *pastio villatica*, prevalent in the sources, would leave few obvious traces for the archaeologist to identify, although the remains of fishponds and dormouse hutches have been found.[102]

Three main stages, therefore, can be identified in the development of the landscape of this region over the period in question. The first is related to the impact of Roman expansion between the fifth and third centuries B.C. Some parts of the region, like the Ager Veientanus and the area around Cures, show little sign of disruption. In the Ager Faliscus, Crustumerium, Fidenae and Collatia there was a dramatic decline both in the number of rural sites and in the size of the main urban centre (in the case of Falerii Veteres, of course, complete destruction). The most plausible explanation of this decline is that it was due to a combination of factors: the immediate effects of military conquest, involving the forcible reduction of some towns; continuing military activity leading to the disruption of farming and other economic activity; a tendency to respond to unsettled rural conditions by moving to more nucleated settlement (as happened in Collatia) or to the city of Rome itself.

The second phase centres around the second century. In Crustumerium and Fidenae the decline in rural sites continued and even accelerated, while areas of South Etruria which had previously escaped disruption now experienced considerable impoverishment, if not actual depopulation. Once again we are faced with the various theories on the agrarian crisis of post-Hannibalic Italy and the decline of the peasantry. The idea that rural depopulation (the *Italiae solitudo* of the sources) is directly attributable to the ravages of Hannibal's army has been convincingly demolished by Brunt, partly on the grounds of probability and partly for the simple reason that South Etruria escaped such ravages entirely while Latium escaped fairly lightly.[103] The theory that peasants were expropriated from their land to make way for slave villas can be queried in general terms: there is a considerable gap between the onset of the 'crisis' and the arrival of the villas, in both the Ager Cosanus and most parts of

---

[101] The advantages and disadvantages of slave labour are discussed in the next chapter.
[102] References in Purcell (1995), 174 n.17.   [103] Brunt (1971), 269–77.

the *suburbium*; villas and peasant farms are by no means exclusive; a free population survived in the countryside, to provide both casual labour for the villas and migrants for the city of Rome.[104]

Rathbone suggests that the unprecedented demands on manpower of the unrelenting military activity of the previous century was a sufficient explanation of demographic decline among the *assidui*, if one assumes a 7 per cent casualty rate and a 25 per cent chance that the death of the man would lead to the abandonment of the holding. The Hannibalic War, with still greater levels of casualties, would simply be the final straw, and recovery could take a long time. To this may be added the possibility of migration to the city of Rome, which began its great expansion in this period. Residents of the *suburbium* were in an excellent position to make the move, and what might have begun as a response to unsettled conditions may have continued as the newly resurgent city offered more attractions to the peasantry than a still convalescent countryside.[105]

The third phase is one of recovery and increasing prosperity. It began as early as the second century in Collatia, Tibur, Cures and the eastern *suburbium*; settlement became more dispersed, larger and better appointed sites appeared (often lacking continuity with earlier periods, suggesting that they represent the arrival of a new population), and the overall quality and quantity of finds increase. The process was delayed until the end of the second century in Crustumerium and Fidenae, and until the middle of the first century in South Etruria. It culminated in the first and second centuries A.D. with the intensive settlement and exploitation of all parts of the region.

The driving force behind this recovery must have been the growth of the city of Rome and its demands for goods which could be supplied only from its immediate hinterland. Inseparable from this development was the arrival of a class of wealthy landowners, beneficiaries of Rome's successes, whose expenditure in the capital supported the expansion of the urban market, and who had the money to invest in suburban properties for relaxation and profit. Two other factors which may have contributed to the process should also be mentioned: the settlement of veterans in some areas in the first century B.C. and the expenditures of those made rich through the Sullan proscriptions.

Water

The city of Rome depended on its immediate hinterland for supplies of various foodstuffs and other goods like wood and building materials. It

[104] Rathbone (1981); Garnsey (1980b).
[105] Cf. Livy 25.1.8, 26.35.5; Brunt (1971), 272.

obtained these in a number of ways; by market exchange, as rent taken by landowners, and by owners moving supplies between their suburban and urban properties. The result was the intensive exploitation of the region, and increasing prosperity. The city sometimes added to the pressure on the supply of land by using it for building and burials, but in general the relationship may be said to be one of mutual advantage.

In the case of another important resource, however, city and country were in direct competition. Water was an essential feature of civilised existence for the Romans, and the city daily consumed vast quantities for drinking, washing and recreation, in baths, fountains and private houses. It was also in great demand in the *suburbium*. Vegetables, fruit trees and flowers all require irrigation, and Varro recommends that aviaries, even those for non-aquatic birds, should have a regular water supply.[106] Running water also had an important place in the residential part of the suburban villa, with bath houses, fountains and ornamental gardens.[107] Given the normal pattern of rainfall in the region, water was in short supply for much of the year; the Tiber and the Anio were perennial rivers, but most watercourses were seasonal, and there was a limited number of perennial springs.

The city's response to this situation was to take what it required and to introduce laws to protect its supplies. Perennial springs were tapped and the water transported to Rome in aqueducts, which were built on land obtained through forced purchase and subject to strict regulation – as were estates adjacent to the course of the channel.[108] In a single case, the water of a spring near Tusculum was restored to the use of local proprietors, after being tapped illegally by the *aquarii*.[109] We may surmise that other areas were not treated so generously; for example, four of the greatest aqueducts were supplied from springs which had previously fed into the Anio, doubtless to the detriment of users at Tibur and other places along the course of the river.

Frontinus, *curator aquarum* under Nerva and Trajan, regarded his duties as concerning 'not merely the convenience, but the health and even the safety of the city', 'that the public fountains may deliver water as continuously as possible for the use of the people'.[110] His priority, as well as that of the aqueduct builders and the emperor, was the urban supply.[111] Most of his comments about what goes on in the countryside are about abuses which threatened to disrupt this supply; illegal tapping of the conduits, damage to the channels and refusal to allow workmen onto the land.[112] The elder Pliny also objected to the appropriation of

[106] Col. 10.23–6; Pliny, *HN* 19.20, 19.60; Varro, *RR* 3.5.2; Hodge (1992), 246–7.
[107] Purcell (1987b), 192–3.   [108] Frontinus, *Aq.* 127–9; Ashby (1935).
[109] *Aq.* 9.   [110] *Aq.* 9, 104.   [111] Cf. Corbier (1984).   [112] *Aq.* 65, 75, 126–9.

the city's water, so that 'private ambition and avarice diverts what should be a source of public health into villas and suburban estates'.[113] The notion that the city was in fact stealing water that properly belonged to the countryside is not considered. Frontinus states that he intends to sort out these abuses informally, by intimating to those responsible that they should seek the emperor's pardon, but he had a considerable weight of legislation behind him if required.[114] Other laws covered 'public' rivers like the Tiber (which was important not only for water but for the transportation of supplies to Rome): farmers were forbidden to change the course of such waterways, or even to take water from them to irrigate their fields if this was likely to impair navigation.[115]

Some aqueduct water was distributed in the countryside, about a third of the total capacity of the system.[116] The Aqua Alsietina was notoriously muddy and was therefore used entirely outside the city; the Anio Vetus was similarly used 'for watering the gardens, and for the meaner uses of the city itself'.[117] This distribution was made possible only by Frontinus' diligence in stopping water being taken illegally; it is the disposal of a surplus once the needs of the city have been met from the purest water, like that of the Aqua Marcia.[118] Rights to aqueduct water might be obtained either through a direct grant from the emperor – Statius received one in recognition of his poetic endeavours – or through a more formal system: 'As soon as any water rights are vacated, this is announced and entered in the records, in order that vacant water rights may be given to applicants.'[119]

Clearly the advantage in obtaining water rights lay with those who had regular contact with Rome and links with the networks of patronage and influence; in other words, the wealthy villa-owners rather than their tenants. The only place definitely known to have been supplied with aqueduct water was the luxurious villa of Manlius Vopiscus at Tibur, fed from the Aqua Marcia by a siphon under the Anio.[120] Archaeologists have found that the Anio Novus has two channels when it passes through the region of Tibur; this must have made it easier to clean, but it is also likely that one of these was a special branch line to supply properties in the area.[121] The cisterns in many Tiburnian villas seem too small to supply the needs of such complexes, suggesting that they had access to aqueduct water.[122]

In the minds of those who administered the water supply there was a clear divide between city and countryside, with the city having an

---

[113] *HN* 30.41.   [114] *Aq.* 130; Robinson (1980).   [115] *Dig.* 8.12.1.
[116] *Aq.* 78.   [117] *Aq.* 11, 92.   [118] *Aq.* 103.
[119] *Aq.* 105, 109; Statius, *Silv.* 3.1.61.   [120] Statius, *Silv.* 3.1.
[121] H. B. Evans (1993), 453.   [122] *Ibid.*, 455.

overwhelming advantage in obtaining what it required. A few privileged residents of the *suburbium* also benefited from the system; the remainder were left to assert their objections through water-stealing or vandalism, and to compete amongst themselves for the water that remained after the city had drunk its fill. This competition, for both productive and leisure uses of water, must have been fierce, especially in a dry year. The Roman jurists produced a detailed set of rulings on the administration of water rights, which must reflect the likelihood of litigation in this area; the word 'rivals' derives from *rivales*, those who drew water through the same channel and who were thereby liable to come to blows.

Water rights were attached to the land rather than the owner. They could be forfeited if water was taken at the wrong time without prior arrangement, or if the right was not regularly exercised; the emphasis throughout is on continuity, that everything should be done 'as it was last summer'.[123] The main problem with this philosophy is that it assumes a constant supply of water every year; in the event of a drought, a man taking his legitimate share of water might still be depriving a neighbour of *his* rights. The legal response was that both men should be placed under an interdict.[124] The jurists also provide evidence for likely conflicts through the examples they give to illustrate points of law; for example, the man who sent slaves to prevent his neighbour from channelling water.[125] Another set of laws covered the problem of drainage and erosion, presumably as a response to the sorts of arguments that would arise following the heavy spring rains; at certain times of year, too much water could be as awkward as too little.[126]

There is evidence for the existence of more organised schemes of water distribution in the areas around Rome. Frontinus writes of the Aqua Crabra near Tusculum that 'this is the water which all the estates of the district receive in turn, dealt out to them on regular days and in regular quantities', and Cicero paid a rent to the *municipium* of Tusculum for water rights to this stream.[127] There are two inscriptions from the *suburbium* relating to the distribution of water, one showing a plan of channels and properties with the water allotted to each, the other (from Tibur) listing the times during which water might be taken from an unspecified source.[128] A comparable inscription from Numidia relating to water rights includes a preamble stating that it was set up after the traditional system of distribution had broken down and outside intervention was necessary to enforce a compromise.[129] The Italian inscriptions

[123] *Dig.* 8.3.1, 41.1.17, 43.13.1, 43.20.1, 8.6.10–18.   [124] *Dig.* 43.20.1–3.
[125] *Dig.* 8.5.18, 8.3.25, 8.6.16.   [126] Hodge (1992), 252.
[127] Frontinus, *Aq.* 9; Cicero, *Leg. Ag.* 3.2.9, *Fam.* 16.18.
[128] *CIL* VI:1261, XIV:3676.   [129] Shaw (1982), (1984).

may be the products of similar events, or they may relate to an organised scheme like that at Tusculum (the water of the aqueduct at Venafrum was also sold to farmers by the municipal authorities). It may be strongly suspected that demand for water in the *suburbium* was such that sizeable rents could be charged for its use, and carefully regulated distribution schemes were necessary to keep the peace.

Summary

The demands of Rome for perishable goods like fruit and vegetables and for luxury foodstuffs supported the development of particular forms of production in the *suburbium*, resulting in intensive exploitation of the land and in increased prosperity. This led in turn to dramatic changes in the social landscape, seen above all in the fate of urban centres in the region.[130] The fortunes of the *suburbium* became increasingly bound up with those of Rome, an orientation embodied by the roads and aqueducts which radiated out from the city and drew in people and resources from the region. The relationship between the metropolis and its immediate hinterland was not a simple one – one need only think of the conflict generated by the urban demands for water, burial space and leisure as well as for food – but it was undoubtedly intimate and enduring.

Appendix of classical sources

1.	Near Falerii	bees (*RR* 13.16.10–11).
6.	Sabine country	fieldfares (*RR* 3.2.15, 3.4.2).
10.	Crustumerium	pears (*HN* 15.53; Col. 5.10.18).
11.	Nomentum	wine (Mart. 1.105, 13.119; *HN* 14.23, 14.48; Col. 3.2.14, 3.3.3); fruit (Mart. 13.42).
13.	Tibur	fruit (*HN* 17.120; Col. 10.138); mulberries (*HN* 15.97); apples (Hor. *Sat.* 2.4.70–1); figs (*HN* 15.70; Col. 5.10.11); wood (Mart. 7.28); wine (Mart. 7.28; *HN* 14.38); flowers (Mart. 9.60).
14.	Caere	wine (Mart. 13.124).
18.	Rome	turnips (*HN* 19.77); mulberries (*HN* 15.97); figs (Ath. *Deip.* 3.75e).
22.	Praeneste	flowers (Mart. 9.60); nuts (*Agr.* 8.2; *HN* 15.90).
23.	Ostia	leeks (*HN* 19.110); mulberries (*HN* 15.97); *pastio villatica* – bees, boars etc. (*RR* 3.2.7).
26.	Aricia	leeks (Mart. 11.19; *HN* 19.110; Col. 10.139); cabbage (*HN* 19.140); wine (*HN* 17.213, 14.12).
27.	Alba	wine (*HN* 14.25, 14.64; Col. 3.2.16); almonds (*HN* 15.90); *pastio villatica* (*RR* 3.2.17).
28.	Tusculum	flowers (Mart. 9.60); onions (*HN* 19.105); wild boar (*RR* 3.3.8); birds (*RR* 3.4.3, 3.5.8).
29.	Laurentum	boar (Mart. 9.48, 10.45); *pastio villatica* (*RR* 3.13.2); winter pasture, milk and wood (Pliny, *Ep.* 2.17).
32.	Velitrae	wine (*HN* 14.65).

[130] See below, Chapter 7.

Beyond a certain distance from the market it is no longer profitable or practical to specialise in exotic, perishable foodstuffs; farms outside the immediate hinterland of the city will tend to grow the standard mixture of cereals, vines and olives. However, according to our model it is likely that many farmers in the succeeding zone will still alter their methods of cultivation in response to the demands of the market. Within a region extending up the Tiber Valley and along the Tyrrhenian coast, the price of land – at any rate the price of the most fertile land, and of land with good access to transport arteries – will be high enough to persuade farmers to intensify production, whether by increasing inputs of land, capital and labour, by introducing improved technology and techniques or by making changes in the organisation of labour.

Our most important literary sources for the development of agriculture in central Italy are once again the works of the Roman agronomists. Invaluable though these writings are, a number of problems should be noted. The treatises contain a mixture of description and prescription, and in many cases it is impossible to say how far the advice may have been followed by farmers. The way in which the agronomists illustrate their precepts with anecdotes and examples, and above all their clear awareness of the innumerable different situations which may be encountered in the field, suggest that their works are not merely theoretical or rhetorical exercises, but this may still be farming as practised by an enthusiast with the income to support his hobby. At the very least, however, the works of Cato, Varro and Columella serve to illustrate the potential of Roman agriculture, the extent to which it could develop given favourable conditions.

The agronomic textbooks are limited in their geographical scope. All three writers are concerned with Italy alone, and Cato's attention is confined to Latium and Campania. His successors are more wide-ranging (which may indicate a widening of the interests of the Roman elite), but the majority of their references to arable farming pertain to the same region of central Italy. This was certainly the main area of interest of their elite audience; not only on account of its proximity to Rome but because of its political importance and its history of colonisation, centuriation and *ager publicus*, which left them with extensive land-holdings there. It is more difficult to decide whether this marks the limit of the distribution of the particular forms of cultivation which the agronomists describe, a question which will be considered in the next chapter.

The most serious problem with using the agronomists as sources for the development of Italian agriculture is the fact that they are concerned exclusively with the estates of the rich, and above all with a particular form of estate, the villa. They have little to say about tenancy (and that exclusively from the perspective of the landlord) or about small farmers, except for moralising comments about Cincinnatus and his 4-iugera plot.[1] The archaeological evidence for the persistence of small farms during this period will be examined below, but it cannot wholly compensate for the silence of Varro and Columella on the subject. We remain ignorant of the manner in which such small- and medium-sized farms were exploited, how far production was oriented towards the market and whether new technology and techniques were adopted as a result; we can only note the existence of various possibilities, bearing in mind the earlier discussion of the availability of capital and the mentality of the small farmer.[2]

There is a tendency, based on the works of the agronomists though doing considerable injustice to their subtlety, to assume that there was such a thing as 'the villa'.[3] In the broadest possible terms, we can identify a few features common to most of the estates they describe: the 'typical' villa is a medium-sized, market-oriented enterprise using slave labour. However, the agronomists were well aware of the wide variety of different types of estate to be found in reality, and constantly emphasise the need to adapt the style of cultivation to local conditions. They offer advice which may be applicable to most estates, though their initial comments on the selection of a farm, emphasising fertility and access to the market, suggest that their recommendations may be of little use on an isolated estate with poor soils. In so far as they conceive of an ideal villa, there is no suggestion that this form of estate will be profitable anywhere (and, as Purcell suggests, the fact that the villa of Settefinestre seems to conform so closely to the model might have caused its excavators to wonder

[1]   Col. 1.7, 1 *pr.* 13.
[2]   See above, Chapter 3; on peasants generally, cf. Garnsey (1976c), J. K. Evans (1980) and Halstead (1987).
[3]   Cf. Carandini (1985a); recently, however, he has offered a more nuanced picture – (1994), 167–9.

rather than celebrate their good fortune).[4] The practice of identifying all large scatters found by field survey in any part of Italy as 'villas', assumed to be organised along the same lines as those described by the agronomists (in particular, assumed to be based on slave labour), is still more dubious.

The development of agriculture in central Italy, and above all the development of the villa and the 'slave mode of production', has received a great deal of attention in recent years. The aims of this chapter are threefold. The first is to emphasise the vitality of agriculture during this period, and its ability to respond to the incentives offered by the market. The second is to restore the demands of the city of Rome to their rightful place in the scheme of development, against an undue emphasis on the export trade as the driving force in the transformation of agriculture in this region. The third is to emphasise how complicated this process of change was, with the emergence of new forms of estate management alongside traditional methods and the persistence of a variety of types and sizes of farm. Although the evidence is in certain respects inadequate, this is the history of the development of regional economies in all their aspects, not just the development of the villa estate.

Production for the market

In von Thünen's original model of agricultural location, each zone is characterised by a particular crop. This is an unrealistic expectation for Roman Italy. An individual estate might be able to afford to specialise in a cash crop, especially if it lay near the coast and so could draw on imported staples if the local harvest failed, but in general variations in fertility, the uncertainty of the weather and the limitations and cost of transport meant that polyculture, aiming at self-sufficiency in most respects, was the most rational strategy.

This applies still more strongly at the regional level. Exclusive specialisation in wine production or arboriculture, rather than the traditional Mediterranean polyculture, is a very recent development in parts of southern France, Spain and Italy.[5] It is the product of technological developments that have permitted the production of massive agricultural surpluses and their cheap transport between regions. Most parts of England were self-sufficient in cereals until the late seventeenth century; the development of genuine regional specialisation, rather than marketed specialities, was a slow process.[6] Even in the *suburbium* of Rome, the region best placed to draw on the imports of staples into the city, literary

[4]   Purcell (1988), 196.   [5]   Grigg (1974), 141–51.
[6]   Kussmaul (1990), 98–125.

sources and material remains indicate that some farmers continued to produce their own wine, oil and grain. Outside this immediate hinterland, what varies with distance from the market is not the type of crop grown but the proportion of total production oriented towards the market, and the relative importance of certain crops within the standard mix.

The ideal estate described by the agronomists contains a variety of soil types and is devoted to polyculture.[7] Cato's olive plantation of 240 iugera also produced grain, beans, lupins, wine, wood, pork (his list of slaves includes a swineherd) and meat and wool from a flock of a hundred sheep.[8] His 100-iugera vineyard is similarly equipped for a mixture of crops, and his advice on matching crops to soils implies that any estate will be devoted to polyculture.[9] Varro's description of farm buildings, including storage space for wine, oil, beans, lupins and grain, stalls for cattle and a pond for geese and pigs, also suggests that mixed cultivation is envisaged.[10] Columella specifically recommends an estate containing a variety of soils which can be used for grain, wine, oil, wood and meadows.[11] It is possible to argue that differences between the agronomists indicate changes in attitudes or circumstances: the growing importance of animal husbandry, for example, or the need to defend viticulture against its critics.[12] The basic ideal remains the same: the medium-sized estate aiming at self-sufficiency through polyculture, perhaps concentrating on one crop for the market but selling any surpluses it produced.

The twin aims of minimising costs and maximising profits (the latter mainly achieved through the former) were essential in managing an estate. Cato advises buying a farm with a plentiful supply of labour nearby and a handy local market or easy access to transport arteries.[13] His obsession with cost-cutting is such that he recommends selling not only the surplus grain and wine but also worn-out oxen and old slaves.[14] Varro notes the importance of having a market nearby, or suitable means of transporting products from the farm; a farm is rendered more profitable if there are roads on which carts can easily be driven, or navigable rivers nearby.[15] He does modify the doctrine of self-sufficiency (or admit its impracticability), observing that one can sometimes buy farm equipment and hire specialised technical services from local towns or other estates.[16] Several times he emphasises the advantages of keeping produce until it rises in value, and praises Cato for advising that the farm

---

[7]   K. D. White (1970), 384–412; Carandini (1985a).
[8]   *Agr.* 10; but cf. Foxhall (1990), 114, on its grain storage capacity.
[9]   *Agr.* 11, 6–9.   [10]   *RR* 1.13.   [11]   1.2.3–5.
[12]   *RR* 1.8.1; Col. 3.3; K. D. White (1970), 397.
[13]   *Agr.* 1.3–5.   [14]   *Agr.* 2.5–7.   [15]   *RR* 1.16.1–3, 6.
[16]   *RR* 1.16.3–4.

should have enough storage space to make this possible.[17] He even offers an explicit philosophy of farm management:

The farmer should aim at two goals, profit and pleasure ... The profitable plays a more important role than the pleasurable; and yet for the most part the methods of cultivation which improve the aspect of the land, such as the planting of fruit and olive trees in rows, make it not only more profitable but also more saleable, and add to the value of the estate.[18]

Columella praises agriculture as the only morally and socially respectable way for a gentleman to make a living, but he is clearly concerned with its profitability, arguing that it is poor husbandry alone that is responsible for low returns from farming.[19] He too recommends a farm near the sea, a navigable river or a convenient road, because of the 'convenience for bringing in and carrying out the necessaries – a factor which increases the value of stored crops and lessens the expense of bringing things in'.[20] In discussing the farm buildings he pays particular attention to storage facilities, and in his advice to the *vilica* he offers numerous precepts on the preservation of wine, presumably looking to the profits to be made by storing produce until market prices are favourable.[21]

'Si è detto che l'economia schiavistica e la villa erano orientate verso la produzione per il mercato. Ma quale mercato?'[22] There is little indication in the writings of the agronomists of where they expected to sell their produce. Some of it was sold locally, if there was a town nearby, but there is no mention of the destination of goods shipped out by road, sea or river. It is the contention of this book that the city of Rome was the most important market for estates in central Italy; however, much recent work has emphasised the role of exports to other parts of the empire, especially to Gaul.[23]

The evidence for Italian exports is archaeological rather than literary. Wine produced on the Tyrrhenian coast between the middle of the second and late first centuries B.C. was transported in a characteristic type of amphora, the Dressel 1.[24] This had a wide distribution in Western Europe during this period, above all in Gaul; furthermore, a number of shipwrecks discovered on the south coast of France contained vast numbers of these amphorae.[25] For all the uncertainties involved in using maps of distribution, there can be no doubt that large quantities of wine

[17]   *RR* 1.22.4, 1.69.1.   [18]   *RR* 1.4.1–2.   [19]   Col. 1 *pr.*, 1.4.5–8, 3.3.
[20]   1.2.3, 1.3.3.   [21]   1.6.9–20, 12.18–28.
[22]   Pucci (1985), 20.   [23]   Panella (1981); Carandini (1989).
[24]   Peacock and Williams (1986), 86–90.
[25]   Lequément and Liou (1975); Tchernia *et al.* (1978); Parker (1992), esp. 552 fig. 8.

were exported to Gaul from central Italy over the last two centuries B.C.[26]

Few Dr. 1 amphorae have been found at Rome; in fact, few amphorae of any description dating to the republican period are known, and it is only with the development of Ostia under the Julio-Claudians that the origins of the city's imports can be studied in this way.[27] Clearly it is impossible to compare the Roman and Gallic markets on the basis of material remains; it is necessary to turn instead to speculative estimates of the levels of demand. Tchernia has made an attempt at quantifying exports to Gaul, using the size and number of known shipwrecks to produce an estimate of the average number of voyages per year over the century in which Dr. 1 amphorae were in use.[28] The total comes to around 60,000 hectolitres per annum; since the figure takes account only of known wrecks, the true amount may be more than double this, of the order of 120–150,000 hl p.a. The population of Rome in 100 B.C. was about half a million. For an average level of consumption, Purcell suggests taking the amount that Cato allocated to his slaves, about 250 litres p.a., which should be modified by giving half rations for women and children.[29] This gives a total for consumption of over 800,000 hl per annum. If the level of consumption is halved, and the estimate for the population reduced to 300,000, the figure is 250,000 hl p.a., still appreciably higher than the proposed level of exports to Gaul.

Carandini does not deny that Rome was a large consumer of wine, but his articles have continually placed the emphasis on the Gallic market; in part as a reaction against historians who deny that any large-scale inter-regional trade took place in antiquity, in part due to an over-emphasis on exports as the prime mover in economic development.[30] Trade with Gaul was certainly important, above all as a means of obtaining slaves and metals.[31] Some landowners exported their produce, and some doubtless made fortunes by doing so; it is conceivable that the Gallic market absorbed most of the wine production of a region like the Ager Cosanus and was the main influence on its development. However, as the differing levels of demand show, many more farmers sold their produce in Rome. The metropolis offered little in the way of a return cargo, but the journey was easier, prices were high and demand insatiable – on one occasion shortage of wine provoked popular disturbances.[32]

Those who emphasise the role of the export trade in the development

---

[26]   Tchernia (1983) and (1986), 74–94.
[27]   Tchernia (1986), 66–7; Hesnard (1980).
[28]   (1986), 85–7.   [29]   Purcell (1985), 13–15.   [30]   (1989), 511–14.
[31]   Diodorus Siculus 5.26.3; Tchernia (1983), 95–104.
[32]   Sue. *Aug.* 42; on prices, Duncan-Jones (1982), 364–5.

of villas in Italy also underestimate the place of crops other than vines in this type of estate. Viticulture could indeed be very profitable, although both Varro and Columella had to defend it against those who argued that the costs outweighed the returns.[33] Other estates, however, concentrated on producing olive oil or cereals, and it has yet to be suggested that these also were predominantly exported to southern Gaul. The demands of the urban market for both products was vast. Oil was used not only for cooking but for washing and lighting; estimates for consumption range between 20 and 30 litres per head per annum, while Rome at its apogee would have required over a million litres every year for lighting alone.[34]

Little is known of the containers in which oil was carried until Spanish products started to appear in Ostia in the Augustan period.[35] Oleoculture is not well suited to the labour-intensive villa, which may account for its modest position in the works of the later agronomists and the apparent triumph of provincial production under the Principate.[36] Earlier, however, Italy must have supplied the bulk of Rome's needs; Cato clearly believed in the likely profitability of olive cultivation, putting an olive yard fourth in his list of the best uses of land and describing the necessary equipment for one of 240 iugera.[37] Olives were particularly important in a system of polyculture; Columella praises them because they can be maintained with very light cultivation and respond promptly to any attention.[38]

The contribution of Italy to Rome's grain supply declined in importance as Africa and Egypt were added to the empire.[39] This need not imply any decline in production; the agronomists make it clear that cereals retained an important place in villa agriculture, and grain production was quite compatible with the use of slave labour.[40] Food crises continued to occur periodically in Rome under the Principate; if provincial suppliers could not necessarily be relied upon, Italian farmers were well placed to fill the gap. Campania remained famous for cereal cultivation into the first century A.D.[41] In earlier centuries, Campania, northern Etruria and Latium all made significant contributions to Rome's grain supplies.[42]

The villa estate prescribed and described by the agronomists produced a large surplus of cereals, wine or oil for the market; above all, for the

---

[33] *RR* 1.8; Col. 3.3.
[34] Mattingly (1988a), 33–4, and (1988b), 159–61.
[35] Hesnard (1980); Peacock and Williams (1986), 26.
[36] Mattingly (1988a).   [37] *Agr.* 1.7, 10.   [38] 5.8.
[39] Garnsey (1988a), 188–91.   [40] Spurr (1986), 133–46.
[41] Pliny, *HN* 18.109–14; Jongman (1988a), 100–5.
[42] Cf. Erdkamp (1995), 178 n.23; Appian, *BC* 1.69.

Roman market. The extent to which this type of estate dominated agriculture in Tyrrhenian Italy, and its relation to other types of farm, will be considered in later sections. First, we may consider how far the incentives offered by the market led to an intensification of production or to changes in the technology and techniques involved in cultivation.

Technology and techniques

Roman agriculture, like other sectors of the ancient economy, is generally characterised as technologically backward, especially when compared to later periods; there were few radical advances, and many of these (the water-mill, for example) were not widely adopted.[43] The explanations offered for this stagnation generally emphasise the absence of conditions which are seen as essential for innovation in the modern world; the availability of capital, a close relationship between pure science and technology, an expanding market for products, new sources of power and social self-consciousness.[44] Ancient science was prone to abstraction, divorced from – indeed, disdainful of – practical applications.[45] The climate of thought was pessimistic and backward-looking, not conducive to progress.[46] The wealthy classes, who had the wherewithal to invest in new technology, were predominantly agricultural, with a consumptive rather than productive mentality and no conception of 'productivity'.[47] Above all, the wide availability of dependent labour meant that there was no incentive to develop labour-saving devices; slavery was profitable enough on its own, and the servile status of most workers led to a general disdain for manual labour.[48]

It is certainly true that the ancient world did not experience an industrial revolution; it remained wholly dependent on organic sources of power (human and animal muscle, above all), which set strict limits on the extent to which productivity could be increased.[49] The important question is how the ancient world compares with other pre-industrial agrarian societies; and this should be assessed not in terms of the presence or absence of particular innovations (whose significance is often assumed because of their role in the development of Western Europe) but in terms of whether the existing level of technology was appropriate for its context.[50]

43   Finley (1965); Reece (1969).
44   K. D. White (1959), 82; cf. Greene (1990), 209–11.
45   Finley (1965), 32–3.   46   Reece (1969), 34–5; L. White (1980).
47   Reece (1969), 36; Finley (1965), 40.
48   Finley (1965), 43–4; Pleket (1967), 1–2.
49   Wrigley (1988), 17–30, 34–67; K. D. White (1984), 49–57.
50   Greene (1993) and (1994).

The level of technology sets limits on agricultural growth. For example, if inputs of land are to be increased, previously uncultivated land must be brought under the plough; if a certain level of technology is not available (say, tractors with caterpillar tracks), the effort required to exploit marginal land may be greater than the eventual rise in output. Similar limits are set on the productivity of labour and capital. However, it is not technology alone that sets these limits, but technology and the environment in combination. Machines and techniques are not intrinsically useful and progressive; in a different context – transplanted from northern to southern Europe, or from Europe to other parts of the world – they may be ineffective, or even detrimental.[51]

Histories of technology often lay particular stress on inventions which save time and labour; however, in a pre-industrial economy time and labour may not be conceptualised, let alone commoditised, in the same manner.[52] The extent to which it is important to economise on time and labour also varies between different agricultural regimes. For example, in northern Europe the threat of poor weather meant that the grain harvest had to be gathered in as quickly as possible, and the cost of the requisite amount of labour (under a capitalist mode of production where labour was commoditised, rather than a feudal system) provided an incentive for mechanisation. The task was usually much less urgent in countries like Italy which enjoyed a Mediterranean climate.

It is interesting to note that a Roman reaping machine is known from Gaul, where the weather and possibly a shortage of labour made it a practical investment, while the invention was not widely adopted in Italy.[53] Pliny also contrasts the mowing of hay in the two regions – in Gaul they economise on labour by using larger scythes and cutting only the longer stalks – and in the section on threshing notes that 'the size of the crops and scarcity [or cost] of labour cause various procedures to be adopted'.[54] Mechanised harvesting would be little suited to the inter-cultivation of crops, which was commonly practised in Roman agriculture, or to the irregular terrain which characterises much of Italy.[55]

One area in which speed could be important was the harvesting and processing of grapes and olives; judging the right moment for picking the crops was a fine art, and the fruit should not then be left on the ground for too long.[56] However, the picking of grapes and olives is little suited to

[51]   Alvares (1979); Busalla (1988), 207–18.
[52]   Greene (1993), 41.
[53]   Pliny, *HN* 18.296; Pleket (1967), 15; K. D. White (1970), 448–9.
[54]   *HN* 18.261, 18.300 – different manuscripts read *caritas* and *raritas*; Kolendo (1980), 155–77.
[55]   Cf. K. D. White (1970), 452.
[56]   Cato, *Agr.* 64.1; Varro, *RR* 1.54–5; Col. 11.2.67–71.

mechanisation, and the growth of specialisation of production in the north-west Mediterranean in the twentieth century was achieved without any major improvements in technology.[57] As for processing, the Roman world did in fact see improvements in the design of oil and wine presses between 150 B.C. and A.D. 50.[58] Wine presses were made more efficient with a change from ropes and levers to a screw press, an innovation which Pliny dates to 'within the last hundred years', with a further refinement 'within the last twenty'.[59] Columella talks of the superiority of the oil mill over the oil press or *trapetum*, which is the only type mentioned by Cato.[60]

As Mattingly notes: 'It is worth stressing that mills and presses are not necessary for making oil. The involvement of a press is generally an indicator of a higher form of social or economic organisation.'[61] The mill or press was a capital investment designed to increase surplus production, and it is significant that innovation did take place and was (albeit to an unknown extent) adopted in one of the few areas of agricultural production suited to it.[62] Similarly, while technological innovation in cereal agriculture in Italy was limited to the diffusion of iron tools (not necessarily an insignificant advance), there were notable improvements in the processing of grain with the development of the 'Pompeian' donkey-mill in the early second century B.C.[63]

Improvements can also be seen in techniques of cultivation and seed selection. Comparison of lists of varieties in Pliny and Columella with those in Cato and Varro points to the diffusion of a wider range of crops over this short period, especially tree crops, olives and vines, which are carefully matched to local conditions.[64] Techniques of grafting and transplanting, originally developed by the Greeks, were widely adopted and are described in detail by the agronomists.[65] They also recommend careful seed selection – albeit on the basis of maximising seed weight and yield in terms of seed sown, which would not necessarily have a positive effect on yield per unit area.[66] While these techniques may not in fact have increased the productivity of the land, they are evidence for a concern, if only on the part of the agronomists, to maximise yields. A

---

[57] Grigg (1974), 145.
[58] Kolendo (1980), 180–1; K. D. White (1984), 68–72.
[59] *HN* 18.317.
[60] Col. 12.52.6; *Agr.* 22; Drachmann (1932); Amouretti *et al.* (1984).
[61] (1988b), 157.
[62] For the archaeological evidence for mills and presses in Italy, see Rossiter (1981); cf. Frier (1979) on the uneven spread of new technology.
[63] Moritz (1958), 62–90; K. D. White (1984), 72; Greene (1990), 216.
[64] E.g. *Agr.* 6; Col. 3.1.5–7, 3.2; K. D. White (1970), 224–71.
[65] *Agr.* 40–2; Col. 4.29.
[66] *RR* 1.52; *HN* 18.195; K. D. White (1970), 188–9; Sallares (1991), 341–6.

variety of wheats and other grains was always grown; partly as a buffer against the weather, partly so as to make best use of different soils and partly because the market itself demanded variety.[67]

Columella's discussion of grape varieties offers interesting evidence of important changes in Italian viticulture since the second century B.C.[68] Cato was concerned solely with choosing the correct vine for the soil, and his advice is quoted verbatim by Varro.[69] In Columella, however, there is a new tension, between quality and quantity. His ideal is a grape that produces large quantities of first-rate wine, but he is well aware that in some regions the best choice may be a variety commended for fruitfulness alone:

A vine of this sort [producing a quality wine], though only moderately fruitful, should be our choice, if only we have a piece of ground where the flavour of the wine is distinguished and costly; for if it is of poor quality or low in price, it is better to plant the most prolific vines, so that our revenues may be increased by the greater quantity of the yield.[70]

It may be deduced that the demand for wine was such as to encourage the planting of vines on land not best suited to viticulture and to promote the cultivation of low-quality, high-yield varieties for the mass market.[71] Columella denounces this tendency to plant the worst quality land with vines, to stint on the provision of essential equipment and to work for short-term yields; his preferred approach is one of intensive cultivation, obtaining better returns in the long term.[72] It is impossible to say how far his advice may have been followed (the goal of combining quality and quantity was in fact more or less unattainable), but both tendencies in Italian viticulture are evidence for changes in practice in response to the demands of the market.[73]

The area of Roman agriculture which is most often dismissed as stagnant and primitive is cereal cultivation. This condemnation appears to be based on the fact that ancient agriculture did not develop along the same lines as the 'early medieval agricultural revolution' proposed by a number of historians.[74] White and Duby disagree on the date of this revolution (the sixth to the ninth centuries and the eighth to the twelfth respectively), but stress similar changes in systems of rotation, ploughs and the use of horses in farm labour. The key to increased production is intensification; more land is brought under cultivation each year through

---

[67] Col. 2.6; Spurr (1986), 1–22, 41–65; cf. Sallares (1991), 359, 369.
[68] Purcell (1985), 16–19.   [69] *Agr.* 6.4; *RR* 1.25.
[70] Col. 3.2.5, 3.2.19–20, 3.2.25, 3.7.2; cf. Pliny, *HN* 14.48–52.
[71] Tchernia (1986), 172–9, 197–256.   [72] Col. 3.3.
[73] On quality v. quantity, cf. Purcell (1985), 18.
[74] L. White (1962); Duby (1976); cf. Pleket (1990), 71–2.

the change from the two-field system of biennial fallow that characterised the Mediterranean to a three-field system of rotation, oats–wheat–beans. These changes permitted a large increase in population and in the volume of trade, and contributed to a shift in the focal point of European economy and society from the Mediterranean to the north-west.

There are three main objections to this picture and its low estimation of Roman agriculture.[75] Firstly, the success of the revolution, at either date, may be disputed. Adoption of the innovations was very slow: the ox remained the key agricultural animal until well into the thirteenth century, while legumes were not regularly incorporated into rotation schemes until the seventeenth.[76] It is not clear that output per head increased significantly, and the change to a three-field system may in fact have led to decreasing yields in the long term.[77] Comparison of yield ratios, while of limited value (a high yield ratio may still mean a low return per acre) suggests that Roman yields compare well with those achieved in France, Italy and Spain in the early modern period, and some particularly fertile regions may be comparable with southern England and Holland.[78] Pleket concludes that 'the early medieval growth meant a return to a "normal level" after the period of the Dark Ages, rather than an alleged agricultural revolution'.[79]

The observation that Roman agriculture was apparently quite successful despite the absence of these innovations leads to the second point, that many aspects of the revolution were simply not appropriate for agriculture in the Mediterranean environment. The changes were not confined to north-west Europe merely by chance, they were necessary only in regions with a wet climate and heavy soils. The light, ox-drawn Mediterranean plough could cope with most Italian soils, and in many cases a heavier plough might have been detrimental to the soil.[80] The heavy alluvial soils of the valley bottoms, which were not easily cultivable with light ploughs, were used for the lucrative pursuit of grazing: there was no incentive to grow cereals there.[81] Horses were not only much more expensive and difficult to feed and maintain than oxen, but were in the Roman period greatly inferior in strength: 'What mattered in the course of the development of the ecological mutualism between man and horse was not alleged innovations in harness technology, but biological evolution of the horse.'[82]

The third objection is that Roman agriculture was not, *pace* Boserup

[75]   Pleket (1993a); Greene (1994).
[76]   Langdon (1982) and (1984); Pleket (1993a), 323–4.
[77]   Grigg (1982), 177–81.
[78]   Spurr (1986), 82–8; Pleket (1993a), 327–8.   [79]   (1993a), 323.
[80]   Kolendo (1980), 57–70; Jongman (1988a), 82.   [81]   Cf. Col. 6 *pr*. 4.
[82]   Sallares (1991), 399; Langdon (1982).

and others, entirely dominated by a two-field system of biennial fallow, light ploughs and a shortage of animals. A variety of ploughs was available for different soils and different farming operations: light and heavy, sometimes with detachable plough-shares.[83] Columella explicitly recommends investing in strong oxen and heavy ploughs, since this will be repaid by higher yields.[84] There is no suggestion in the agronomists that any soils were completely unworkable: the second-best type in the eyes of Columella was the combination of rich and dense, 'which rewards the expense and toil of the husbandman with rich yields'.[85] If areas of plain were left as meadow rather than being drained and cultivated, it was because meadows were a prized asset.[86]

It is equally inaccurate to say that Italian agriculture was dominated by a system of dry-farming using two-field fallow. In the writings of the elder Pliny six different systems of crop rotation are described, with a further two in Varro.[87] The great misconception is that fallow was necessary to conserve two years' worth of moisture in the soil, a standard technique of dry-farming.[88] Italy, with the possible exception of two small areas, is not semi-arid, and therefore does not demand dry-farming techniques; the agronomists show no awareness of a need to conserve water. Rather, fallow is supposed to rest the land; if it is used as winter pasture, allowing animals to graze the weeds growing there, the soil benefits further from their manure. This was not the only option: some areas were fertile enough to be cropped every year, or could even bear several crops in a single year (Campania's famous fertility); annual cropping could also take place where there was an ample supply of manure; finally, various legumes could be grown which both restored nutrients to the soil and provided fodder for animals.[89]

These last two are linked: fodder crops provided for more animals, whose manure increased the fertility of the land. According to Spurr's calculations, which combine Columella and comparative evidence, a farmer could manure 35–42.5 per cent of an estate of 200 iugera every year from the manure produced by the draught oxen, four asses and a flock of 100 sheep.[90] This is by no means a superabundance of fertiliser, but neither is it scarcity; if both the poorest land and the continually cropped land were manured regularly, and the average land every so often, there would be little need for biennial fallow. Such a system would also support more animals, especially working animals, than is generally

[83] Spurr (1986), 28–30.   [84] Col. 2.10.24.
[85] 2.2.5; Spurr (1986), 38.   [86] E.g. Varro, *RR* 1.7.10.
[87] *HN* 18.187, 191; K. D. White (1970), 110–24; Spurr (1986), 117–22.
[88] Spurr (1986), 23–7.   [89] K. D. White (1970), 125–45.
[90] Spurr (1986), 126–32.

thought typical of Mediterranean farming. Smaller farms could support fewer animals and so had far less manure available, but even so it would be possible to intensify production to a limited extent.[91]

In short, the Roman agronomists recommend a number of techniques of cultivation and land use that permit more frequent cropping and a greater employment of animal labour. The two aspects of the medieval revolution which had no place in ancient agriculture were clover, a useful fodder crop which is not suited to the Mediterranean, and the horse, which in its stronger, evolved form was faster, if also fussier and weaker, than the ox, and therefore more adaptable to tasks other than ploughing. The picture offered of Roman agriculture by the agronomists is much more varied and sophisticated than the traditional caricature, with considerable potential for the intensification of arable cultivation.

Certainly Columella would have been surprised that Roman agriculture should be described as 'stagnant'. At the beginning of his work he observes that many of the precepts of earlier authorities were no longer relevant – 'the agricultural practice of our times is at variance with the ancient principles' – a circumstance which he tentatively attributes to environmental changes, but which may be taken as evidence for the notable development of Italian agriculture over the previous centuries.[92] The agronomists prescribe and describe (as ever, the balance is uncertain) the adoption of a number of techniques and technologies designed to increase the volume of production, the quality of the produce, the speed of processing crops and the cost of the whole process. The aim is to increase the profitability of the estate; the changes are clearly a response to the incentives offered by the market, and it was observed above that the chief market for the produce of most of these estates was the city of Rome.

Such developments were not possible on all farms. Only the wealthy could afford to invest in expensive equipment like oil and wine presses, to hold back produce from the market until the price was right or to draw upon technical and scientific knowledge rather than relying on traditional methods. This applies above all to the use of animals for power and manure. On a smallholding, labour requirements could be met from the family; an ox could raise productivity threefold, but it competed with the family for food and made their labour redundant.[93] Peasants might be able to pool resources and share an ox between a number of families, but full integration of animals and arable cultivation was possible only on estates above a certain size, which could produce a large surplus above what was needed to feed the labourers.[94]

[91] Cf. Alcock, Cherry and Davis (1994), 145–57.
[92] 1.1.3–6; cf. Kolendo (1980), 183.   [93] Jongman (1988b).
[94] On the pooling of resources, see Lirb (1993).

Organisation of labour

De Neeve characterised the Roman villa as a form of 'plantation', organised in a similar manner to estates in nineteenth- and twentieth-century colonial contexts.[95] If the comparison is valid, it has important implications. Specialisation in certain crops on a sufficiently large scale permits division and specialisation of labour on the plantation; workers can be trained in particular skills and allotted specific tasks within the production process as part of an 'industrialisation' of cultivation, resulting in greater productivity per head.[96] Careful management and supervision of the work force, co-ordinating the different sectors of the plantation, also contribute to the notable efficiency of such estates. It is worth considering how far these elements were indeed present in the estates described by the agronomists.

Some farms were large enough to support a considerable division of labour. Cato's ideal olive yard and vineyard include slaves with special responsibility for looking after different animals, and in the latter case an expert in working willow.[97] Varro envisages villas which might have spinners, weavers and other artisans, and notes that some rich men had their own smiths and physicians on distant estates.[98] A passage of the *Digest* lists workers who might be found on an estate, including gardeners, foresters, bakers, barbers and masons; however, the jurists are concerned with the kinds of workers who may be included in the *instrumentum* of an estate *besides* the men involved in cultivation, and therefore have little to say about the division of labour among the latter.[99]

Columella is aware that there are advantages in the division of labour, and stresses the need to select the right sort of men for particular tasks.[100] Admittedly, he tends to think in terms of choosing diligent and thrifty men to keep the flocks, and strong but gentle men as ploughmen. However, his lengthy discussion in Book 4 of the techniques involved in the planting, pruning and grafting of vines shows that this was a highly skilled practice. An estate which was large enough to support a number of specialist vine-dressers could well benefit from their experience. A strict division of labour also made it easier to see whether each section of the labour force was performing adequately: 'For this reason ploughmen must be distinguished from vine-dressers, and vine-dressers from ploughmen, and both of these from men of all work.'[101]

[95] (1984b), 75–82.
[96] Courtenay (1980), 36–43; Graham and Floering (1984), 7–32.
[97] *Agr.* 10–11.   [98] *RR* 1.2.21, 1.16.4.
[99] *Dig.* 33.7.8.1–2, 33.7.12.5; cf. 33.7.19.1.   [100] Col. 1.9.   [101] Col. 1.9.6.

Modern plantation agriculture is associated with a restricted range of crops, whose cultivation does not involve any major seasonal peaks; with other crops, either the labour force would not be fully employed over the whole year, or it would be unable to concentrate its efforts or skills narrowly enough to reap the benefits of specialisation.[102] In the Mediterranean, however, all crops show considerable seasonal variation in their demands for labour. The villa work force could be fully employed only through the cultivation of a range of crops peaking at different times, with additional labour hired for the harvest: full 'industrialisation' along the lines of a modern plantation is not a practical option. Columella's division of labour, between ploughmen and vine-dressers (who could be employed in those tasks for most of the year) and *mediastini*, who were used for a variety of different tasks, is eminently practical. It does mean that the likely benefits of specialisation of labour were fairly limited.

More significant is the careful management of all elements of cultivation advised by the agronomists: deciding on the mix of crops to be grown, closely monitoring income and expenditure and directing labour to ensure that all tasks are carried out properly.[103] Land and labour are each to be employed in the most effective manner and to the greatest possible extent. Comparative evidence suggests that it is possible for close supervision to serve as an alternative to the employment of skilled adaptive labour, especially in fairly mechanical tasks.[104] Labourers were deployed in groups under close supervision for various tasks in the Roman villa, above all in viticulture, and this may have led to greater efficiency.[105] However, what is arguably the most important feature of villa agriculture has as yet scarcely been mentioned; the fact that the majority of those labourers were slaves.

Although the institution of slavery is recognised as immensely important (one has only to look at the volume of material written on the subject), there is little agreement on how it actually affected Roman agriculture.[106] On the one hand, there are those who see slavery as inefficient, unprofitable and an impediment to economic and technological development.[107] On the other hand, slaves are seen as the most important technological breakthrough of antiquity; the development of the 'human tool' led to a dramatic rise in the productivity and profitability of agriculture, at least until internal contradictions and/or external pressures brought an end to the 'slave mode of

---

[102] Graham and Floering (1984), 16.   [103] *Agr.* 2; *RR* 1.23; Col. 1.8.8–11, 1.8.20.
[104] Graham and Floering (1984), 17–18.   [105] Col. 1.9.4–8.
[106] Westermann (1955); Brockmeyer (1968) and (1979); Finley (1985a), 62–94; Yavetz (1988).
[107] Štaerman (1964), 34–5, 90–1; cf. Finley (1985a), 83; Kolendo (1980), 193–200.

production'.[108] The choice of slave over free labour has been attributed to a concern for social status, rational economic considerations, the low estimation of waged labour and a shortage of any free labour which might be employed.[109]

The agronomists take slave labour entirely for granted. Columella does discuss the relative merits of tenancy and direct exploitation, concluding that the latter invariably yields a higher return but that tenants should be employed on poor land in unhealthy districts and on distant estates, especially those under cereals.[110] What is lacking is any debate on what type of labour should be employed on the estate.[111] Columella himself blames the state of Italian agriculture on the fact that the elite have handed the cultivation of estates over to the worst of their slaves – but this is a plea for greater involvement on the part of the owner, not for a change in the organisation of labour.[112] All his advice on managing the farm is concerned with slaves, and later in the work he is anxious to defend himself against the accusation that he prefers to till his fields with criminals rather than honest men.[113]

It is clear from the sources that the villa was expected to be profitable. Part of this profitability is unconnected to the form of labour employed: the owner could afford to invest in processing equipment and to store produce until the market was favourable; above all, an estate of 100 iugera worked by sixteen people produced a far greater marketable surplus (and could support more animals) than 100 iugera farmed by ten or more tenant-farmers who had to feed their families. The question remains as to why those sixteen workers should be slaves rather than free men: for reasons of status, by default (in the absence of a sufficient supply of free labour), or because slaves were more productive and their use did indeed represent a technological advance. The ancient evidence for the productivity of labour is poor, to say the least.[114] It is therefore helpful to turn to the comparative example provided by the slave plantations of the American South, and the lengthy debate in recent decades over their economic efficiency.[115]

Two points can be made immediately. The first is that slave estates were profitable, far more so than either northern farms or free farms in

---

[108] Giardina and Schiavone (1981); Carandini (1980), (1985a), (1985b); cf. Rathbone (1983) and Wickham (1988), 187–90.

[109] K. Hopkins (1978a), 99–132; Finley (1980), 67–92; de Ste Croix (1981), 133–74; Rathbone (1981).

[110] Col. 1.7; cf. Varro, *RR* 1.17.3; de Neeve (1984b), 75–117; Foxhall (1990), 100–4.

[111] And there is no reason to suppose that tenants did not themselves use slaves and cultivate the land intensively – e.g. Pliny, *Ep.* 3.19.7, *pace* de Neeve (1984b), 126, 158.

[112] Col. 1 *pr.* 3, 11–12.   [113] 1.9.5.   [114] K. D. White (1965).

[115] Cf. Yeo (1952); K. Hopkins (1978a), 99–102; Carandini (1985c).

the South.[116] The second is that it is impossible, despite the large amount of statistical evidence at the disposal of historians, to determine the precise causes of this profitability, or to measure the productivity of slave labour.[117] The profitability of the plantations was based on cotton, a cash crop for which there was a large demand in the world market; northern farms could not produce cotton at all, and southern free farms produced only marginal quantities.[118] The plantations were large enough to permit greater specialisation for the market and a basic division of labour. Any comparison of the productivity rather than the profitability of free and slave labour founders on the fact that the contexts in which they were employed were so different.

Fogel and Engerman argue that the efficiency of the plantation was based not only on its size and the advantages of specialisation but on the intensity of labour and its close supervision.[119] Slaves worked harder than free men, partly because they could be coerced with force or the threat of force, partly because they responded to incentives. Free labourers were unsuitable for plantations, because the 'nonpecuniary disadvantages' of working in gangs were too great – that is, landowners would have to pay much higher wages to attract workers into such an undignified job. Various elements of this argument have been heavily criticised, above all the image of a 'Protestant work ethic' among slaves, and the over-optimistic view of their treatment at the hands of owners.[120] However, the idea that slave labour could be more productive specifically within the context of the plantation has found support even among critics of Fogel and Engerman's *Time on the Cross*.

Force or the threat of force could compel a greater intensity of labour in relatively simple tasks like cotton-picking.[121] The slave was property, and treated as such; owners sought to maximise the return on their investment through coercion and close supervision, while providing the bare minimum of food and clothing to keep the slave healthy enough to work. Free labour simply could not be treated in the same way; in addition, there was little surplus labour available, as the great majority of poor southerners preferred the status of land-owning to wage labour. Within the context of the plantation, therefore, slave-owning was immensely profitable; however, the risk of slaves dying and the cost of replacement meant that this investment in 'human capital' had to be exploited as intensively as possible, and the enterprise was dependent on the existence of a healthy market for its products.[122]

---

[116] Fogel and Engerman (1974), I, 59–106; Ransom (1989), 41–81.
[117] David *et al.* (1976).   [118] Wright (1976), 302–36.   [119] (1974), I, 191–257.
[120] Gutman (1975); David and Temin (1976a) and (1976b).
[121] David and Temin (1976b), 202–9.   [122] Butlin (1971), 104–28; Ransom (1989), 42–7.

In Carandini's opinion, the important question is not what the slave is, but how he is employed.[123] There were slaves in Italy before the second century, and slaves were always employed in large numbers in places other than villas, but it is the combination of slaves and plantation-style agriculture that constitutes the 'slave mode of production'. The two are intimately linked: villa agriculture is inconceivable without slave labour, and the slave can achieve his full economic potential as a pre-industrial 'computer-robot' only within the context of the villa.[124]

It has already been noted that the emergence of the villa is closely linked to the events of the second century B.C.[125] The Romans captured large numbers of slaves in the course of the Hannibalic War; however, Finley argues that they did so because a demand for slaves already existed, rather than the short-term availability of slaves leading to the establishment of the villa system.[126] Far more important was the influx of wealth into Rome, which supported its expansion (and therefore the growth of a large market for food) and permitted the emergence of large estates. 'The "conquest theory" thus helps to explain the specific character of the Roman slave society, not its emergence.'[127] The fact that, as seen in the archaeological record, the emergence of villas was a lengthy process extending over several centuries adds more weight to this argument.

Finley suggests that there are three necessary conditions for the emergence of a slave society: private ownership of land, the existence of a suitable market and the absence of an internal labour supply (or a labour supply that can be exploited sufficiently).[128] He is scathing about the possibility that ancient landowners might have compared the efficiency, profitability or productivity of slave and free labour, since they lacked the conceptual tools for such a comparison.[129] Slavery was simply the only possibility, since for political reasons free citizens could not be exploited to a sufficient degree.[130] However, the extent to which free Roman citizens were exploited by the elite through their liability for military service must lead to doubts about their immunity to economic exploitation.[131] The decision to employ slaves may therefore be explained in one of two ways: an actual shortage of alternative sources of labour, or the positive advantages of slave labour.

In the course of his critique of the traditional narrative of the crisis of the second century B.C., Rathbone offers a calculation designed to demonstrate that a slave-run villa estate, specialising in viticulture but

---

[123] (1981), 249–50; cf. Spurr (1985), 123–4.   [124] Carandini (1985c), 197.
[125] Gabba (1989); K. Hopkins (1978a), 1–96.   [126] (1980), 83–6.
[127] Ibid., 84–5.   [128] Ibid., 86.   [129] Ibid., 91–2.
[130] See also K. Hopkins (1978a), 111–15.   [131] Garnsey (1980b), 2.

growing cereals to feed its work force, would produce a lower return on investment than an estate worked solely by free labour which could be devoted entirely to non-subsistence crops.[132] Slave labour is not significantly cheaper than free, and therefore its adoption in Italy must be due to the lack of a suitable free labour force (he notes earlier in the article that peasant farms disappeared from the Ager Cosanus long before the arrival of the villas) and to social factors like the status accorded to slave-owning.

Rathbone rejects outright the suggestion that slave labour might, within the context of the villa, be more productive than free labour; his figures for wine yields are therefore the same throughout. The figure chosen for the daily wage, which is taken from the rate for casual seasonal labour, may also be questioned. As Fogel and Engerman suggested for the American South, the social disadvantages of working on a plantation must be compensated for by higher wages, which would clearly affect any calculations of relative profitability. Roman sources – all from an elite perspective, of course – are convinced that wage labour involves 'slavish' dependence on an employer.[133] The jurists count free labourers among slaves: they may plead superior orders if they damage someone else's property, and they are not subject to actions for theft from their employers – which implies that instead they are liable to punishment, like slaves.[134] It is impossible to tell whether these prejudices were shared by the population at large. The steady stream of migrants seeking paid labour in the city of Rome suggests that they were not; however, it was one thing to work in the city, or on a casual basis at the harvest, and quite another to work full time as part of a gang under close supervision.

At any rate, there is little evidence that free labour was ever considered as a realistic option by the agronomists, except as a supplement to slave labour at certain seasons, and in conditions where the risk of losing slaves was too great.[135] Slaves were not liable to be called up for military service, and their employment 'freed' peasants for the army; slaves could be forced to work, perhaps resulting in a greater intensity of labour per hour, especially when employed in fairly simple tasks in closely supervised gangs, and surely resulting in a greater number of hours worked per day; finally, their ownership conferred status.[136] The little that is known of slave prices suggests that they were an expensive investment, except immediately after a battle or the conquest of new territory.[137] In an asset-pricing model, the amount paid reflects the expected income

---

[132] (1981), 14–15.   [133] de Ste Croix (1981), 179–204.
[134] *Dig.* 43.16.1.18, 47.2.90; Crook (1967), 179–205.
[135] *RR* 1.17.3.   [136] K. Hopkins (1978a), 108–11.   [137] *Ibid.*, 110.

over the life of the slave (which may of course include non-monetary 'income' like social status): high prices therefore suggest that owners expected to derive considerable profit from the intensive exploitation of their slaves.[138]

The evidence is simply not available to calculate the efficiency of slave-run plantations. Columella offers the information that 9.5–10.5 man-days per iugerum (14.5–16 per acre) were required for cereal cultivation, which compares with 12.5 man-days per acre in sixteenth-century England and 20–4 in early modern Cordova.[139] This, combined with the equally sketchy figure for yields, suggests that Roman cereal cultivation was fairly efficient. This can plausibly be linked to the use of animal power and the availability of manure rather than the status of the workers.

The crucial test of a plantation would be in viticulture, where cultivation was based on slave gangs working under close supervision. Columella's figure is 63 man-days per iugerum, which compares with 66 on a modern vineyard in the Rhône Valley.[140] There is, however, a problem with the figures for ancient wine yields: Columella's suggestion of three *cullei* per iugerum is nearly three times the average for Italian vineyards in the early twentieth century.[141] Much lower figures for yields can be quoted from the medieval and early modern periods.[142]

The search for average or typical yields ignores the effects of different terrain, and above all of different cultivation methods (in particular, whether the owner's goal is quantity or quality), on the volume that could be produced in a good or average year.[143] A single passage in an ancient author, in the context of a polemical advocacy of viticulture, cannot prove that Roman vineyards regularly produced such vast quantities of wine, but equally the comparative evidence for yields is insufficient to disprove the contention that Roman viticulture may have achieved a higher level of productivity than vineyards of later periods.[144]

In Tchernia's opinion, Columella's detailed figures are basically worthless but the general intentions of the passage are still revealing. 'Varron présentait les records historiques de productivité dans l'Ager Gallicus et l'Ager Faventinus comme des curiosités qui entraient dans le cadre d'une éloge de la fertilité de l'Italie. Pour Columelle ce sont des modèles à atteindre.'[145] The minimum figure quoted by Columella, Graecinus' estimate of one *culleus* per iugerum, is what may in his opinion be

[138] Cf. Ransom (1989), 42–7.   [139] K. D. White (1965) and (1970), 370–4.
[140] K. D. White (1970), 373.   [141] Col. 3.3.11; Duncan-Jones (1982), 39–48.
[142] Purcell (1985), 13.   [143] Tchernia (1986), 211–14.
[144] Cf. Bergqvist (1992), who argues from the storage capacity of the (very intensive) vineyard within Pompeii that Columella's suggested yields were perfectly possible.
[145] Tchernia (1986), 217.

obtained from the very worst sort of vineyard, planted on the wrong soil and not properly tended; if the vineyard is treated as a long-term investment, planted on the best soils and cultivated intensively, higher yields are inevitable. One *culleus* per iugerum is roughly the same as the average figure from early modern Italy.[146] While Columella's figures cannot have been typical of all vineyards every year, it would seem that labour-intensive viticulture could achieve a high level of production and profit. The great advantage which modern Californian and Australian wine production has over most Italian viticulture is said to lie in the size of the farming units and in the intensity of labour.[147]

To recapitulate: the villa estate described by the agronomists was large enough to allow some division of labour and specialisation, which, especially in viticulture, may have led to improvements in the productivity of labour and the volume of production. The use of slave labour may also have led to higher yields, since slaves could be compelled to work harder through the threat of force, and worked under conditions of close supervision which might not have been tolerated by free men. Slave labour had positive advantages over free; its adoption was not simply a response to the lack of any alternative. Of course, slaves were not suitable for all estates; they were an expensive investment, to be deployed where they could be most productively exploited.[148] If the 'slave mode of production' is seen as dominant in central Italy, it is not because this type of estate was the only way of exploiting the land but because it was the most efficient means for landowners to extract surplus production from labourers.

The archaeology of the villa

We may now turn to the archaeological evidence for the emergence of the villa in two regions of central Italy. Before turning to the areas in question, the Ager Cosanus and the Albegna Valley on the coast of northern Etruria and the Ager Falernus in northern Campania, it is worthwhile reiterating some of the points made in the previous chapter concerning the use of survey evidence. The pitfalls involved in comparing the results of different surveys are clearly seen in the case of the Ager Cosanus, where surveys covering the same region found entirely different patterns of site sizes and chronologies.[149] The variations may be accounted for by differences in sampling strategy, size classification or chronology, but they certainly indicate the need for caution. The two surveys in the Ager Falernus were both carried out by individuals, with

[146] Jongman (1988a), 132 n.3.   [147] Grigg (1974), 128, 130.   [148] Cf. Col. 1.7.
[149] Dyson (1978); Carandini and Settis (1979); Millett (1992), 1, 5, fig. 1.

an uneven coverage of the territory, and there are substantial differences in the patterns of site distribution and dating that emerge from each study.[150]

The classification and interpretation of artefact scatters is as ever a problem. To divide them into 'villas' and 'peasant farms' is more or less to beg the question, following too slavishly the historical tradition and ignoring the possibility of a wide variety of different sizes and types of farm.[151] In particular, the identification of large scatters, including building materials and mosaic tesserae, with the particular form of estate described by the Roman agronomists is at best arguable. This holds true even when a site has been excavated, as at Settefinestre. The ranks of small rooms found in the *pars rustica* were identified by the excavators as slave quarters; however, as Purcell observes:

> It is important to remember that that is a supposition, and that Varro and Columella are in the end behind it: an alien archaeologist would spot the menial status of the majority of the occupants, but would not be able to deduce the phenomenon of slavery from the remains of Settefinestre ... The literary tail wags the archaeological dog.[152]

The argument can be taken further: the elaborate architecture, bath houses and decoration by which most 'villas' are identified are entirely unconnected to the way in which production was organised. It is true that the agronomists recommend that the villa estate should include a suitable residence for the owner, to encourage him to visit it more often, but 'the opulent villa is the result not of a particular mode of production but of a decision to display existing wealth in a particular way'.[153] The establishment of a slave-based form of production may precede by decades the construction of a villa using the proceeds of successful farming. This has obvious relevance to the argument over the dating of the emergence of the villa and its relationship to earlier forms of rural settlement.

The Ager Cosanus lies on the Tyrrhenian coast about 140 km to the north of Rome. It was originally part of the territory of Vulci, confiscated after that city's defeat in 280 B.C.; the colony of Cosa was founded in 273 and the land centuriated.[154] The territory consists of an alluvial plain along the coast and up into the Valle d'Oro, surrounded by rolling hills with light soils.[155] The area has been covered by two different surveys.

---

[150] Arthur (1991a) and (1991b); Vallat (1987a); Fentress (1993).
[151] Rathbone (1993).
[152] Purcell (1988), 197; Carandini (1985b), 121–1, 157–60.
[153] Millett (1992), 2; Col. 1.4.8.
[154] Brown (1980); Celuzza and Regoli (1982), 37–41; Carandini (1985d).
[155] Attolini *et al.* (1991), 142.

The first, carried out by the Wesleyan University, intensively 'sherded' sites which had been located previously; its coverage of the whole area was therefore somewhat uneven, and even the smallest of the sites surveyed was fairly substantial.[156] The second was carried out in conjunction with the excavation of the villa at Settefinestre, and covered both the Ager Cosanus and the Albegna Valley to the north.[157] This survey aimed at a more systematic coverage of the region, based on a sampling strategy of surveying kilometre-wide tranches running E–W and N–S at 5 km intervals; it has tended to find a larger number of smaller sites, leading to different reconstructions of the region's history, in addition to offering the opportunity of comparing settlement patterns in the coastal regions with those found further inland.

Neither survey found much evidence for third-century occupation of the territory; the patterns of centuriation are clear, but the great majority of republican sites date to the second or first century, and can plausibly be linked to the recolonisation of the area in 199 B.C.[158] The invisibility of the original colonists may be attributed to the short life of their farms, to the fact that many of them lived in the town and walked out to their fields or to poverty, so that they left few material remains; at any rate, the fact that it was necessary to recolonise Cosa shows that the territory was already experiencing problems in the period immediately after the Hannibalic War.[159] Shortly afterwards, however, the town was flourishing and its immediate hinterland was densely occupied with small sites (although still far fewer are known than one would expect from the number of colonists).

At some point in the next two centuries there was a dramatic change: the imperial landscape is dominated by a small number of large sites, interpreted as villas along the lines of Settefinestre, each with a number of small satellite sites which may be smallholdings, tenant farms or outlying farm buildings (the importance of free labour in the villa economy suggests that one of the first two possibilities should be preferred).[160] The difficulty lies in dating this change more precisely. The Wesleyan survey dated sites to 'Republic' or 'Early Empire', without attempting to sub-divide the former category.[161] It also found far fewer of the smallest republican sites, which are precisely those that disappear most dramatically from the archaeological record; according to Celuzza and Regoli, 90 per cent of the small sites were abandoned by the middle

[156] Dyson (1978), 253–5.
[157] Carandini and Settis (1979); Celuzza and Regoli (1982); Attolini et al. (1982), (1983), (1991).
[158] Celuzza and Regoli (1982), 37–41.   [159] Rathbone (1981), 16–18.
[160] Celuzza and Regoli (1982), 41–4; Rathbone (1981), 20–2.
[161] Dyson (1978), 257, 259–61.

of the first century. In the second half of the previous century Tiberius Gracchus had passed through Etruria, probably along the Via Aurelia, and had been shocked by the state of the countryside, seeing a dearth of inhabitants and the land being cultivated by slaves.[162]

The first 'villas' – large, rich sites with remains of building material and decoration – began to appear in the late second century, although many date to the first, and Settefinestre itself was built around 40 B.C. At the same date, evidence for the large-scale production and export of wine appears; a large dump of Greco-Italic amphorae dating mainly to the second century was found just to the north of Cosa, but the great boom in production came with the arrival of the Dressel 1 around 130 B.C. Vast numbers of these amphorae, and several kiln sites, are found in the territory, especially along the coast.[163] Such was the quantity of Dr. 1 in the region that sherds were used extensively in construction work. Wine was not the only product of the region – the size of the granary at Settefinestre suggests that cereals may have been at least as important in the villa's economy – but it is the most visible in the archaeological record.[164]

Amphorae finds provide a better basis for establishing the beginning of market-oriented wine production than villa sites, which may simply represent the culmination of several decades' successful viticulture. What the changing pattern of settlement suggests is that the process was a gradual one, rather than a single dramatic displacement of the small farmer in favour of slave plantations. The villas appear intermittently over the course of a century; the decision to build a luxurious residence might be based on a chance windfall – a particularly good harvest, for example, or the aftermath of the Sullan proscriptions – but it is not stretching the imagination too far to suggest that the establishment of medium-sized slave plantations was an equally drawn-out affair. The demography of the expansion of Rome argues against a single cataclysmic change in the rural economy in the early second century in favour of a gradual drift from the land, and suggests that the free population was never wholly displaced.

Some small farms had clearly been experiencing difficulties at the very beginning of the second century, and the new settlers of 199 had little more success. Over the next two centuries many of them despaired of agriculture or were tempted by the delights of city life, and their holdings were amalgamated to create the medium-sized estates best suited to market-oriented production. 'Expropriation', with all its overtones of the Enclosures in early modern England, is perhaps too emotive a label for

---

[162] Plutarch, *Tib. Gracchus* 8.7.   [163] Attolini *et al.* (1991), 146–51.
[164] Cereals at Settefinestre: Purcell (1988), 197.

this process. The rich were, of course, in an excellent position to exert pressure on their poorer neighbours through the manipulation of credit, to offer higher rents for public land (as described in Plutarch's account of the Gracchan crisis) and to buy up vacated holdings.

By the end of the first century A.D., however, the villas of the Ager Cosanus were themselves experiencing difficulties. Several sites were abandoned during the Flavian and Trajanic eras, and two thirds disappeared under the Antonines; only seven villas continued in occupation. No new sites are known, although some of the other villas were reoccupied spasmodically; instead, the landscape was increasingly dominated by *vici*, villages. There are also signs of changes in the economy of the region. The Dr. 2–4 amphora, which had replaced the Dr. 1, was not itself replaced by any new type, while the villa at Settefinestre apparently tried to diversify its system of production by building pigsties. This is the 'crisis of the slave mode of production', which will be discussed below.

There is a striking contrast between the history of the coastal Ager Cosanus and that of the interior.[165] The Albegna river is navigable as far as its confluence with the Elsa, south of the town of Heba (a Roman colony, probably founded in the middle of the second century); the area between this point and the sea followed a similar line of development to the Ager Cosanus, with villas on the lower slopes of the hills, large dumps of amphorae and kilns. Further inland, the terrain is less hospitable except for a fertile basin around Saturnia (colonised in 183). This area was characterised by a notable continuity of settlement; the small, presumably colonial, sites did not suffer the same decline in the first century B.C., while some larger sites seem to have stayed in the hands of the pre-Roman elite. The region was also far less affected by the 'crisis' of the second and third centuries A.D., and it is tempting to connect this to the fact that it was less closely involved in the wine trade – amphorae are found in the area, but no kilns. The terrain may be less suitable for viticulture, but the crucial factor is its relative inaccessibility, far from the sea and lacking a navigable river. The villa – meaning the slave-based unit of production, rather than simply a well-appointed rural residence – is found only in a narrow strip of land along the coast of Italy.

A similar contrast between coastal and inland areas is found in the region of northern Campania that contained the Ager Falernus, the Massico and the territories of Suessa Aurunca and Sinuessa.[166] The Ager Falernus was famous for its wine (Falernian was an expensive vintage of

---

[165] Attolini *et al.* (1982), (1983), (1991).
[166] Arthur (1991a), (1991b); Vallat (1987a), (1987b), 201–4; generally on Campania, Frederiksen (1981).

high quality), while Campania in general was renowned for fertility, producing both wine and cereals.[167] The area was confiscated by Rome after the defeat of the Samnites and subjugation of Capua in 313/12, the land was centuriated and colonies were founded at Suessa, Minturnae and Sinuessa. In the early second century more colonies were established to the south, at Puteoli, Liternum and Volturnum.[168]

The original colonists seem to have favoured nucleated settlements on the uplands (plausibly explained by the hostility of the previous occupants of the land); in the second century, and above all in the first, there was a notable dispersal and intensification of rural settlement. The southern slopes of the Massico were particularly densely occupied; rather fewer sites have been found in the area around Suessa. Epigraphic and literary sources identify a number of Roman senators who owned land in the Ager Falernus, although this is hardly to be compared with the vast numbers who bought property on the Bay of Naples.[169] Much less is known about those who farmed the territory of Suessa, which supports the idea that inland sites were less attractive to men who wished to establish market-oriented enterprises.

The sites in question show less evidence of luxury than the villas of the Ager Cosanus, except for some elaborate terracing, but are nevertheless interpreted as 'Catonian' slave villas. Two comparable sites are known at Francolise, to the east of the Ager Falernus.[170] Both were platform villas of modest proportions (one dating to the second century B.C., the other to the beginning of the first) which were rebuilt on a much more impressive scale around 30 B.C. The first contains no evidence for its productive activities until an olive oil separating vat was added in the remodelling; the second contains a threshing floor, along with rooms in the *pars rustica* suitable for an overseer and family as well as other labourers.

In the Ager Falernus there is much more evidence for oil production, and above all for viticulture. Greco-Italic amphorae appeared in the region from the early second century, and the appearance of Dr. 1 was accompanied by the development of kilns along the coast. Many sites have the remains of wine or oil presses, and Arthur's survey also found ancient vine trenches.[171] The main evidence for the use of slave labour in the region is literary; after a slave rising in 133 B.C., 500 slaves were crucified at Minturnae, and 4,000 at Sinuessa.[172]

The first century A.D. was the period of maximum occupation of the

---

[167] Pliny, *HN* 3.60.   [168] Frederiksen (1984), 264–80.
[169] Arthur (1991b), 66–9; cf. D'Arms (1970).
[170] Cotton (1979); Cotton and Métraux (1985).
[171] (1991b), 71–8.   [172] Orosius 5.9.4.

countryside in this area, doubtless in part attributable to the settlement of 300,000 veterans by Augustus in Minturnae, Suessa and the Ager Falernus.[173] However, study of the architecture of the villas shows that there was little new building during this period. Few sherds of African Red Slip have been found in the region, which suggests that the abandonment of sites may have begun at the end of the first century. One of the Francolise villas has an ARS sherd from around A.D. 160, which is followed by a lengthy gap until the building was apparently reoccupied by squatters in the fourth century; the other villa was abandoned towards the end of the second century. Production of Dr. 2–4 amphorae came to an end in the Trajanic period; the coastal kiln sites had been replaced early in the first century by kilns further inland, which now began to concentrate on the production of domestic pottery. The town of Sinuessa also seems to have declined in the second century; Suessa and its territory show a greater degree of continuity and prosperity into later centuries. Once again, inland areas follow a different rhythm of prosperity and decline.

Provincial competition and economic crisis

In A.D. 92, the emperor Domitian issued an edict which prohibited the establishment of new vineyards in Italy and ordered the destruction of half the vineyards in the provinces.[174] This action, taken with Columella's comments about the state of farming in his day, Pliny's complaints about his difficulties in finding suitable tenants and the Trajanic alimentary schemes, has been used to support the idea that Italian agriculture was in crisis by the end of the first century A.D.[175] Rostovtzeff attributed this crisis to provincial competition, as imports of wine and oil from Gaul and Spain put medium-sized, market-oriented estates in Italy out of business and pushed their owners towards tenancy and extensive cereal agriculture.[176] Štaerman argued instead for an internal 'crisis of the slave mode of production' due to the inherent contradictions of this form of economic organisation; the growth of large estates, *latifundia*, driven by the owners' insatiable desire to increase their profits, led to the downfall of the system because of the escalating costs of supervising production.[177]

In the last two decades, archaeological evidence has been used to support this theory of crisis (albeit a 'crisis' that extends over a century

[173] Keppie (1983).   [174] Suet. *Domitian* 7.2; Statius, *Silv.* 4.3.11–12.
[175] Col. 1. *pr.* 1–20, 3.3.4–6; Pliny, *Ep.* 9.37; Garnsey and Saller (1987), 59–61; Vera (1995).
[176] (1957), 70–5, 91–105, 192–204.
[177] Štaerman (1964); Štaerman and Trofimova (1975).

or more). As seen above, sites in both the Ager Cosanus and the Ager Falernus began to be abandoned from the late first century. Still more important is the evidence of amphorae, especially those uncovered in excavations at Ostia.[178] Although Italian wine containers make up 60 per cent of the amphorae found in a deposit dating to the Augustan era, Tarraconensis and Baetica were already making an important contribution to Rome's imports. Meanwhile, the scarcity of Dr. 2–4 amphorae in Gaul, compared to the heyday of Dr. 1, suggests that Italian growers had lost their monopoly of this market. As the century progressed, provincial imports played an increasingly important role in Rome's supplies; the total numbers of Dr. 2–4 amphorae produced seem to decline in the Trajanic period, and the type was not replaced when it finally went out of use in the middle of the second century. Carandini originally echoed Štaerman in offering an internal structural crisis as the explanation for the decline of the slave-run villa and the associated trade in wine; he has since moved towards the Rostovtzeff model of provincial competition.[179] The effects remain the same: a move from intensive viticulture using slave labour to less intensive cereal cultivation and tenancy, implying a decline in the profitability and productivity of agriculture and hence leading to a crisis in Italian society and economy as a whole.

The picture of crisis has clearly been overdrawn. Domitian's edict is concerned with the over-production of wine in the context of a shortage of cereals; Tchernia plausibly suggests that too many vines had been planted earlier in the century after the eruption of Vesuvius had wiped out the vineyards of Pompeii and the surrounding area.[180] Provincial vineyards are treated unfairly, but this is hardly a protectionist measure to support Italian agriculture against provincial competition. Trajan's scheme for feeding children in Italian towns cannot be taken as evidence for crisis in the countryside, falling instead within a long tradition of local civic patronage, while Pliny's complaints about the lack of decent tenants are hardly specific to this period.[181]

The apparent disappearance of Italian amphorae from the archaeological record and the decline of the villas do demand some explanation. Italian wine continued to be produced; a number of varieties appear in Diocletian's Edict on maximum prices, and in the medical writers.[182] The lack of a replacement container for the Dr. 2–4 amphora may be explained in part by the use of barrels, which would not be preserved, while it remains possible that a new amphora type has simply yet to be identified (one is known from the Ager Falernus, although it seems to

---

[178] Panella (1970), (1973); Hesnard (1980).
[179] (1981), (1989); cf. Wickham (1988), 187–90.   [180] Tchernia (1986), 221–53.
[181] Woolf (1990a); Garnsey and Saller (1987), 60.   [182] Vera (1995), 197.

have been produced in fairly limited quantities).[183] Considerable quantities of wine came down the Tiber, and so left no record at Ostia. Many areas of Italy were entirely unaffected by any decline in rural settlement.[184] Slaves continued to be used in large numbers in agriculture into the later Empire.[185] What appears to be at stake is a crisis in a limited sector of the economy, the intensive, slave-run villa producing wine for the market (the importance of amphorae in arguments about the crisis means that other crops are rarely discussed). However, given the importance of this type of estate in supplying the city of Rome and its importance (even dominance) in the production of a marketable surplus for the elite, this may indeed have a wider significance than the comparatively small number of farms affected would suggest.[186]

Two of the theories put forward to explain the crisis have already been mentioned. Štaerman argued that the growth of large estates meant that it became uneconomical to supervise intensive slave labour on them; however, 'concentration of ownership does not automatically entail an increase in the size of units of exploitation', and there is no reason why large estates could not continue to be managed intensively as 200-iugera farms.[187] The existence of provincial competition, the preferred theory of Rostovtzeff and of Carandini's most recent publications, is not a sufficient explanation of any crisis.[188] Spanish viticulture had certain advantages over its competitors, using low-cost methods and producing large quantities of lower quality wine; however, although Spanish vineyards were located close to the sea, Italian growers still had the advantage of proximity to the market and lower transport costs.[189] The Roman market was vast enough to need supplies from many areas, vast enough to absorb the produce of both Italy and Spain; it was this huge demand that promoted the development of *cépages d'abondance* in both countries in the first century. Italian wines did lose their monopoly of the Gallic market, which may have been a serious blow for some regions (such as the Ager Cosanus), but the export trade was relatively unimportant compared with the demands of the city of Rome. Moreover, there is too great a gap between the decline in exports (marked by the change from Dr. 1 to Dr. 2–4) and the decline of the villas for the loss of this market to be the critical factor.

Neither theory offers a satisfactory explanation of why Italian vineyards, with easy access to a large and lucrative market and a fair amount

[183] Tchernia (1986), 285–92, 295–9; Arthur (1982); cf. Panella (1989), esp. 161–6.
[184] Patterson (1987).
[185] Finley (1980), 123–4; Whittaker (1987); MacMullen (1987); Samson (1989).
[186] Cf. de Ste Croix (1981), 52; Wickham (1988), 187.
[187] Finley (1980), 133.   [188] Cf. Tchernia (1989).
[189] Tchernia (1986), 179–84.

of experience in viticulture, should have run into problems. A third suggestion, that the price of slaves had risen to uneconomic levels after the Roman empire ceased its expansion, is equally untenable; the evidence for slave prices is too poor to support the argument, which ignores the possibility of a peacetime slave trade and of breeding on the estate.[190] Finley sees the causes of the end of ancient slavery in the decline of commodity production and the market for the products of slave labour, with the growth of a command economy and the increasingly inward-looking behaviour of the elite; a theory which may well work for the third century and beyond, but which is little help for understanding earlier changes.[191]

The mere existence of competition is an insufficient explanation; there needs to be a reason why Italian viticulture, or at any rate intensive slave-run viticulture, should have succumbed to such competition if, as has been suggested, it was a successful and profitable way of managing an estate. One possibility is suggested by the comparative example of the plantations of the American South. Slavery there was profitable, but slaves were expensive; owners had to extract as much labour from them as possible to make their investment pay.[192] Moreover, slave plantations were profitable because the prices they could obtain for their crops were high. The 1850s were a period of high demand for cotton; if the American Civil War had not intervened, a fall in world demand might have brought about the collapse of slavery of its own accord.[193] Such an assertion is unproveable – Wright's main aim in his article is to cast doubt on the use of the 1859/60 census as evidence for the 'normal' profitability of the southern plantation, rather than to suggest alternative lines of historical development – but it does offer a new perspective on the internal pressures of an intensive, slave-based form of production.

The agronomists had no doubt that an estate managed in the way they advised would be profitable, but one of the most important themes in their writings is an almost obsessive concern with the cost of farming and above all of labour. Cato's approach to cultivation was to minimise all costs, avoiding certain types of land: 'Remember that a farm is like a man – however great the income, if there is extravagance but little is left.'[194] Varro is generally concerned with the cost of equipment for the vineyard rather than the cost of labour, but in a later passage he writes: 'When the harvest is over the gleaning should be let, or the loose stalks gathered with your own force, or, if the ears are few and the cost of labour high, it should be pastured. For the thing to be kept in view in this matter is that the expense should not exceed the profit.'[195] Columella,

---

[190] Finley (1980), 128–30.   [191] *Ibid.*, 139–40.   [192] Ransom (1989), 42–7.
[193] Wright (1976).   [194] *Agr.* 1.6–7.   [195] *RR* 1.53.

who is wholly convinced of the benefits of intensive cultivation, praises the olive, 'because it is maintained by very light cultivation and, when it is not covered with fruit, it calls for scarcely any expenditure; also, if anything is expended upon it, it promptly multiplies its crop of fruit'.[196]

The elder Pliny, in contrast, observes that olives are rarely worth cultivating, and that intensive cultivation may be disastrous:

Moderation is the most valuable criterion of all things. Good farming is essential, but superlatively good farming spells ruin, except when the farmer runs the farm with his own family or with persons whom he is in any case bound to maintain. There are some crops which it does not pay the landlord to harvest if the cost of labour is reckoned, and olives are not easily made to pay; and some lands do not repay very careful farming.[197]

The main cost in olive cultivation was the hiring of pickers for the harvest; waiting for the olives to fall or knocking them down with poles was a false economy.[198] Elsewhere, Pliny repeats Cato's advice about 'extravagant' land.[199] In discussing the timing of vine pruning, he notes that 'all this depends on calculations regarding labour on large estates', and later observes that 'another mistake is made with the vines near the city of Aricia, which are pruned every other year, not because that is beneficial for a vine but because owing to the low price at which the wine sells the expenses might exceed the return'.[200]

The second major concern of the agronomists is with the slave labour force: the need to exploit it as intensively as possible, combined with considerable insecurity about its use. 'It is of the greatest importance that farm-workers should begin work at early dawn and should not proceed slowly with it through laziness.'[201] Slaves are to be worked all the time, indoors if wet and on maintenance tasks on feast days.[202] Two sets of tools should be kept, so that no time is wasted if something is broken.[203] All slaves must work, so old women and boys are set to look after the hens.[204] Cato adjusts the slaves' rations according to their labour, so that the chain-gang receive more and the sick receive less.[205] Slaves might be given larger rations, or clothing, or even allowed to cohabit with female slaves, as incentives to work harder.[206]

Alongside this advice, which must surely reflect the wish to obtain an adequate return on a large investment, there is clear evidence of fear. This is less pronounced in the agronomists, who regard their slaves with paternalistic condescension, than in other Roman authors.[207] If the

---

[196] Col. 5.8.1.   [197] *HN* 18.38.   [198] *HN* 15.11.   [199] *HN* 18.28.
[200] *HN* 17.192, 213.   [201] Col. 11.1.14.   [202] *Agr.* 2.2, 5, 39.2; Col. 2.21.
[203] Col. 1.8.8.   [204] Col. 8.2.7.   [205] *Agr.* 56–7.
[206] *RR* 1.17.7, 2.1.26; Col. 1.8.18–19; cf. Plutarch, *Cat. Mai.* 21.2–4.
[207] Bradley (1984).

slaves are worked all day, it is suggested, they will not have the energy to be troublesome.[208] Privileges should be granted 'so that, if some unusually heavy task is imposed, or punishment inflicted on them in some way, their loyalty and kindly feeling to the master may be restored'.[209] Masters should keep a careful eye on slaves who are regularly punished:

> When smarting under cruelty and greed, they are more to be feared ... In fact, I now and again avenge those who have just cause for grievance, as well as punish those who incite the slaves to revolt, or who slander their taskmasters ... Such justice and consideration on the part of the master contributes greatly to the increase of his estate.[210]

Taken in isolation, such statements might suggest the relatively humane treatment of slaves by their masters, who received loyal service in return. They can be seen in a different light if set alongside statements like those of the younger Pliny: 'Slaves lose all fear of a considerate master once they are used to him'; 'No master can feel safe because he is kind and considerate; for it is their brutality, not their reasoning capacity, which leads slaves to murder masters.'[211] Varro and Columella write of an ideal world, in which it is possible to find slaves who are 'neither cowed nor high-spirited', and to keep them under control with kind words rather than whips; it is perfectly clear that they still expected laziness, discontent and outright opposition, and that physical punishment, chaining and imprisonment were an important part of estate management.[212] Pilfering was to be expected, and even deliberate damage to tools or clothing.[213]

The solution to these problems, according to the agronomists, was careful supervision. The *vilicus* and his wife should keep an eye on slaves inside and outside the house, making sure than none of them is malingering.[214] The slaves should be quartered close together, so that they may more easily be supervised.[215] Competition between them should be encouraged; even mutual suspicion and informing.[216] The problem was that most of this supervision was carried out by another slave. The agronomists give copious advice on the selection of a *vilicus* and equally copious lists of things that he should not do, both of which suggest the vast scope for things to go wrong.[217] The privileges granted with respect to food and family life, the prospect of eventual freedom and the effects of a lifetime in slavery presumably meant that many

---

[208] Col. 1.8.11.   [209] *RR* 1.17.7.   [210] Col. 1.8.17–19.
[211] *Ep.* 1.4, 3.14.
[212] *RR* 1.17.5; Col. 1.6.3, 1.8.10–11, 1.8.15–19, 1.9.4, 1.9.7–8.
[213] Col. 8.4.6, 11.1.21.
[214] Col. 12.3.7.   [215] Col. 1.6.8.   [216] Col. 1.6.7–8, 1.9.8.
[217] *RR* 1.17.4–7; Col. 1.8.1–14; cf. Maróti (1976).

overseers carried out their duties loyally, but there could be no substitute for direct supervision by the master.

Columella blames the decline of Italian agriculture on the neglectful attitude of land-owners; he quotes with approval Mago's advice that the farmer should sell his town house, and failing that urges him to buy estates near the city, 'for it is certain that slaves are corrupted by reason of the great remoteness of their masters'.[218] Cato describes the way that a careful master should inspect his farm, going through the accounts, interrogating the overseer if the amount of work done seems unsatisfactory and making decisions about selling and leasing; the expectation throughout is that without such care the overseer will try to shirk or cook the accounts.[219] In part this is an ideological posture, agriculture as the only respectable profession for a gentleman; in part, it is another expression of concern with getting the most out of an expensive investment.

'Le grand domaine esclavagiste est fragile, soumis à des contrites économiques. Il utilise une main-d'œuvre chère à acheter, à entretenir, à reproduire. Il exige donc d'importants investissements en capitaux.'[220] The slave-run villa could be immensely profitable under certain conditions – the right soils, access to the market and close supervision by the owner. Like any agricultural enterprise, it was subject to vagaries of climate, although the average estate was large enough to keep a sizeable surplus in storage, sufficient to weather at least one poor year. The intensive vineyard was more precarious, and it is significant that both Varro and Columella felt the need to defend it as a worthwhile enterprise. Costs were higher, especially for labour, and the potential for losses in a poor year greater. This was compensated for by higher yields, if the vineyard was considered as a long-term investment, but it can also be argued that intensive cultivation depended on high market prices to offset the high costs of labour and supervision.

It is impossible to support this hypothesis with any figures; the critical price would depend on the attitudes of landowners and the return they expected on investment, as well as on what kind of wine was being produced – quality wines and *vins communs* are produced in different ways and compete in different areas of the market. Nevertheless, it does offer a possible explanation for the crisis of the villas in the late first and second centuries A.D. Demand for wine in the city of Rome stabilised as the city ceased to expand; the level of demand remained huge, and prices remained high, but the appearance of Spanish and Gallic wine on the market might lower prices just enough to cause problems for Italian

---

[218] Col. 1.1.18–20.   [219] *Agr.* 2, 5.3–4.   [220] Corbier (1982), 111.

villas. This need not entail a sudden crisis; rather, the margins of error simply became a little tighter, so that a bad year had more serious consequences than before. In such circumstances, marginal land might be abandoned, and alternative means of exploiting the land might begin to seem more attractive; for example, the exploitation of tenants rather than slaves might not entail any less work for the landowner, but it was less capital-intensive and less risky.[221] The result was a decline, not of Italian agriculture or Italian viticulture in general, but of a particularly intensive form of cultivation which had previously flourished under the exceptionally favourable market conditions offered by the growth of Rome.

Summary

The demands of the metropolis led to a number of changes in agricultural practice on estates in central Italy. There were changes in the techniques and technology of cultivation, in the use of animal power, in systems of fallow and manuring and in the organisation of labour, all of which permitted an intensification of production, squeezing the maximum returns from land and labour. These changes came together in the villa, a market-oriented, medium-sized estate based on the systematic exploitation of slave labour. The emergence of various forms of villas in different parts of central Italy is the clearest evidence for the power of the urban market to transform the productive landscape of its hinterland, although it is clear that that there were strict limits on how far this development could progress.

[221]   Cf. Finley (1976), 117–18.

6   Exploiting the margins

Centre and periphery

With distance from the market, transport costs rise and the price of land falls. It becomes less economical to intensify production by increasing inputs of labour or capital, except on land which either is very fertile or has particularly good access to transport arteries. It may therefore be predicted that the intensive, slave-run villa will be successful and profitable only within a limited area of central Italy. Farms outside this region may still sell their surplus production to the metropolis. However, it becomes increasingly unlikely that there will be dramatic changes in agricultural practice in response to the demands of the market; at most, we may expect to find that regional specialities, distinctive local products which could be sold in Rome, would have a prominent place within the standard mixture of crops. In many areas of Italy, farming practices were determined purely by local environmental conditions; in other regions, the stimulus to change was provided by the demands of markets other than the metropolis.[1]

It is possible, however, that this picture of the steady decline of metropolitan influence with distance from the city is misleading. In the 'world-systems theory' of Wallerstein, the periphery is not left to its own devices by the more advanced countries that form the core of the world-system; rather, it is exploited in a different manner.[2] The periphery serves as a source of raw materials and as a market for goods manufactured by the core nations, and it is in the latter's interest to maintain this state of affairs. The failure of most modern Third World countries to develop modern industrial economies reflects the imbalance of power within the capitalist world-economy, as the periphery is prevented from competing with the core on equal terms and is instead kept in a state of 'underdevelopment'.

Wallerstein argues that his theory is applicable only to the capitalist

[1]   Cf. Paterson (1991).
[2]   Wallerstein (1974) and (1980); discussed by Woolf (1990b).

world-economy, but this has not prevented a number of archaeologists from making use of such ideas in studying pre-industrial societies.[3] With some obvious modifications, the notion of the underdeveloped periphery raises interesting questions about the way in which the demands of the Roman market may have affected more distant regions of Italy. In von Thünen's model of agricultural location, the outermost zone is turned over to ranching. Land at the margins is cheap, and grazing requires little investment once land and animals have been bought; its products can fetch good prices, making it a more profitable activity than leasing the land to tenant-farmers. Rather than the simple model of declining metropolitan influence, therefore, in which remote regions are left largely untouched, the demands of the city may instead tend to keep peripheral regions underdeveloped, with good arable land turned over to pasture.

It is interesting to note that the historical tradition does indeed portray Apulia and other parts of southern Italy as deserted, with the old population driven out to make way for extensive, slave-run cereal estates (*latifundia*) and grazing.[4] As we have already seen, the traditional picture of Italian development can rarely be trusted; it must be set alongside the archaeological evidence for changes in agricultural production and patterns of settlement in such marginal regions. First, however, we should examine in more detail the evidence for the diffusion of intensive villa agriculture outside central Italy.

The limits of villa cultivation

The Roman agronomists were well aware that different farming conditions required different approaches to cultivation. Varro says that one of the particular concerns of any farmer was 'whether the land would yield a fair return for the investment in money and labour ... For no sane man should be willing to undergo the expense and outlay of cultivation if he sees that it cannot be recouped.'[5] He notes elsewhere that it is necessary to use both experiment and imitation to determine how many slaves should be employed on a particular farm, since the rule for a farm in Gaul does not necessarily hold good for a farm in the mountains of Liguria.[6] Varro is particularly concerned about the quality of the soil, whether it would repay the effort of cultivation; however, access to the market is included as an important criterion in choosing an estate, showing that he was aware how this factor could affect the profitability of an investment. If a farm was not bringing in an adequate return,

---

[3]   E.g. Rowlands *et al.* (1987) and Champion (1989).
[4]   Toynbee (1965), 286–95; summary of tradition in Lomas (1993), 13–17.
[5]   *RR* 1.2.8.   [6]   *RR* 1.18.6–8.

Varro's ideal farmer would adapt his style of cultivation, equipping and managing the estate in the manner best suited to its soils and situation. The logical conclusion is that few landowners would attempt capital-intensive villa agriculture in regions where the cost of transporting produce to market would eat too far into the profits.

Varro's concern with the natural conditions of the farm, its soil and situation, is an important reminder that many parts of Italy are ill-suited to the cultivation of the crops usually associated with the villa. Olive trees are confined to the plains and the lower slopes of mountains; vines can be grown at higher altitudes, but the quality and quantity of the wine they produce make it best fitted for local consumption rather than export. The third major crop, cereals, can be grown successfully in most areas of the highlands (especially in the pockets of fertile land often found in upland valleys), but the cost of transporting bulky goods overland makes it highly improbable that cereals were grown for the Roman market in mountain regions. If the crops best suited to intensive cultivation are absent from or relatively unimportant in such regions, it is logical to conclude that intensive slave agriculture and the innovations associated with it were also absent. The question of the diffusion of the villa is concerned exclusively with the thin strip of land along the Tyrrhenian and Adriatic coasts, and the fertile plain of the Po Valley.

The agronomists offer no direct evidence for how far villa agriculture spread beyond Etruria and Campania. This is simply because their perspective is that of the metropolitan elite. For example, Columella recommends that 'far distant' estates, especially land under grain, should be leased to tenants, since the owner cannot adequately control his slaves at such a distance.[7] This advice is inspired by the rising costs and difficulties of supervision, not by the cost of transporting the surplus to market; clearly it is relevant only to a Rome-based landowner who had to be persuaded to spare even a little time from his business in the forum. A local landowner faced no such problem of supervision; Columella's comment is no proof that *all* estates in 'far distant' regions were cultivated in this manner, and the same can be said of the younger Pliny and his tenants.[8] On the other hand, the presence of slaves in a region, attested for the south of Italy by several sources, is not evidence for intensive slave villas; what matters is how the slave was employed, in highly organised intensive cultivation or in some other manner.[9]

Archaeology is little help in this regard, since, as observed in the case of Settefinestre, it is impossible to infer the status of the labourers or the organisation of labour from the material remains.[10] Surveys from all

---

[7]   Col. 1.7.6.   [8] *Ep.* 9.37.   [9] Cf. Lepore (1981).   [10] Purcell (1988), 197.

parts of Italy (and elsewhere in the Roman world) continue to label large, rich rural sites as 'villas', but this need imply nothing about the way in which the estate was managed. A 'villa' in this sense is simply a convenient label for a site which is noticeably larger than others in the region; it often has more architectural remains, and sometimes evidence of decoration (painted plaster, mosaic tesserae); generally it has more sherds of imported fine wares than smaller sites.

Several surveys have observed that these 'villas' clearly stood out from other sites on account of their size and apparent complexity.[11] As Lloyd suggests for Samnium, this relative prosperity implies the production of a surplus for the market, while the presence of imported pottery (and, at S. Giovanni, 70 km from the sea, oyster shells) shows that these sites were tied into wider networks of trade and distribution.[12] The major crops of the estate clearly varied from region to region. Samnite villas were mainly involved in cereal cultivation and pastoralism, to judge from the floral and faunal remains; farms in the Piacenza region tend to be found on land best suited to arable cultivation, while the large sites in Lucania apparently practised traditional mixed farming.[13]

Excavation of several sites in highland regions has revealed buildings of a variety of sizes; none includes any equivalent of the accommodation for the labour force found at Settefinestre, and none compares with the Cosan villa in its luxury elements.[14] This is scarcely surprising; the situations and economies of these villas are wholly dissimilar. Moreover, the decision to construct an elegant residence is not necessarily connected to the success of the productive side of the estate; the wealth of Settefinestre may have been drawn from other sources, and the land-owners of Molise may have preferred to live in towns rather than on their estates.[15]

Neither archaeology nor the literary sources are able to substantiate the theory that intensive slave cultivation was generally profitable in only a limited area of Italy. It is possible, however, to illustrate the likelihood of this assertion with an attempt at speculative quantification, along the lines suggested by Jongman.[16] Taking the total demand for wine at Rome as about 169 million litres p.a. (population one million, 250 l. per head p.a. with half rations for women and children), which is high, and the yield of vineyards as 2,000 l./ha (one *culleus* per iugerum), which is relatively low, we can see that 84,500 ha under vines will produce enough

[11]   E.g. Gualtieri and de Polignac (1991), 198, 202 on Lucania; Barker *et al.* (1978), 41–2 on Molise.
[12]   Lloyd (1991), 182–4; Lloyd and Rathbone (1984); Small (1985).
[13]   Dall'Aglio & Marchetti (1991) on Piacenza.   [14]   Dyson (1985); Lloyd (1991), 182.
[15]   Cf. Lloyd and Barker (1981), 301–3.   [16]   (1990), 50–2.

wine for the city's needs; less than 1 per cent of agricultural land in Italy. If the wine is produced on 100–iugera estates, with 20 iugera of vines on each, the area needed is 422,500 ha, 4.2 per cent of cultivable land in Italy. A similar calculation for olive oil, at 20 l. per head p.a. and a yield of 440 l./ha, suggests that another 2.3 per cent of Italian farmland would be occupied by oil-producing villas (many of which also produced wine, not to mention other marketable goods). In other words, Rome's demands for wine and oil could be met from less than 7 per cent of Italy's agricultural land – and this takes no account of the contribution of provincial imports.

Of course, intensive slave villas could thrive in the hinterlands of towns elsewhere in Italy, and the expansion of urban centres from the first century B.C. surely went hand in hand with the diffusion of villa agriculture. However, it seems clear that villas dependent on the Roman market were limited in number, and also in geographical distribution. Doubtless the picture changed over time, as high prices in the urban market (especially while the city was still expanding rapidly) encouraged the extension of the zone of intensive cultivation – only for farms in more distant regions to run into problems when prices stabilised or fell.

Regional specialisation

That is not to say that other regions of Italy did not supply Rome, only that intensive villa agriculture was uneconomical there; estates cultivated in the traditional manner could still produce a sizeable surplus for sale to the city. Evidence for the marketing of regional specialities comes from a mixture of literary and archaeological sources. Descriptions of Italy, like that of Strabo, often mention local products, sometimes stating that they were exported; the agronomists mention varieties of crop named after or associated with particular places, suggesting that these varieties were familiar to their elite audience; passing references in writers like Martial – to olives from Picenum, for example – imply that the products in question were well known at Rome.[17] On the archaeological side, the presence of large 'villa' sites or oil and wine presses in a region implies the production of a surplus for the market, though without showing which market was involved; archaeology is here best suited to tracing the distribution of 'visible' products like wine and oil, which were transported in distinctive and imperishable containers.

Most crops leave no such trace in the material record. It is impossible to say whether Rome imported grain from Apulia, Picenum or the Po

[17]   Loane (1938), 11–43 for references.

Valley, all areas which were known in antiquity for cereal cultivation.[18] Apulia was a long way from Rome to have been a regular supplier, and the other regions are still more distant.[19] Varro and Strabo clearly imply that Apulian grain was exported, without mentioning its likely destination, and in the fourteenth century at least 45,000 tons every year were shipped to towns like Venice, Florence and Naples.[20] However, Sardinia, Sicily and North Africa (regions on which medieval Italian cities could draw much less frequently than the Romans could) are all closer to Rome than Apulia; it seems better to regard the region as one possible source of supplies in the event of harvest failure in one of Rome's usual granaries. The development of cereal agriculture in the Po Valley – attested also by the location of farms on land suited to intensive arable cultivation – can be plausibly linked to the growth of the region's famously large and wealthy cities, and to the market provided by the army to the north.[21]

Varieties of fruit and vegetables are known from areas outside the *suburbium*, especially less perishable and more easily transported produce like cabbages (all over Campania) and turnips (Amiternum and Nursia, as well as the land north of the Po).[22] Campania is particularly well represented in the lists, which probably reflects the familiarity of the Roman elite with this region as much as export of its produce (which included quinces, figs, chestnuts and myrtles).[23] However, more distant regions are also mentioned. Tarentum seems to have been especially fruitful, producing leeks, pears, figs, almonds, chestnuts and myrtles.[24] Paestum was famous for its flowers, Apulia produced edible bulbs and Bruttium contributed cabbages and pears.[25] Finally, there is a rather improbable passage in Athenaeus: 'I hold in greatest esteem the apples sold in Rome and called Matian, which are said to come from a village situated in the Alps near Aquileia.'[26] Although it is not mentioned, it is likely that most fruit being transported over such distances was preserved or dried, in the manner described by Columella.[27]

The export of fish products, particularly *garum*, can be traced in both literary and archaeological evidence. Velia, Pompeii and Thurii all had 'factories' for the salting of fish; in the case of the first, Strabo states explicitly that this was due to the poverty of the soil in the territory of the

[18] Spurr (1986), 8 n.21 for references.   [19] Garnsey (1988a), 190.
[20] *RR* 2.6.5; Strabo 6.3.9; Abulafia (1981), 382.
[21] Dall'Aglio and Marchetti (1991), 162–5; Chilver (1941), 132–6; Chevallier (1983), 233–4.
[22] Col. 10.125–140, 421; Pliny, *HN* 19.77, 18.127.   [23] *HN* 15.38, 70, 94; 17.62.
[24] Col. 5.10.18, 8.11.14; *HN* 15.61, 71, 90; 17.62.
[25] Martial 9.60; Col. 10.139; *HN* 19.140, 15.55.   [26] Athenaeus, *Deip.* 3.82c.
[27] 12.10, 12.14–16.

town.[28] *Garum* amphorae from Pompeii, and possibly also from Antium and Puteoli, have been found at Rome; by the first century A.D., however, the trade seems to be dominated by Spanish products, even in Pompeii itself (although the presence of imports does not necessarily imply a crisis of local production).

The majority of literary references to olive cultivation are concerned with central Italy: with the famous oil of Venafrum, on the border between Campania and Samnium, and with the Sabine hills.[29] Olive oil is mentioned as one of the exports of Apulia, and Picenum produced olives for eating.[30] This pattern of distribution seems to be confirmed by the finds of olive presses in excavated villas; the vast majority are found in Latium and Campania, with the rest divided between Apulia, Picenum and Lucania/Bruttium.[31] The survey is of course incomplete; it reflects a regional bias in excavations, and takes no account of the remains of presses found in many areas of Italy by survey projects in the last ten years. Olive cultivation was common to most areas of Italy which had a suitable climate (which basically means those parts lying below a certain altitude), and surplus production might find a market in upland areas as much as in Rome or other towns.[32]

Evidence for exports to Rome is provided by the distribution of amphorae. Degrassi's argument that Istrian amphorae must have contained oil since the local wine was heavily criticised by Pliny is effectively contradicted by inscriptions on the containers themselves.[33] This leaves the oil amphorae from Brundisium, which are widely distributed in Gaul, Spain, Italy (with three known from Ostia) and even Palestine and Egypt.[34] The trade is concentrated in the first half of the first century B.C. and ceases altogether after Augustus.

Wine production in Italy follows a similar pattern to that of oil, with one significant exception. The vast majority of named varieties of wine, *grands crus*, come from central Italy, especially Latium and northern Campania.[35] The same regions produced wines of lesser quality, as did Apulia and the long stretch of the Adriatic coast between Picenum and the Po delta. This is confirmed by archaeology; Brundisium produced a version of the Lamboglia 2 amphora from the middle of the second century B.C., as well as a variation on the Dr. 2–4 type, while the north

[28]   Curtis (1991), 85–96; Strabo 6.1.1.
[29]   *RR* 1.2.7; *HN* 15.8; Strabo 5.3.10, 5.3.1; Col. 5.8.5.
[30]   *RR* 3.7.1; *HN* 15.16; Martial 5.79.   [31]   Rossiter (1981).
[32]   Cf. Strabo 4.6.2. and 4.6.9, on Liguria and Istria.
[33]   Degrassi (1962); Baldacci (1967–8).
[34]   Hesnard (1980), 148; Cipriano and Carre (1989), 68–74; Volpe (1990), 65–70.
[35]   Tchernia (1986), 108–14.

produced large quantities of Lamb. 2, to be replaced by the Dr. 6 some time towards the end of the first century B.C.[36]

Few amphorae of the republican period are known from Rome, making it impossible to establish the sources of its supplies except from literary evidence or to determine at what date a taste for wine spread among the urban masses.[37] Wine from the Adriatic was certainly exported to the East in this period. For the reign of Augustus there is the deposit at La Longarina in Ostia; over 30 per cent of the amphorae are from Spain, while 23 per cent are Dr. 6 from north Italy.[38] For all the problems with the size of the sample (it represents about one fiftieth of the cargo of a single large ship), this offers clear evidence that the level of consumption in Rome was now such as to attract large quantities of wine from areas beyond the central Italian heartland. It is therefore somewhat surprising that, with a single exception, Apulian wines seem to play no part in Rome's imports, just as Apulian olive oil disappears from the material record around this time. It is true that parts of Tarraconensis are closer to Rome than Brundisium, but any explanation based on the cost of transport has to explain the obvious importance of wines from much further up the Adriatic.

Vines from north Italy, like those from Spain, are characterised by their fruitfulness, and the wine they produce by its ability to survive long-distance travel.[39] Production of Dr. 6 amphorae continued in the region until the second century A.D.; they disappear from the Ostian stratigraphies under the Julio-Claudians, but evidence for their continued export to Rome is provided by the presence in Ostia during the second century of members of the *collegium* of Adriatic shippers and wine merchants.[40] The wide diffusion of the amphorae in the Po Valley also suggests an expansion of the local market, which therefore absorbed a greater proportion of local wine production.[41] Finally, there was a market for wine in the regions to the north, among the Illyrian tribes and the Roman garrisons (although it has been argued that the latter drank *posca* rather than wine).[42] In general, it appears that the economy of the Po Valley became increasingly independent of Rome and the rest of Italy – which is perhaps hardly surprising, given the region's relative isolation.

This leaves the problem of the disappearance of Apulian products from the material record at the end of the first century B.C. Tchernia has

[36] Cipriano and Carre (1989), 68–74, 80–7.   [37] Tchernia (1986), 66–7.
[38] Hesnard (1980); Tchernia (1986), 153–7.   [39] Strabo 5.1.7 on wine from Ravenna.
[40] E.g. *CIL* VI: 9682; XIV: 409; Meiggs (1960), 275–6; Tchernia (1986), 252.
[41] Cipriano and Carre (1989), 85–7; cf. Panella (1989), 165.
[42] Chilver (1941), 136–42, 175–6; Chevallier (1983), 235–9; Strabo 4.6.9, 5.1.8; on wine in the army, Middleton (1983), 75–6 v. Tchernia (1986), 11–19.

suggested that Apulian wine lost out because it could manage neither quality nor quantity, and was therefore confined to a local market.[43] This is compatible with the evidence for continued production of wine and amphorae in the region.[44] Another possibility is that most production was absorbed by local markets; the literary tradition generally emphasises the decadence of cities in this region, compared with the heyday of Magna Graecia, but inscriptions provide evidence for the continuing vitality of urban society.[45] Far from being a sign of the decadence of Italian agriculture in the face of provincial competition, the decline in exports to Rome and other parts of the Mediterranean may indeed be a sign of local prosperity. There is, however, an alternative explanation of the development of Apulia which must be considered; the expansion of pastoralism.

Pastoralism and transhumance

The outermost zone of von Thünen's model of agricultural location is devoted to grazing; this is land which is too far from the market to be worth the effort or expense of cultivation. The rearing of animals for their meat is made yet more economical by the fact that the produce walks itself to market. Milk and wool have to be transported in the usual manner; the former is often made into cheese, while in the latter case much of the processing may be carried out locally, to reduce the bulk of the product.[46]

Many areas of Italy are ill-suited to arable cultivation; a large part of the highland regions of Italy was given over to grazing of one form or another long before the expansion of the city of Rome. The question is how far the products of this pastoralism reached the urban market, and whether the mountain economies saw any changes as a result. Outside the highlands, the main question is whether the demands of the city kept regions at the periphery in a state of 'underdevelopment'. A small farmer, aiming for self-sufficiency, could make a reasonable living from land at the 'margins' of Rome's economic hinterland; however, wealthier landowners could make greater profits by turning arable land over to winter pasture than by leaving it to be cultivated by tenants. Such a development might have serious consequences for the health of a region's economy and society.

By the third century A.D., when Aurelian included pork in the state distributions, the consumption of meat had to some extent become routine in the city of Rome, even if its place in the popular diet remained

---

[43] (1986), 166–8.   [44] Volpe (1990), 65–70.   [45] Lomas (1993), 143–87.
[46] Cf. de Ligt (1991a), 33–5 on Alfred Weber's theory of industrial location.

modest from the point of view of nutrition.[47] Taverns and *popinae* sold cooked meats of various kinds (and were subject to occasional imperial legislation for their pains), street-vendors offered other delicacies, and sacrifices and banquets added to the demand for meat in the city – a demand which simply cannot be quantified, however roughly, since it depends on the amount of surplus income possessed by the urban populace rather than on its nutritional requirements.[48] The same must be said of products like milk and cheese. The demand for wool, meanwhile, would be affected by the efficiency of the second-hand clothing trade; Thompson therefore takes a low figure of 1 kg per person per year, which nevertheless means that at least a million sheep were needed to fill the city's requirements.[49] If it is accepted that, because of the corn dole, many of the Roman *plebs* did have surplus income for 'luxuries' like wine and meat, even if they bought them only occasionally and in small quantities, the aggregate demand, and therefore the number of animals and the area of pasture involved, must have been considerable.

The excavation of a late-Roman deposit at the foot of the Palatine offers evidence for the relative importance of different animals as sources of meat.[50] Of the total number of animals indicated by identifiable bone fragments, 40 per cent are pigs, 30 per cent sheep or goats, 20 per cent fowl and 10 per cent cattle, with the occasional horse, red deer and cat; considered in terms of the amount of meat per animal, however, cattle make up 40 per cent of the total, pigs 30 per cent and sheep and goats 20 per cent. As Barker notes, this is just one sample from a single deposit, and literary sources (especially the Codex Theodosianus) suggest that pork was the most important meat in Rome. Before considering the geography of Italian pig breeding, two other findings of the Schola Praeconum excavation should be mentioned: that the animals in question were apparently fairly small, and that their average age at slaughter was between one and three years. This suggests that animals of a suitable size for butchering were being raised on a systematic basis, while clearly not being fattened as rapidly as is possible under modern farming methods.

Pig-keeping was, according to Varro, an important part of traditional mixed farming in Italy: 'Who of our people cultivates a farm without keeping swine? and who has not heard that our fathers called him lazy and extravagant who hung in his larder a flitch of bacon which he purchased from the butcher rather than got from his own farm?'[51] Besides this domestic pig-keeping, part of the eternal drive towards self-sufficiency (Cato's farms also included a swineherd), he mentions herds

[47] Corbier (1989).
[48] On taverns, Hermansen (1974) and (1981), 185–205; Martial 1.41.
[49] J. S. Thompson (1989), 147–55.   [50] G. Barker (1982).   [51] *RR* 2.4.3.

of 100 to 150 pigs, animals which are clearly destined for the market.[52] Columella offers more details on how pigs should be reared, particularly noting their willingness to eat more or less anything, and the fact that the best feeding grounds are woods.[53] He provides additional evidence of the importance of the market; near towns, sucking pigs should be sold so that the sow can produce two litters in one year (presumably to recoup the cost of leaving the land as pasture), while 'in out of the way districts where raising stock is the only thing which pays', piglets can be brought up properly and then weaned on stubble and windfalls.[54]

Three areas can be identified as having an important place in the pork supply of Rome. The first, on the authority of Varro, is Gaul: 'The Gauls usually make the best and largest flitches; it is a sign of their excellence that annually Comacine and Cavarine hams and shoulders are still imported from Gaul to Rome.'[55] The Comacine are not mentioned elsewhere, but Pliny identifies the Cavarae as a tribe of Gallia Narbonensis.[56] We might imagine that Gallic ham was something of a luxury; more significant in terms of the volume of production were Cisalpina and the south of Italy.

Varro continues: 'With regard to the size of Gallic flitches, Cato uses this language: "The Insubrians in Italy [the chief tribe in Cisalpine Gaul] salt down three and four thousand flitches; in spring the sow grows so fat that she cannot stand on her own feet".'[57] Polybius wrote of the Po Valley that 'the amount of acorns grown in the woods dispersed over the plain can be estimated from the fact that, while the number of swine slaughtered in Italy for private consumption is very large, almost the whole of them are supplied by this plain'.[58] Strabo modifies this description, adding wine and wool to the list of local products and stating that Cisalpine pork provided only the bulk of Rome's demands, not those of the whole of Italy.[59]

Under the Principate, the focus of the Italian pork trade began to move southwards. A survey of the territory to the south of Piacenza in the Po Valley suggests that in the first and second centuries A.D. the land was being exploited intensively; only land which was effectively uncultivable was unoccupied.[60] This implies that considerable clearing had taken place in the area, with woods (and therefore pigs) giving way to arable cultivation.[61] Certainly by the time that pork became a subject of interest to the imperial authorities, the main source of supply was the south of Italy, the otherwise inhospitable regions of Lucania and

---

[52] *RR* 2.4.22; *Agr.* 10, 11.   [53] Col. 7.9.6; cf. Pliny, *HN* 16.25 on acorns as fodder.
[54] Col. 7.9.3–4.   [55] *RR* 2.4.10.   [56] *HN* 3.34.   [57] *RR* 2.4.11.
[58] 2.15; Chevallier (1983), 242–4.   [59] 5.1.12.
[60] Dall'Aglio and Marchetti (1991).   [61] Giardina (1981), 96–7.

Bruttium (which also supplied beef).[62] From at least the first century B.C. there was a type of sausage known as a Lucanian, while one excavated villa in the region had a very high proportion of pig bones in its middens and is therefore assumed to have been involved in the pork supply of Rome in the fourth and fifth centuries.[63]

A survey of the area around the S. Giovanni villa found that the number of *vici* more than doubled over the second and third centuries A.D., and the slight decline thereafter still left the region more densely settled than it had been in the early Principate. The growing importance of pig-farming did not lead to wholesale abandonment of the land, suggesting that, as we might expect, it had long been an important part of the local economy.[64] Further towards the coast, in western Lucania, the pattern is slightly different. Following an apparent decline in settlement over the last three centuries B.C., the first century A.D. saw the arrival of small farmsteads and three larger 'villa' sites, which suffered only a gradual decline in the later period.[65] It may be suggested that this limited revival was linked to the region's new involvement in Rome's pork supply, as pig-rearing was replaced by arable cultivation in Cisalpina – there is no evidence for any attempt to keep the Po Valley in a state of 'underdevelopment', or to prevent the clearing of woodland there.

Other animals were associated with particular regions: horses with Apulia and the Sabine hills, mules and asses with Reate, goats with the Ager Gallicus in Umbria.[66] Most important, for wool at least as much as meat or milk, was the sheep, whose distribution in Italy can be traced though a variety of literary sources. In his description of the Po Valley, Strabo claims that Patavium's prosperity was founded on the export of clothing to Rome, while other cities in the region also produced different wools; Pliny confirms that the white fleeces from the Po Valley fetched high prices, and Columella says that Gallic sheep were in his time regarded as superior to other breeds.[67] Strabo also mentions wool from Brundisium and northern Apulia; Tarentine 'jacketed' sheep were famous for the quality of their fleeces, and Varro himself owned flocks in Apulia.[68] Finally, Strabo and Columella refer to sheep in Liguria, while the latter mentions the Calabrian breed as having once been highly regarded.[69] Frayn argues that other areas can be identified on the basis

---

[62] Cassiodorus, *Var.* 11.39.
[63] Varro, *LL* 5.111; Cicero, *ad Fam.* 9.16.8; Barnish (1987).
[64] Small (1991), 208–12.   [65] Gualtieri and de Polignac (1991).
[66] E.g. Strabo 5.3.1; Varro, *RR* 2.1.14, 2.3.9, 2.71.
[67] Strabo 5.1.7, 5.1.12; *HN* 8.190; Col. 7.2.3.
[68] Strabo 6.3.6, 9; Martial 4.155; *HN* 8.190; *RR* 2 pr. 6, 2.1.16, 2.2.9, 2.2.19; Col. 7.4.
[69] Strabo 4.6.2; Col. 7.2.3–4.

of their suitability for pastoralism, or their lack of suitability for arable cultivation; inland Samnium, Umbria and Picenum and the southern parts of Lucania and Bruttium fall into this category.[70]

Sheep, like pigs, were a standard component of the medium-sized estate devoted to mixed farming described by the agronomists; indeed, only Varro mentions forms of pastoralism other than that fully integrated with arable cultivation.[71] Cato's ideal olive yard included a flock of 100 sheep, and he gives sample contracts for leasing winter pasturage and for selling the increase of the flock.[72] The agronomists are well aware of the beneficial effects of manure, which helps to explain their commitment to keeping animals on the farm.[73] The other main reason is clearly the contribution that wool, meat and cheese could make to farm income. As with pigs, the form of exploitation depends on how close the estate is to the market:

After the lambing season, the bailiff in charge of the sheep on an outlying estate reserves almost all the young offspring for pasture; and in an area near town hands over the tender lambs, before they have begun to graze, to the butcher, since it costs only a little to convey them to the town and also, when they have been taken away, no slighter profit is made out of the milk from their mothers.[74]

It is often stated that the climate of the Mediterranean requires that some form of transhumance should be practised, so that the sheep can find pasture in the summer.[75] This may not be necessary if the landowner decides that it is economical to devote land to fodder crops, a luxury which of course only the wealthier landowners could afford.[76] Columella makes no reference to any form of transhumance, while Varro's distinction between the flocks on the estate and those which feed in distant glades implies that the former remained on the farm all year.[77] Alternatively, flocks might be moved very short distances, a few miles up into the local hills making all the difference.[78]

It seems obvious that small-scale pastoralism was the norm throughout most of Italy, whether fully integrated with arable cultivation or as an adjunct to farming, exploiting the more marginal lands in regions like Samnium, Lucania and Calabria. This idea is supported by the results of two surveys from highland regions, covering the upper Biferno valley in Samnium and the area north of Reate in the Sabine hills.[79] In both cases the land was found to be densely settled, something

---

[70] Frayn (1984), 19–20.   [71] Garnsey (1988b), 201.   [72] *Agr.* 10, 149, 150.
[73] J. S. Thompson (1989), 70–84.   [74] Col. 7.3.13.
[75] E.g. Frayn (1984), 45–6; cf. Garnsey (1988b), 203–4.
[76] On fodder, cf. Varro, *RR* 2 *pr.* 5.   [77] *RR* 2.2.9.
[78] J. S. Thompson (1988), 214; G. Barker (1989), 1–3.
[79] G. Barker *et al.* (1978); Lloyd (1991); Coccia and Mattingly (1992).

which in the case of Samnium would not have been inferred from the literary sources. In the early Principate there was a tendency towards fewer but larger sites, situated above all on the boundary between heavy valley soils (in the case of the Rieti survey, beside an area identified as the famous Rosea pasture) and the lighter soils of the lower hills. The obvious conclusion is that these sites were involved in mixed farming, with a heavy emphasis on pastoralism. For the Biferno valley there is the additional evidence of Cicero's *Pro Cluentio*, with its picture of an area dominated by a number of leading families who owned large flocks in the district. For Reate there is the impressive list of local dignitaries who entered the senate from the middle of the first century B.C. As Barker observes of Samnium, 'we are beginning to see the re-shaping of this landscape under the new social and economic conditions of the Empire. At the same time, however, classical farmers in the valley had to have agricultural systems that would work whatever the level of market organisation or decision-making.'[80]

The role of medium-sized estates in regions like Samnium and the Sabine hills in supplying Rome with meat and wool, and the role of Rome in enriching the owners of such estates, must not be under-estimated. However, much more attention has been given in the past to the phenomenon of long-distance transhumance, like that depicted by Varro:

'[Sheep] usually graze far and wide in all sorts of places, so that frequently the winter grazing grounds are many miles away from the summer.' 'I am well aware of that,' said I, 'for I had flocks that wintered in Apulia and summered in the mountains around Reate, those two widely separated ranges being connected by public cattle-trails, as a pair of buckets by their yoke.'

The prominent role accorded to this form of pastoralism is under-standable; it is, after all, more visible in the historical record, leaving traces like the Saepinum inscription.[81] Its importance for the present argument is twofold. In the first place, it is clear that one of the essential preconditions for the emergence of long-distance transhumance is the existence of a large market for its products; most obviously, the city of Rome.[82] Secondly, it is the development of this form of pastoralism that might occasion the conversion of large areas of good arable land into winter pasture in a region like Apulia, resulting in the desolation of the countryside described by various ancient sources.[83]

It is not hard to show that this picture of doom has been exaggerated.

---

[80]   G. Barker *et al* (1978), 50.   [81]   Corbier (1983).

[82]   J. S. Thompson (1989), 145–6; cf. Pasquinucci (1979); Frayn (1984), 54; Gabba (1988), 138–40.

[83]   Cf. Volpe (1990), xv-xvii.

Survey evidence from Apulia contradicts any suggestion that the countryside was entirely deserted; in Daunia, 25–30 per cent of the land shows little trace of settlement and is assumed to have been under cereals or pasture, but the remainder was densely settled and cultivated intensively.[84] It can also be argued that historians have been too eager to associate every reference to large flocks with long-distance transhumance. Many of Varro's comments on the movement of flocks make no reference to the distances involved. It seems likely that he moved his sheep to Reate simply because he owned land there, while other flocks generally travelled much shorter distances.[85]

Nevertheless, there is no doubt that long-distance transhumance did take place on a considerable scale; besides the literary references and the Saepinum inscription there is further epigraphic evidence relating to rules for transit on the *calles*, the cattle-trails.[86] To this must be added the evidence for increases in the sizes of flocks from the second century B.C., known mainly through fines levied for breaking the rules governing the use of *ager publicus*, and for the growing importance of the *pecuarius*, the professional manager of flocks for profit.[87] The growth of the city of Rome, coinciding as it did with an influx of wealth into Italy (flocks were a large and risky investment), the establishment of peace and political control over the peninsula and the expansion of *ager publicus*, led to the development of market-oriented pastoralism on a notable scale.

The effects of this development on regions like Apulia, where flocks were pastured during the winter months, were serious, even if they did not amount to complete desertion of the countryside. Large amounts of land had been confiscated in Apulia after the defeat of Hannibal, and much of this eventually fell into the hands of the metropolitan elite; over a quarter of arable land in Daunia was apparently turned over to pasture or extensive cereal cultivation.[88] Most of the rest of the region was occupied by innumerable small farms, whose numbers were swelled by extensive veteran settlement: farms which were too small and too far from overseas markets to compete successfully in the export trade, except for a brief period during the expansion of the city of Rome in the first century B.C. Pastoralism was the main activity whose products could find a market outside Apulia. Some of the profits probably remained in the region and supported the continuing life of Apulian cities (providing a market for local wine and oil), but a large proportion of the revenue

---

[84]   G. D. B. Jones (1980); Volpe (1990), 46–60, 72–5, 77–8.
[85]   Garnsey (1988b), 201.   [86] *CIL* I²: 585; IX: 2826.
[87]   Gellius, *Noct. Att.* 6.3.37; Livy 33.42.10, 35.10.12; Frayn (1984), 45–65; J. S. Thompson (1989), 27–50.
[88]   Volpe (1990), 40–5; Lomas (1993), 119–20, 122.

from flocks like those of Varro went to the city of Rome. To a limited extent, the development of this peripheral region was indeed restricted to cater for the demands of the metropolis and the avarice of the metropolitan elite.

Summary

Long-distance transhumance was a restricted phenomenon, the preserve of a few wealthy men, confined to a limited area of Italy. It was by no means the only way of managing flocks, even if it is the most obvious example of the power of the Roman market to promote new forms of economic organisation in Italy. Other forms of sheep-raising (the sedentary pastoralism of the upper Biferno valley, or pastoralism integrated with arable cultivation) played an equally important role in supplying the city – and served to enrich their regions, whether by the effect of manure on arable cultivation or by the influx of revenue. Long-distance transhumance tended to have a less positive effect, and it is probably fortunate for regions like Apulia that it did not become more widespread.

Rome's demands, whether for wine, oil, meat or wool, were not infinite. The intensive market-oriented villa was found only in a limited area of central Italy. In a similar manner it can be argued that there was no need to turn the whole of Apulia over to pasture; Rome's demands could be met from a combination of a few large flocks and the smaller-scale pastoralism of Samnium and the Sabine hills. There was no incentive to keep the Po Valley in a state of underdevelopment, preventing the extension of arable cultivation, when alternative supplies of pork could be obtained from southern Italy.

The main difference between the Roman Empire and the capitalist world-economy of Wallerstein lies not in the imbalance of power between core and periphery – that is clear enough in both cases – but in the different levels of demand in pre-industrial and industrial systems. In the modern world, the underdevelopment of the periphery ensures the supply of cheap raw materials and a market for manufactured goods. Rome had no manufactured goods to sell and far less difficulty in obtaining adequate supplies – it could, after all, draw on the resources of most of the Mediterranean – and so had little reason to prevent areas of its hinterland from developing as they wished.

7   Marketing and urbanisation

The marketing of villa produce

In the course of his account of the duties of the *vilicus*, Columella warns that the man should not become involved in buying and selling using his master's money, 'for doing this diverts him from his duties as a *vilicus* and makes him a *negotiator* rather than a farmer'.[1] To judge from the lack of attention paid to the subject, the idea that marketing was not one of the proper concerns of a farmer pervades the entire work. There is little doubt that in Columella's opinion the ultimate aim of cultivation was profit, and numerous passing comments make it clear that the bulk of the estate's produce was intended to be sold.[2] The means by which this produce was turned into money, however, are barely hinted at. Varro, meanwhile, having stated that the final part of his sixfold division of the farmer's year was the marketing of produce, dramatically interrupts the dialogue after the fifth part (storage) with the news of the murder of the *aeditumus*.[3] As in Columella's work, it is clear that the crops are to be sold, but Varro neatly (and, we must conclude, deliberately) evades discussion of the mechanisms involved.[4]

It is left to Cato, whose avariciousness is highlighted in Plutarch's biography, to offer a set of sample contracts for the sale of estate produce.[5] The succeeding centuries saw an increase in the volume of advice offered on cultivation, important changes in agricultural practice and a new unwillingness on the part of Roman authors to address certain issues. The marketing of produce is a job for the master, not the *vilicus*, and the master declines to discuss the subject.[6] Clearly this makes it more difficult to offer an account of the development of marketing systems in response to the demands of the city of Rome. The evidence for changes in practice provided by inscriptions and legal texts will be examined later;

[1]   Col. 11.1.24.   [2] E.g. 1.6.9, 3.2.1, 3.3.10, 3.21.6, 7.3.13.
[3]   *RR* 1.37.4, 1.69.2.   [4] Sale of produce: e.g. *RR* 1.62, 1.69, 3.2.14–15.
[5]   *Agr*. 146–8; Plutarch, *Cat. Mai.* 21.5–8; R. Martin (1971), 87, 90–3.
[6]   On the *vilicus*, cf. *Dig.* 14.3.16.

first, we should consider the various options open to the landowner in selling the produce of his estate or estates.

Some of this produce never entered the market; instead it was consumed by the owner and his dependants.[7] It is impossible to assess the relative importance of the redistribution of produce between estates and urban residences (or other estates). Neither amphorae stamps nor *tituli picti* indicate whether the container's contents were sold or consumed by the *familia urbana*, nor is it possible to tell whether the amphora was shipped by the producer or by an independent merchant.[8] We are left to speculate on the basis of the attitudes and behaviour of the elite. On the one hand, there is the Roman ideal of self-sufficiency, taken to a ludicrous extreme by Trimalchio.[9] On the other hand, the agronomists make it clear that most farm produce was sold, and the expenses of a political career and the maintenance of a comfortable existence made a cash income indispensable.[10]

The landowner who wished to sell his surplus produce had three main options.[11] Firstly, he might oversee the entire process, transporting the goods to the market and selling them through his dependants, as Lichas of Tarentum does in the *Satyricon*.[12] The architecture of houses in Pompeii points to close links between elite residences and shops, while the legal sources show that *tabernae* were a source of income for the elite, either rented out or managed by slave or freedman *institores*.[13] Secondly, he might transport the goods to the city and sell them to middlemen in one of the urban markets, thereby avoiding the legal liability involved in managing businesses through *institores* but presumably making a smaller profit.[14]

However seriously we take the idea that it was demeaning for members of the elite to be involved in trade, it is clear that the marketing of one's own produce was exempt from censure. Discussions of the *lex Claudia* of 218 B.C. show that many members of the elite owned ships for the purpose of exporting produce; the limit on the size of ships that senators and their sons might legally possess was set at three hundred amphorae, since 'this was reckoned to be sufficient to transport the crops from one's fields'.[15] Vessels *quae exportandorum fructuum causa parantur* ('which are provided for carrying away produce') counted as part of the *instrumentum* of a farm.[16] In 179 B.C., a magistrate was criticised for building

---

[7]   Whittaker (1985), 58.   [8]   Peacock and Williams (1986), 10–13, 54–66.
[9]   Petronius, *Sat.* 38, 48.   [10]   Shatzman (1975), 84–98.
[11]   Cf. de Ligt (1993a), 163–5.
[12]   *Sat.* 101.   [13]   Wallace-Hadrill (1991); *Dig.* 14.3.4 *pr.*, 5.1.19.
[14]   Liability: e.g. *Dig.* 14.3.5.12.
[15]   Livy 21.63.4; cf. Cicero, *II Verr.* 5.44–6; D'Arms (1981), 31–9.
[16]   *Dig.* 33.7.12.1.

a mole near Terracina, where he owned property; clearly the provision of local harbour facilities at no cost to himself would add greatly to the profits of the estate.[17]

Alternatively, the landowner could hire a ship to carry the produce, or send it as part of a mixed cargo, although in general the legal sources assume that the owners of such cargoes will be *negotiatores* or *mercatores*.[18] On land, the owner might use his own draught animals and wagons, or hire carriers – or, in the case of animals, hire shepherds and dogs to lead the flocks to market.[19] One passage in the *Digest* discusses a contract for the transport of wine from Campania; others examine the likely problems in hiring carriages, draught animals and muleteers.[20] The same possibilities – investing in the means of transport or hiring them when necessary – were open to the merchant who bought produce at the estates and arranged for its transport to the market himself.

This was of course the third option open to landowners; to sell the crops at the farm gate, passing the costs of transport on to the middleman. In the writings of Varro and Columella, it is generally impossible to tell where the sale is taking place; when Seius sells his boars or Columella hands over new-born lambs to the butcher, it is unclear whether the *macellarius* has come to wait on them or whether they have sent the animals to town themselves.[21] The brothers Veianius, successful bee-keepers, are said to have profited by bringing in (*admitterent*) the merchant only when the time was right, which implies that he would come to the farm to buy the honey.[22] Varro also mentions the merchants in Apulia bringing produce down to the sea on mules, having presumably bought it at the farm.[23] Given the difference in status between landowner and trader, it seems likely that this would be the standard practice, and this is confirmed by Cato and other sources.

Cato offers sample contracts for the sale of olives on the tree, grapes on the vine, wine in jars and the increase of the flock.[24] In the first two cases, the purchaser assumes responsibility not only for transporting the crops but for harvesting and processing them, even if this is carried out by the landowner (Cato also includes contracts for the gathering and milling of olives).[25] The crops were sold to the highest bidder in an auction; the first contract stipulates that the purchaser should pay the auctioneer's fee, while the fourth notes that the owner should receive payment from the *coactor*, a member of a profession devoted to

---

[17]   Livy 40.51.2   [18] *Dig* . 14.1.1.3, 19.2.13.1, 19.2.31, 19.2.61.1.
[19]   Col. 1.3.4, 10.309–10; Varro, *RR* 2.9.6.
[20]   *Dig.* 19.2.11.3, 19.2.60.8; S. Martin (1990).
[21]   *RR* 3.2.11; Col. 7.3.13, 3.2.1, 7.9.4.   [22] *RR* 3.16.11.   [23] *RR* 2.6.5.
[24]   *Agr.* 146–8, 150.   [25] *Agr.* 144–5.

collecting payments due after auctions.[26] The contracts for the sale of grapes and wine make provision for storage on the farm until the following October. In the case of wine sold in *dolia*, the transaction is completed only after tasting to check that only wine which is neither sour nor musty is sold; if the grapes are bought on the vine, it seems that the risk of the wine going off falls on the purchaser. Even in the former case, the contract is strongly weighted in favour of the seller: it stipulates that the *degustatio* must take place within three days, and that the decision on the wine's quality should be made *viri boni arbitratu*, according to the opinion of a reasonable man, rather than being left entirely to the buyer.[27]

Evidence that these sales continued to be normal practice after Cato's time is offered by legal sources, which mention the sale of olives on the tree and go into considerable detail on the sale of wine.[28] There is also an anecdote in the elder Pliny, referring to the sale of grapes on the vine, and a letter of his nephew which illustrates the relative advantages and disadvantages of such sales for landowners and merchants. 'I had sold my grape harvest to the *negotiatores*, who were eager to buy, when the price quoted at the time was tempting and prospects seemed good. Their hopes were frustrated ...'[29] By buying grapes on the vine, the *negotiatores* gambled on the size and quality of the harvest, and on the state of the market when the wine was ready. Large profits could be made; but if the harvest was disappointing, as seems to have happened in this case, they were left with full liability for the price agreed with the landowner and nothing to show for it. The landowner, meanwhile, was assured of his income regardless of the vagaries of the climate, as all risk was passed on to the purchaser as soon as the agreement was concluded.[30]

It is clear that the vendor had no legal obligation to give a rebate in such cases. The sale of grapes on the vine might be classified in Roman law as *emptio rei speratae* (sale of something expected to come into existence) or *emptio spei* (sale of something which may or may not come into existence – the example generally quoted is the sale of a fisherman's next catch).[31] In the latter case, the sale was valid and the buyer liable for the full price even if the thing to be sold failed to materialise; in the former case, the sale was void if there was nothing to sell – but a poor harvest, as opposed to a non-existent one, would not invalidate the contract, unless it included special conditions to take account of such an eventuality. Even in later Roman law the speculator could expect no

---

[26] Andreau (1984), 105.   [27] Cf. Yaron (1959), 75.
[28] On olives, *Dig.* 18.1.39.1; on wine, see below.
[29] *HN* 14.50; *Ep.* 8.2; Sherwin-White (1966), 448–50.   [30] de Zulueta (1945), 30–5.
[31] Dig. 18.1.8; de Zulueta (1945), 14–15; Thomas (1976), 281–2.

redress if his gamble failed. Pliny's complicated scheme of compensation, rewarding those who had invested large sums and those who had paid up promptly, was inspired by other considerations:

This seemed a suitable way both of expressing my gratitude to each individual according to his past merits, and of encouraging them not only to buy from me in future but also to pay their debts ... The whole district is praising the novelty of my rebate and the way in which it was carried out, and the people I classified and graded instead of measuring all with the same rod, so to speak, have departed feeling obliged to me in proportion to their honest worth.[32]

It is in the landowner's interest to maintain good relations with the merchants and to personalise exchange, building up ties of dependence and obligation; but the disparity between their social and economic situations is stressed.

The advantageous position of the landowners in such transactions can be seen equally clearly in the development of the institution of credit at auction sales, managed by the *argentarii* and the *coactores argentarii*.[33] The *coactores* collected money from the purchaser and passed it on to the vendor; it remained the responsibility of the vendor to sue in the case of non-payment. The *argentarii*, however, took this risk upon themselves; they extended credit to the purchaser, paying the vendor immediately. This gave the purchaser, who was a wholesaler or retailer, the opportunity to sell the goods to raise the money with which to pay for them, and it is likely that this short-term credit increased the speed of circulation of goods; the chief beneficiary, however, was the landowner, who was thus relieved of another of the risks usually involved in market transactions.[34]

From the first century B.C. onwards, there is an increase in the number of professions involved in money-lending and in the number of people involved in these professions, as recorded in inscriptions, especially in ports like Ostia and Puteoli and in the capital. It has been argued that this reflects an increase in the total volume of commercial transactions, which can plausibly be linked to the expansion of the metropolitan market.[35] However, it is uncertain how often this form of credit was involved in the sale of the produce of villa estates. Our main source for the business of the *argentarius*, the tablets of 'Monsieur Jucundus' found at Pompeii, deals mainly with *ventes occasionnelles*, often involving dealings with other freedmen, although the distribution of auctions over the year does exhibit seasonal peaks coinciding with important dates in the agricultural calendar.[36] The sums involved in Iucundus' dealings,

[32] *Ep.* 8.2.6–7.   [33] Andreau (1984), 99–107; (1987), 110–16, 359–400, 528–606.
[34] Andreau (1987), 643–70, esp. 659.
[35] Andreau (1984), 104–5; cf. de Ligt (1991b), 495–6.
[36] Andreau (1974), 109–15.

some as large as 30,000 sesterces and many around the 10,000 mark, are quite compatible with those mentioned in Pliny's letter.[37] The system is weighted so much in the vendor's favour that surely only some over-whelming social stigma attached to dealing with *argentarii* (for which there is no evidence) could have dissuaded farmers from taking full advantage.

Apparently the only point in which the advantage of the landowner was not wholly overwhelming lay in the legal protection accorded to those who purchased wine in jars. The jurists exercised considerable ingenuity in dealing with the problem of 'vinegar sold as wine'; that is, what happens if the wine deteriorates while still in the keeping of the vendor, probably a fairly common occurrence in the case of cheap wines.[38] Cato's contract included provision for the tasting and measure-ment of the wine, with the onus on the purchaser to protect himself by taking these precautions.[39] Columella says nothing of tasting, but he does note that 'care should also be taken so that the must, when it has been pressed out, may last well, or at any rate keep until it is sold'.[40] This last comment does not reflect too well on Columella's *bona fides*.

The early classical jurists sought to protect the buyer by questioning the validity of the sale on the grounds of *error in substantia*; their successors rejected this formulation, putting the emphasis on the vendor's warranty that the wine was fit for sale and on the need for the buyer to protect himself by tasting the wine.[41] If the vendor had guaranteed the quality of his wine, he was liable if it was found that it had turned to vinegar; if he remained silent, the purchaser shouldered the risk 'because, if he had not tasted the wine, or, tasting, injudiciously approves it, he has only himself to blame' – unless it could be proved that the vendor knew that it was likely to deteriorate and failed to warn the buyer.[42] This judgement was the outcome of centuries of legal argument, complicated by the fact that vinegar had a marketable value of its own.

The jurists also concerned themselves with the storage of the wine after it had legally been sold, and with its removal from the farm. To be exact, they offered guidelines for cases where no other arrangement had been made; the contracting parties were at liberty to stipulate whatever conditions they desired.[43] It is generally assumed that, in the absence of other arrangements, storage will be provided until the vessels are required for the next vintage (as in Cato's contract); an exception is made when the vendor is a wine merchant, and therefore needs to empty his casks to receive more wine on a regular basis.[44]

---

[37]   *Ibid.*, 88–95.   [38]   Yaron (1959); Frier (1983).   [39]   *Agr.* 148.
[40]   Col. 12.19.1.   [41]   Frier (1983); *Dig.* 18.6.1 *pr.*, 18.6.4.1.   [42]   *Dig.* 18.6.16.
[43]   Cf. *Dig.* 18.1.71.   [44]   *Dig.* 18.6.1.3–4, 18.6.2 *pr.*

Finally, there is the question of what damages should be imposed if either party is responsible for a delay in delivery, or even actively prevents collection; in particular, how far consequential damages – losses incurred because of non-delivery – should be imposed on top of interest on the sums involved.[45] The *Digest* is somewhat unhelpful on this, probably because the jurists disagreed and Justinian edited out their controversies.[46]

When the seller is responsible for non-delivery of an object, every benefit to the buyer is taken into account, provided that it stands in close connection with this matter. If he could have completed a deal and made a profit from wine, this should not be reckoned in, no more than if he buys wheat and his household suffers from starvation because it was not delivered; he receives the price of the grain, not the price of the slaves killed by starvation. An obligation does not increase because it is carried out slowly, although it would grow greater if wine were worth more today.[47]

The intention is to avoid unduly speculative damages, including any profits that a wine merchant could have made if he had been able to sell the wine at an earlier date. The jurists show no particular sympathy, and certainly make no special provision, for those whose income was subject to the vagaries of market prices and therefore dependent on their ability to sell the goods at the right moment.

In general, as Frier observes, 'the jurists display considerable doctrine, but little dogmatism, in adapting the scaffold of Roman private law to the peculiar needs and usages of the wine trade'.[48] This may be due to the unique quality of wine, that its deterioration produces a new product with its own value, or to the importance and profitability of the wine trade, but no other product receives such attention from Roman lawyers. Two additional points should be noted. Firstly, the prevailing standard of trade assumed by the later jurists appears to be one in which regular and repeated orders, rather than simple one-off transactions, are the norm.[49] Secondly, there is still a great deal of emphasis on the *bona fides* of the vendor, with the buyer encouraged to rely on him for quality, prompt delivery and so forth. Despite the extension of legal protection to cover one of the more problematic areas of the wine trade, and the assertion that the vendor 'has to display greater care than he might show in his own affairs', it seems clear than landowners remained in a commanding social and economic position.[50]

The sale of produce at the farm gate relieved the landowner of the cost

---

[45]   *Dig.* 19.1.3.3–4, 19.1.25.   [46] de Zulueta (1945), 41.
[47]   *Dig.* 19.1.21.3; the final sentence refers to vintage wines, which do increase in value over time.
[48]   Frier (1983), 290.   [49] *Ibid.*, 291.   [50] *Dig.* 18.6.3.

and trouble of transporting his crops to market. He made a smaller profit than might otherwise have been possible, but received a more certain income. As Cato observed: 'It is true that to obtain money by trade is sometimes more profitable, were it not so hazardous … The *mercator* I consider to be an energetic man, and one bent on making money; but, as I said above, it is a dangerous career and one subject to disaster.'[51] The landowner who sold his crops in advance to speculators had a yet more assured income, avoiding even the risk of a poor harvest. The sale of produce at the farm gate is assumed to be the norm in Cato's work, and it is taken for granted by the younger Pliny and the jurists; despite their silence on the subject, it is likely that Varro and Columella disposed of most of the produce of their estates in the same way.

Two important points follow from this conclusion. Firstly, the fact that a sizeable proportion of Rome's supplies reached the market by private channels rather than through town markets must be taken into account when considering the effect of the metropolis on urbanisation in Italy; we might compare the declining importance of market towns in the supply of London in the early modern period.[52] Secondly, the decision of many landowners to pass most of the risks of marketing their produce on to others led to the emergence of a class of middlemen who were prepared to shoulder these risks: not only urban retailers but also wholesalers who bought from villa estates and then sold the goods to retailers in places like the *forum vinarium* at Rome.

Peasant marketing and the *nundinae*

Short-cycle periodic markets, known by the Romans as *nundinae* because they were originally held every eight days, catered above all for peasant producers, especially those normally resident in the countryside.[53] This is made clear by the fact that *nundinae* continued to take place in the first century A.D. in Italian towns which possessed permanent facilities for daily trade, including *tabernae* and often a *macellum*.[54] Roman sources stress the multi-functional aspects of the weekly markets, and in doing so make it clear that their expected clientele is the country-dwelling population; the *nundinae* are an opportunity for peasants to 'arrange matters concerning both town and countryside', 'to visit the market' and 'to take cognizance of new legislation'.[55] Varro observes that the Romans'

---

[51] *Agr. pr.* 1, 3.   [52] Everitt (1990), 55–65; Chartres (1990), 157.
[53] de Ligt (1993a), 106–54.
[54] Inscriptions in Degrassi (1963), 300–4; MacMullen (1970); on *macella*, de Ruyt (1983), 17–222; generally, Shaw (1981), 41–4.
[55] Macrobius, *Sat.* 1.16.33–4; de Ligt (1993a), 112.

virtuous ancestors had 'so divided the year that they attended to their town affairs only on the ninth days and dwelt in the country on the remaining seven'.[56]

The rationale of such high-frequency periodic markets is related to the density of rural demand and supply:[57]

For traders, periodic markets are a means to make a living on products for which insufficient demand exists to make a permanent establishment in one place viable. Or they may be a means for them to buy up surpluses which are available only periodically. For consumers, periodic markets have the effect of reducing the distance they have to go to obtain the desired goods and services. Finally, in primitive economies producer and seller often coincide. In that case the seller finds periodicity profitable even if he only sells at one market: he spends most of his time producing the goods to be sold.[58]

There are two ways in which these *nundinae* might be involved in urban food supplies. The first, obviously enough, is that farmers might sell their surplus produce to urban consumers or retailers when they visited the market. Peasants in Italy did not need to raise money to pay the land tax, but many of them had to pay rents in cash, and they certainly needed to sell some produce so as to buy goods that they could not produce themselves.[59] Few small farmers would be willing to risk specialising in cash crops and relying on the market for their subsistence; rather, we are dealing here with the sale of the comparatively small surplus left after subsistence needs had been met.[60] Nevertheless, they might still make a significant contribution to urban food supplies: in a case mentioned by the younger Pliny, the municipal authorities opposed the establishment of a market on a local estate, apparently because of their concern for the effect on urban consumers if peasants no longer sold their produce in the town market.[61]

The second possibility is that the *nundinae* might be frequented by middlemen, making a living by buying up peasant surpluses and shipping them to more distant markets, larger cities which were dependent for part of their food supply on the production of farmers who lived outside the catchment areas of their own markets. From the trader's point of view, it is clearly more economical to collect these surpluses at the market rather than having to visit a large number of different farms; merchants might still have to visit several markets in a week to make the exercise profitable. The practice has been observed in modern periodic

---

[56]   *RR* 2 *pr.* 1.   [57]   C. A. Smith (1974), 181–6; de Ligt (1993a), 6–9.
[58]   de Ligt and de Neeve (1988), 401.
[59]   de Ligt (1990), 36–9, 47–9; (1993a), 136–42; on monetary rents in Italy, Pleket (1990), 91–2 and Duncan-Jones (1990), 187–98.
[60]   de Neeve (1984a), 32–3; de Ligt (1993a), 136–8, esp. n.125.
[61]   de Ligt (1993b), esp. 247–8, on Pliny, *Ep.* 5.4 and 5.13.

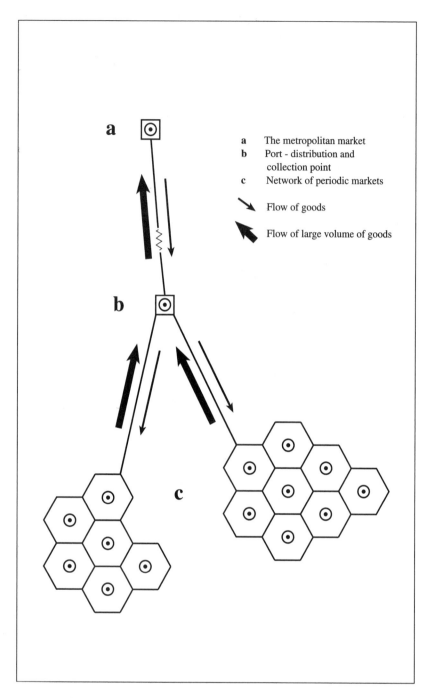

a   The metropolitan market
b   Port - distribution and
       collection point
c   Network of periodic markets

     Flow of goods

     Flow of large volume of goods

Figure 3   Dendritic central place system.

markets, for example in Nigeria and in Barcelos in northern Portugal.[62] The result may be envisaged as a form of dendritic central place system, with groups of periodic markets linked to the central market (Figure 3).[63] There is no direct evidence that small farmers in Italy played a significant part in the food supply of the city of Rome. However, if they did, then it is likely that periodic markets had an important role in the collection of their surplus produce. A more detailed study of the *nundinae* of central Italy does offer some support for this theory.

Evidence for periodic markets in Italy is provided by a series of market calendars, known as the *indices nundinarii*, dating from the first century A.D.; four are inscriptions, one a graffito.[64] Each contains the whole or a part of a list of towns, most of which are located in southern Latium, Campania or Samnium; several mention the days on which markets take place at each location, while one has a complicated calendar arranged in the form of interlocking circles with holes for pegs which indicated where the market was being held each day.

There are considerable problems in interpreting these lists. 'There is no logic to the order of names. They do not arrange themselves in an orderly itinerary, nor do they follow a pattern of regular rotation, every eighth day.'[65] Shaw has suggested that the inconsistencies might be explained if it were assumed that some towns held markets several days a week, as they became incorporated into several different market cycles.[66] Certainly the calendars seem to relate to a number of interlocking market networks rather than a single system; however, the evidence is too fragmentary to permit a detailed reconstruction of the various weekly cycles.[67] For the same reason, the absence of certain towns (the most surprising being Venafrum) is not necessarily significant; at least eight names are missing from the inscription from southern Latium, and an unknown number from the calendars found at Allifae and Suessula.

The *indices nundinarii* offer clear evidence for communication between different markets, contrary to the image of Roman cities as self-sufficient solar central places.[68] The very existence of the *indices* suggests that some merchants were in the habit of visiting a number of different markets. It is difficult to imagine why a farmer should need to know about, let alone visit, more than two or three markets; indeed, this would contradict one of the basic functions of the period market cycle, to service as many consumers as possible. The lists would be of most use to craftsmen and

[62]   Prof. M. Chisholm, pers. comm.
[63]   C. A. Smith (1976), 34–6; Hodges (1988), 16–21, 68–73.
[64]   Degrassi (1963), 300–4.
[65]   MacMullen (1970), 340.   [66]   (1981), 66.   [67]   Cf. de Ligt (1993a), 114–15.
[68]   de Ligt (1993a), 115–16, 237–40; Morley (forthcoming).

traders, itinerant or town-based, like the Pompeian *garum* seller in whose shop one of the calendars was found.[69]

A particular problem in the interpretation of the *indices* is the inclusion of the city of Rome in three of the lists. The presence of the equally far-flung Luceria, across the Apennines in Apulia, suggests that the *nundinae* played an important role in trade between the mainly arable coastal regions and the mainly pastoral highlands.[70] Rome, however, is not generally regarded as a centre of manufacture, although Cato mentions it as a source of goods like tunics, blankets, shoes, pots, baskets, ploughs and yokes.[71] Rome had no special advantage (for example, control of scarce raw materials) in manufacturing such items. Moreover, all these goods were comparatively cheap and bought on a regular basis by many farmers, as well as by the *vilici* of slave-run estates. According to the principles of central place theory, such products would be produced and sold locally.[72] The capital can certainly be seen as a centre for the redistribution of imported luxuries through Italy, although we might have expected that most of these goods (at any rate those from the East) would have been off-loaded at Puteoli, rather than carried up to Rome and back again.

Another explanation, offered by Shaw, is that the presence of Rome on the *nundinae* lists is a sign of the city's increasing political and economic control of Campania, which seems to imply that its importance for the market cycle is purely symbolic.[73] There is certainly nothing in the inscriptions themselves to suggest that Rome should be regarded in a different way from other markets on the lists. This leaves us with the final theory, that the city was a market for manufactured goods which were also sold in other *nundinae*, and/or for goods which had been collected at periodic markets – that is, a market for the surpluses of small farmers. This latter theory is quite compatible with the idea that Rome was also the source of certain goods; the city stood at the head of a dendritic network, with goods travelling both ways along the lines of communication.

Some tentative support for this suggestion is found in the spatial distribution of the *nundinae* in Campania and the surrounding area, when compared with the models offered by central place theory.[74] Map 3 shows the towns in question in relation to the region's geography and what is known of the road network; Figure 4 is an attempt at producing

[69] Degrassi (1963), 305; Frayn (1993), 39; cf. Gabba (1975), 148.
[70] de Ligt (1993a), 116; Frayn (1993), 41; cf. de Ligt (1991a), 50–1 for marketing at ecological boundaries.
[71] *Agr.* 135.   [72] de Ligt (1991a), 34–5, 43–4.   [73] Shaw (1981), 44.
[74] C. A. Smith (1974), 168–73; (1976), 10–28; cf. Andreau (1987–9), 182–3.

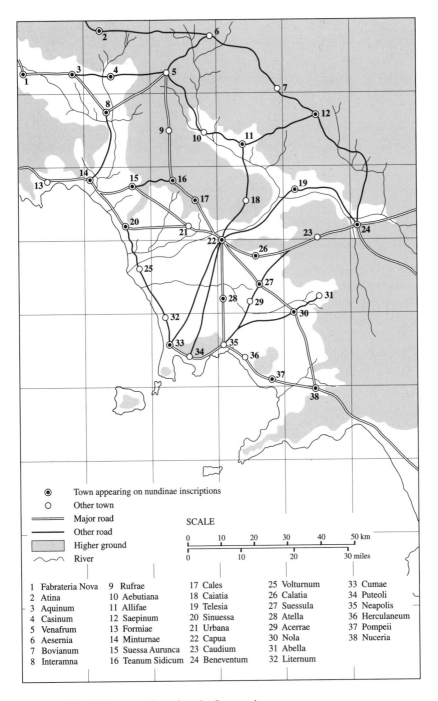

⊙	Town appearing on nundinae inscriptions			
○	Other town			
	Major road			
	Other road	SCALE		
	Higher ground			
	River			

SCALE

0 10 20 30 40 50 km

0 10 20 30 miles

1	Fabrateria Nova	9	Rufrae	17	Cales	25	Volturnum	33	Cumae
2	Atina	10	Aebutiana	18	Caiatia	26	Calatia	34	Puteoli
3	Aquinum	11	Allifae	19	Telesia	27	Suessula	35	Neapolis
4	Casinum	12	Saepinum	20	Sinuessa	28	Atella	36	Herculaneum
5	Venafrum	13	Formiae	21	Urbana	29	Acerrae	37	Pompeii
6	Aesernia	14	Minturnae	22	Capua	30	Nola	38	Nuceria
7	Bovianum	15	Suessa Aurunca	23	Caudium	31	Abella		
8	Interamna	16	Teanum Sidicum	24	Beneventum	32	Liternum		

Map 3 Towns and markets in Campania.

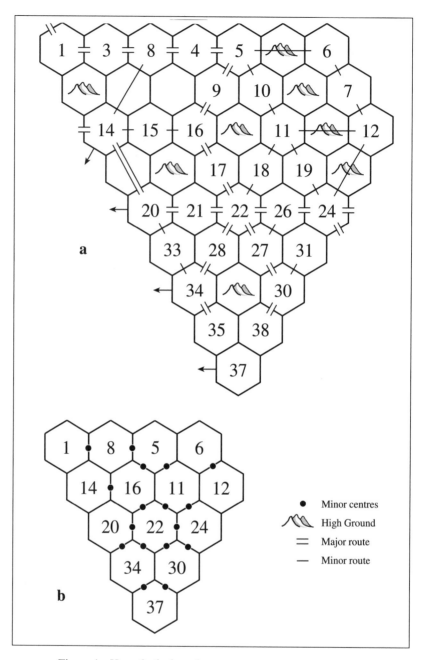

Figure 4   Hypothetical market system.
a is a schematic representation of the Campanian market system, with the numbers corresponding to the market centres shown on Map 3; *b* is a condensed version of *a*, with minor centres shown only as dots.

an abstract model of the relationships between these market centres, based on their locations and their apparent catchment areas.

The towns in which *nundinae* took place – indeed, all the towns in the region – are not evenly spaced. This is not unexpected. The sites of Roman towns were not chosen simply for the convenience of farmers and traders.[75] In addition, central place theory assumes that the landscape in question is featureless and has equal ease of access in all directions, and that population and purchasing power are evenly distributed. If these conditions are met, markets will be evenly spaced; if not – for example, if the population is sparser in highland areas (Samnium) or marshes (the mouth of the Volturnus) – markets will need a larger catchment area to reach their demand threshold, and so will be more widely spaced. Roads can also be a distorting factor; in some cases they will follow the existing marketing system, linking major centres, but in others they help to form the system, promoting some centres at the expense of others. Finally, it should be noted that most attempts at producing abstract models of marketing systems are based on detailed knowledge of the volume and nature of sales in each market, allowing reconstruction of the market hierarchy. In the absence of such information, Figure 4 can only be extremely approximate, besides being based on the arguable proposition that a town's place in the marketing hierarchy can be determined from its political importance, the number of inscriptions found there and a few references in Strabo.[76]

This reconstruction of the Campanian market system resembles the $k = 4$ arrangement in Christaller's original model where k represents the number of settlements served by each central place; that is, a system based on the transport principle, an arrangement which tends to work to the benefit of the inhabitants of higher order centres rather than rural consumers.[77] The importance of roads in organising the landscape has been noted in other regions of Italy.[78] Roads radiating out from Rome, like the Via Appia and the Via Latina, played an important part in establishing control over the peninsula, including Campania. However, these are not the only roads in the region; it can be seen that Capua was well placed to draw in goods from all parts of the surrounding area, and it is not stretching credibility too far to imagine that one of the major influences on the Campanian market system was the development of Capua as a central place, both a high-level supplier

[75] de Ligt (1993a), 12; Ward-Perkins (1964), 19–20; cf. Frayn (1993), 83.
[76] For information on the towns shown in Map 3, see Strabo 5.3.6–10 and 5.4.4–11; Keppie (1983), 136–52; Frayn (1993), 84–91.
[77] Hodges (1988), 64–5.   [78] E.g. Ward-Perkins (1962), 397–9.

of goods to rural consumers and a major consumer of the region's produce.[79]

Also important are the ports; partly as centres for the redistribution of imports, but most obviously as the points where Campanian exports were collected together for shipment overseas. In all likelihood they performed this role also for produce which had been bought privately at the farm gate, but each of the port towns can be seen as lying at a critical point (*b* in Figure 3) in a dendritic network that drew produce from the countryside through periodic markets and sent it on to the city. Pompeii is described by Strabo as the port of southern Campania; Minturnae served the Liri valley, Sinuessa dealt with the produce of northern Campania and the Ager Falernus, and Puteoli was the major port of the Ager Campanus (and perhaps also the point of export for goods like wool, brought down from the highlands via Beneventum and Capua).

This hypothetical reconstruction cannot offer incontrovertible evidence that Campanian *nundinae*, and Campanian peasants and tenant-farmers, were involved in supplying the city of Rome. The theory is certainly not incompatible with the evidence as it stands; indeed, the inclusion of Rome on the *indices nundinarii* is a strong indication that the region's towns had become integrated into a wider system of markets whose function was to funnel produce towards the city, with the secondary effect that certain luxuries and other goods travelled back along the same lines of communication.

Migration and urbanisation

One of the 'laws' of migration identified by Ravenstein in the nineteenth century was that it tends to proceed step by step – that is, people migrate first to local centres and only gradually move further up the urban hierarchy.[80] We have already seen the level of migration necessary to support the city of Rome; it might be expected, therefore, that the growth of the metropolis would be accompanied by an increase in the sizes of other cities in the Italian urban system. However, as the volume of literature on 'primate' cities and 'immature' urban systems shows, the tendency for urbanisation to proceed in a regular, orderly manner is by no means found in every region of the modern world, let alone in past societies.[81]

It is possible to identify two likely constraints on migration to cities other than Rome during this period. The first is related to status and participation in civic life: the fact that migration from one's home town

[79]   Cf. Frayn (1993), 82 fig. 8, 84–7; Cicero, *Leg. Ag.* 2.88.
[80]   Clark and Souden (1987), 19.   [81]   E.g. C. A. Smith (1985a) and (1985b).

involved the loss of certain rights and privileges of citizenship.[82] Clearly this did not apply to someone with Roman citizenship who moved to the capital, and the process by which different parts of Italy were enfranchised must have played an important role in determining the flows of migration to Rome in the last two centuries of the Republic.

The man who moved between two other Italian cities was in a different position. He became an *incola*, entitled to vote in local elections (all *incolae* voting in a single *curia*, determined by lot) but not allowed to stand as a candidate himself.[83] Furthermore, while he became liable for *munera* (local taxes and obligations) in his new place of residence, he remained liable to *munera* in his place of origin; and *origo* was inherited, so that a man remained bound to the place from which his father or grandfather had come.[84] Only in the second century A.D. was the legal principle established that liability to *munera* depended on *domicilium* rather than *origo*.[85] None of the surviving municipal codes includes any provision for adopting immigrants as full citizens; it is not clear whether the principle expounded by Cicero with regard to those who wished to lay aside their Roman citizenship would hold good in such cases: 'A man cannot change his citizenship against his will, and, if he should wish to change it, he cannot be prevented from doing so, provided that he be adopted by that state of which he should desire to become a citizen.'[86]

Although the Roman citizen would retain his status and legal rights anywhere in Italy, the prospect of losing political rights might discourage migration to anywhere but Rome. Three points can be made in this respect. Firstly, in many cases the letter of the law might simply be ignored.[87] It seems unlikely that the civic authorities would assiduously pursue any but the wealthiest of permanent migrants to demand that they perform the necessary *munera*. Furthermore, there are several examples of towns outside Italy electing non-citizens to civic office, and it is quite possible that Italian *municipia* were equally relaxed in their attitude to the law.[88]

Secondly, we may doubt, without the prospect of being able to prove the case either way, how important these political rights were to the mass of the population, who would make up the majority of potential migrants. Thirdly, there is evidence that migration did indeed take place between towns within the empire, despite the political disadvantages. A study of tombstones in the province of Lusitania, which often mention

---

[83] *Lex Municipalis Malacitana* 53 – most evidence on municipal constitutions comes from the provinces. Cf. Livy 25.3.16.
[84] *Lex Coloniae Genetivae Iuliae* 98, 103; *Dig.* 50.1.1, 50.1.6.1, 50.1.29.
[85] Sherwin-White (1973), 312 n. 2.   [86] Cicero, *Balb.* 29.
[87] Sherwin-White (1973), 304.
[88] E.g. Pliny, *Ep.* 10.114; Sherwin-White (1966), 724–5.

the *origo* of the deceased, shows that many had moved from their home town (and not only soldiers and administrators, whose mobility is easily explained).[89] In Herculaneum, at least a third of the *ingenui* named on the membership lists of the local *Augustales* belonged to tribes other than the Menenia, to which all natives of the town belonged; either they or their ancestors must therefore have been migrants.[90]

Questions of status and enfranchisement do not appear to have dissuaded at least some people from changing their place of residence. A more significant constraint on mobility might be the availability of employment; after all, the most common motive for migration is the hope of improving one's economic position. The attractions of the city of Rome are obvious; it remains to be seen whether the other towns of Italy offered such inviting prospects. Smith's explanation of urban primacy in modern Guatemala is precisely that there were few employment opportunities outside the metropolis, so that would-be migrants had little choice but to move to the capital.[91]

In the case of Guatemala, local job prospects were limited because local elites retained a tight hold on production and exchange and discouraged competition, relying on traditional structures of dependence. Italian elites did not assert their dominance through control of the means of exchange; their power was based on control of the means of production, above all land.[92] Within the towns, they invested in urban property, and may have been involved indirectly (through dependent freedmen) in manufacturing.[93] They did not attempt to control directly the activities of craftsmen or retailers, who were equally free from the restrictions imposed by medieval guilds. The limits to the development of manufacturing and exchange (and therefore of urban employment) in the towns of Italy were set primarily by the level of demand for urban goods and services. Given the low level of surplus production in a pre-industrial economy, it may be assumed that the typical city, serving a limited area, was fairly small.

The city of Rome affected the level of demand for goods and services in several ways. Firstly, large numbers of people were employed in supplying the capital with food: not only merchants, but sailors, muleteers, porters and dockers, to say nothing of the tavern-keepers, prostitutes and retailers who provided services for these labourers. The growth of ports like Ostia and Puteoli is closely linked to the demands of Rome.[94] The size of

[89] Stanley (1990).   [90] Ostrow (1985), 80–1.   [91] C. A. Smith (1985b), 131–2.
[92] de Ligt (1993a), 240.
[93] Garnsey (1976a), (1981); D'Arms (1981), 39–45, 66, 142–6; Pleket (1983), 133–4, (1990), 119–27; Jongman (1988a), 172–9.
[94] Meiggs (1960); D'Arms (1974); Frederiksen (1984), 319–58.

Pompeii (even the lower estimates place it well above the average) may be explained by its role as the point of export for produce from its own territory and the rest of southern Campania.[95] Inland cities which lay at important nodes in the marketing network – Capua, for example, or Beneventum – might also benefit from the expansion of trade. New settlements, lacking political institutions but well supplied with taverns, bath houses and other facilities, sprang up along major roads to meet the demands of travellers.[96]

Secondly, the demands of the city for certain goods might stimulate urban manufacturing. Above all, this means textiles: few people in Rome were in a position to produce their own cloth, while it made economic sense to carry out most of the processing of wool before transporting it long distances.[97] There is no reason to assume that these processes could be carried out only in towns, and the idea that the Pompeian economy was dominated by an export-oriented textile industry has been thoroughly demolished.[98] However, Strabo specifically states that Patavium produced clothing for Rome.[99] Other Cisalpine cities were involved in the wool and textile trade, and Garnsey suggests that the apparent openness of the local elite in Mediolanum, with no social stigma attached to uninherited wealth, implies that the economy was diversified rather than exclusively land-based.[100] Cities in other wool-producing regions like Samnium might also have a significant proportion of their population employed in fulling and weaving.

Thirdly, profits made from supplying the city of Rome might be spent on local goods and services, raising the level of demand and therefore supporting more people in non-agricultural labour. In the most optimistic scenario, the demand for agricultural products thus created leads to further increases in rural productivity, thus promoting further urbanisation, and so on. However, the profits of trade were not shared equally among all members of society. The high risks of their profession seem to have left most merchants only moderately well-off, operating on a fairly small scale; the few who made fortunes tended to spend their gains on land as much as they increased their consumption of goods and services. Small farmers at best increased a small surplus by a little – but comparative evidence shows that they might choose to spend their gains on land or conspicuous consumption rather than manufactured goods.[101]

---

[95] Population: Jongman (1988a), 108–12; on exports, Strabo 5.4.8 and Purcell (1990), *contra* Jongman (1988a), 97–137.
[96] Strabo 5.2.10; Potter (1979), 117–20.
[97] A. H. M. Jones (1960); K. Hopkins (1978b), 52–5.
[98] Jongman (1988a), 155–86, *contra* Moeller (1976).   [99] 5.1.7.   [100] (1976b).
[101] de Ligt (1993a), 147–8.

The lion's share of the profits went to the elite, who commanded the land and capital (as well as certain political, social and legal advantages) with which to amass a large marketable surplus. The spending habits of the elite are therefore of critical importance to the process of urbanisation in Italy. For example, changes in the way that the Samnite elites competed amongst themselves led to the growth of towns in the region, which had previously been dominated by a more dispersed pattern of settlement.[102] The great period of expansion of Italian towns was the first century B.C., continuing into the next century, as enfranchisement and municipalisation led to new patterns of elite expenditure.[103] The elite raised the money for such displays through the sale of the produce of their estates, above all to the city of Rome. However, the 'Romanisation' of Italy was a complex process; it is possible that it was regular exchange with the metropolis that served as a carrier of political and social values, as much as it was the adoption of such values (and the consequent need for large amounts of money) that led Italian elites to get involved in the food supply of the capital.

Not every city in Italy blossomed under Rome's influence. Alongside the 'boom towns' like Ostia we must set the centres which were by-passed by the flow of goods and money between Rome and its hinterland. The town of Cosa is a good example.[104] At the beginning of the first century B.C., when its territory was experiencing dramatic changes in its economy, resulting in increased prosperity, the urban centre was abandoned altogether, and an attempted revival under Augustus lasted for barely a century.[105] The port of Cosa continued in use throughout the period, and was clearly the main point of export for the produce of the Ager Cosanus, but the town failed to benefit from this trade.[106] The owners of the villas chose to spend their profits elsewhere; the focus of their political and social lives lay outside the region, most likely in the metropolis, and without the support and expenditure of these magnates Cosa itself was doomed.

A similar process can be seen clearly in the immediate hinterland of Rome. In his description of the region in the Augustan period, Strabo laments the decline of many suburban towns. Sutri is described as a *polis*, but Falerii, Nepi and Nomentum are *polikhnai*, small towns, Eretum is a mere village and Veii and Fidenae 'have been brought low by the Romans'. 'There was Collatia, and Antemnae, and Fidenae, and Labicum, and other such places – then little cities, but now mere villages, or else estates of private citizens.'[107] Cicero echoes the complaint,

---

[102] Patterson (1991).   [103] Gabba (1972), (1987); Gros (1990).
[104] Brown (1980).   [105] Fentress (1994).   [106] McCann *et al.* (1987), 15–43.
[107] Strabo 5.2.9, 5.3.1–2.

contrasting the great cities of Campania with Labicum, Fidenae, Collatia, Lanuvium, Aricia and Tusculum.[108] For Horace, Gabii and Fidenae are examples of desolation.[109] Propertius claims that Veii, once so great, is now given over to cornfields and shepherds.[110]

In many cases this picture can be supported by archaeology; in almost every part of the *suburbium*, the built-up areas of towns and villages shrink steadily from the fourth century onwards. The site of Fidenae was half-devoured by a quarry, while parts of Crustumerium and Antemnae were indeed occupied by villas.[111] Veii produces a number of sherds dating to the late Republic, but the occupied area was clearly very much reduced from earlier periods.[112] There is little evidence of building activity in any of the towns in the north of the *suburbium* in the middle or late Republic, especially when compared with towns like Tibur, Praeneste or Bovillae.[113]

Veii enjoyed a modest revival from the middle of the first century B.C.; it probably received veteran settlement and certainly benefited from the patronage of Augustus, who made it a *municipium*.[114] Lucus Feroniae, Falerii Novi and Sutri also enjoyed some prosperity in the first century A.D.[115] However, unless this is purely a matter of nineteenth-century antiquarian tastes, it appears from the material collected at Veii that this recovery did not last much beyond the Augustan period.[116] The urban nucleus remained modest in size, with other parts of the old city area occupied by villas.[117] Centres like Antemnae, Fidenae and Crustumerium never experienced any such recovery.

In part, this urban decline may be attributed to the spread of more dispersed patterns of settlement after the Roman conquest, as farmers now lived on their estates rather than within the city walls. This hardly applies to places like Collatia and Crustumerium, which suffered simultaneous rural and urban decline, a fate which was to strike South Etruria a century or so later. Rural depopulation or impoverishment reduced the demand for urban goods and services (and the continuation of building activities in towns in the east of the *suburbium* is one indication that the impression offered by surveys of continuity and minimal disruption in the countryside, even in the second century, may be correct). When the countryside began to revive, however, many urban centres failed to benefit.

In the first place, the towns of the *suburbium* had lost much of their

[108] *Leg. Ag.* 2.96.   [109] *Ep.* 1.11.7.   [110] 4.10.27–30.
[111] Quilici and Quilici Gigli (1986), 404; (1980), 294–5, 300–4; (1978), 165–7.
[112] Ward-Perkins (1961), 52–7.   [113] Jouffroy (1986), 333–9, 358–61.
[114] Ward-Perkins (1962), 57–75; Liverani (1987).
[115] Potter (1991), 200; cf. Jouffroy (1986), 333–9, 358–61.   [116] Liverani (1987), 152.
[117] Ward-Perkins (1962), 64.

economic role. Landowners sent their produce direct to the metropolis rather than selling it in the local market. Rome served as a market not only for the region's produce but for its needs, with weekly *nundinae* and three great annual fairs; Cato lists the metropolis rather than local towns as a source of supplies for his villa, and the distribution of fine pottery in South Etruria, declining in quantity with distance from the city, supports the idea that Rome was the original point of distribution.[118] The bulk of traffic passed along the main roads to Rome, which for the most part by-passed the old urban centres.[119] Some towns adapted to a new role – Dionysius of Halicarnassus, describing Gabii, notes that 'today not all parts of it are inhabited, but only those that lie next to the highway and are given up to inns'; some simply declined.[120]

Secondly, and most importantly, the region's wealthy elite, whose expenditure was vital for urban fortunes, had changed; even in towns like Praeneste and Tibur, where the long tradition of building activity tends to disguise the degree of discontinuity. A new population had settled in the *suburbium*, which had few local ties or loyalties. The Veii of the Principate was, in Liverani's words, 'una Veio del tutto de-etruschizzata'; less than 10 per cent of the people mentioned in inscriptions of this period were of Etruscan origin, and even these few may have been newcomers.[121] The division of the citizen body into *intra-* and *extra-murani* may reflect divisions of interest as much as distinctions in residence, which hardly boded well for Veii's survival as an effective municipal unit; there is even an inscription which suggests that the *decuriones* met in the Forum of Caesar in Rome.[122]

Cicero speaks of towns in the eastern *suburbium* like 'Labicum or Gabii or Bovillae, communities which today can scarcely find envoys to send for their share of the victims at the Latin festival'; the problem, as with the shortage of *municipes* at Tusculum, is not one of depopulation but of a lack of native residents.[123] The vigorous epigraphic life of the suburban towns involves for the most part men originally from Rome, merchants, shopkeepers, freedmen and *apparitores*.[124] Some of these newcomers participated fully in what remained of local civic life; many – above all, the great villa-owners – were more concerned with the life of the metropolis, with serious consequences for the urban centres that lay beneath the shadow of the city of Rome.

---

[118] MacMullen (1970); Cato, *Agr.* 135.
[119] Wiseman (1970); W. V. Harris (1971), 161–9; Potter (1979), 101–9; Ward-Perkins (1962), 397–9.
[120] Dion. Hal. 4.53; cf. Quilici (1974a), 36–7.   [121] (1987), 149.
[122] Ward-Perkins (1962), 59; Purcell (1983), 167.   [123] *Planc.* 21, 23.
[124] Purcell (1983).

The Italian urban system

The impact of the metropolis on the towns of Italy was by no means uniform. Most importantly, it changed over time; ideally, discussion of 'the Italian urban system' should focus on the process of continual metamorphosis, as different cities expanded – quite possibly at the expense of other centres – and declined. Unfortunately, evidence for the size of cities at any time, let alone over a period of time, is extremely poor.[125] The difficulties involved in estimating population from the built-up area of a town, or the length of its walls, were discussed in Chapter 2 with regard to the city of Rome.[126] The fact that there was no political separation between town and countryside means that most references to the numbers who benefited from local euergetism may relate to the population of the territory as a whole rather than just the urban centre; in only a couple of inscriptions is it specifically indicated that members of the *plebs urbana* are the recipients of largesse, while in a few others it may be surmised.[127] Writers like Strabo are mainly interested in the political status of urban centres rather than their sizes, while Pliny's account of Italy simply offers a list of the names of towns without any comment.[128]

Any attempt at estimating the urban population of Italy at a given date can only be thoroughly speculative – and, indeed, of arguable utility, except for the purposes of making a rough comparison with the level of urbanisation in other pre-industrial societies. A more productive approach is to concentrate on the process of urbanisation, bearing in mind the factors likely to promote or inhibit urban growth discussed above, and to sketch out a model of the urban system as it eventually developed.

At the top of the urban hierarchy, naturally enough, is the metropolis. The second level of the system is provided by the two major ports involved in supplying Rome, Ostia and Puteoli (Aquileia was also large, but it is highly unlikely that it should be included as part of an Italian urban system centred on Rome). The third level comprises major regional centres, which commanded important junctions, provided higher level marketing functions for a wide area and may also have been involved in manufacturing: Capua, Mediolanum, Patavium. Fourth comes a miscellaneous collection of larger cities: minor ports like Pompeii and Brundisium, marketing centres like Beneventum. The division of specific cities between the third and fourth levels is to some extent arbitrary, but it is difficult to accept the alternative, that cities as different as Pompeii and Mediolanum should be included in the same category. Finally, there are

---

[125] Duncan-Jones (1982), 259–77.   [126] Cf. Nissen (1902), 36–9.
[127] Duncan-Jones (1982), 266–74.   [128] Pédech (1971).

the numerous minor centres of Italy (Polybius names over four hundred cities); *municipia* and *coloniae*, the basic units of local administration, and settlements without independent political status, all providing goods and services for the rural population and an arena for display for the local elite.

Table 1 is an attempt at attaching some tentative population figures to these categories, drawing upon the scattered literary, archaeological and epigraphic evidence for the relative importance of cities (so as to assign them to different levels of the hierarchy) and the size of their populations. If the figures can be related to any actual date, it must be to the middle of the first century A.D., when the system had reached maturity. At first sight, the total figure for the urban population is exceptionally high; apparently nearly 40% of Italians lived in cities (25%, if the city of Rome is excluded), a remarkable figure by the standards of pre-industrial societies.[129] The main contributors to this figure are not the large centres but the medium-sized cities like Pompeii (10–12,000) and Comum (22,500), and the sheer number of small towns.

Table 1 *Urbanisation in Roman Italy*

(i)	The city of Rome	1,000,000
(ii)	Major ports: Ostia, Puteoli; 30,000 each	60,000
(iii)	Regional centres: Mediolanum, Patavium, Capua	
	25–40,000 each: average 30,000	90,000
(iv)	About 25 major cities: 5–25,000, average 15,000	375,000
(v)	400 minor cities: 1–5,000, average 2,000	800,000
	Total	2,325,000

Note: Major cities (iv) include Verona, Ravenna, Placentia, Cremona, Parma, Mutina, Bononia, Dertona, Genua, Spoletium, Comum, Teanum, Corfinium, Teate Marrucini, Pompeii, Beneventum, Tarentum, Brundisium, Rhegium and Canusium (based mainly on Strabo's account of Italy, with Duncan-Jones (1982), 266–77).

Of course, these figures relate only to residence, not to occupation, which may be considered more significant (although high levels of urban mortality affected craftsmen and town-dwelling farmers alike). If it is assumed that a thousand people in every city were involved in agriculture, the proportion of non-agricultural employment in Italy was 18% excluding Rome, 31% including the capital.[130] If only 500 people in the average small town were involved in crafts and services, the figures are 14% and 28%. It is also worth noting that centres of one or two thousand people would not be counted as urban by most studies of

[129] Cf. de Vries (1984), 39; Rozman (1973), (1976).
[130] Cf. Garnsey (1979), 4–7, 10, 19 on peasants in towns.

urbanisation in other periods.[131] If only cities of 10,000 or more inhabitants are counted, the level of urbanisation is 11% (25%), which still compares favourably with many areas of early modern Europe.

The urban system is clearly heavily primate: the capital is over twenty times as large as cities on the second level of the hierarchy. Before dismissing it as hopelessly immature, however, we might consider the wider context. It can be argued that the city of Rome was part of a Mediterranean-wide urban system, the higher levels of which (cities like Alexandria and Antioch) were not so drastically overshadowed by the metropolis. Once Rome is set aside, the Italian urban system seems to be well integrated, with several levels of urban centre ranging from regional central places to centres of local marketing and administration; in regions less densely settled than Campania and Latium, the demands of local consumers were met by rural *nundinae* and domain markets.[132]

This argues against Rozman's characterisation of the Roman Empire as a society at 'Stage D' in his scheme of urban development, its urban network still dominated by the demands of administrative centralisation and political control.[133] With four or five levels of urban centre, the Italian urban system rather resembles his 'Stage E', when 'commercial centralization' takes over as the dominant force in the urban network.[134] For what it's worth, this places Roman Italy on a level with eighth-century China and thirteenth-century Japan.[135] It seems more important to stress the degree both of horizontal integration between markets (at any rate in densely settled areas like Campania), and of vertical integration between different levels of the urban hierarchy. The driving force of the system was the need to channel supplies upwards to the capital, but the structure thus created also served as a means of distributing goods, information, ideas and customs downwards from the metropolis, and of drawing different parts of the peninsula closer together.

The demands of the city of Rome contributed to the erosion of traditional structures of society, just as they helped to transform traditional agriculture. In some regions, the result was a blossoming of urban society on the Roman model (which may still be seen in negative terms, as regional diversity was replaced by a uniform 'Romanisation'); in other regions, towns were forced to adapt to new circumstances, losing their old economic and political roles, and many failed to weather this transition. Whether we choose to emphasise the positive or negative aspects of this process of integration, both tendencies are evidence of the crucial importance of the city of Rome in the development of Italian society.

[131] E.g. de Vries (1984), 21–2.   [132] de Ligt (1993a), 116–17.
[133] Rozman (1978–9).   [134] Rozman (1976), 36.   [135] *Ibid.*, 76.

Conclusion

It is no coincidence that Dickens never writes about agriculture and writes endlessly about food. He was a cockney, and London is the centre of the earth in rather the same sense that the belly is the centre of the body. It is a city of consumers ...

(George Orwell, 'Charles Dickens')

Whether or not Orwell believed that a body could survive without a digestive system, the implications of the simile are clear: it would be better off without one. London is inhabited by people who are 'deeply civilised but not primarily useful'; it contributes nothing of any worth to the life of the rest of the country. The need to feed this belly is a heavy burden, a distraction from more important activities. What might human beings, or nations, not achieve if they were relieved of the necessity of devoting most of their days to filling the insatiable gut?

Such remarks are part of a long tradition of debate over the place of the city, and above all of the great metropolis, in the economy and society of the country that supports it. The Western city is the embodiment of modernism and modernisation, and praised or reviled as such. At the present time, the dominant image is the urban dystopia of films like *Blade Runner*. In the past, the city was seen both as the symbol of the brave new industrial civilisation and as one of the agents that brought it into being, overcoming the reactionary forces of feudalism and ignorance.

This line of thought has had a significant effect on the way in which cities in other societies, pre-modern and non-Western, have been studied. It has sometimes been argued that all urbanisation is progressive, and that all cities transform their surroundings. This can be disputed easily enough, and various writers within the substantivist tradition have done so. The more subtle argument, often put forward by these same scholars, places the emphasis on the progressive qualities of a particular type of city. The towns of medieval Europe are seen as central to the rise of capitalism and the modern world; other cities are measured against them, and generally found wanting. The ancient world failed to develop, for all its art and culture, because its cities were 'consumers' rather than 'producers'.

Rome was an insatiable consumer of bodies, food and drink; it subsisted on the taxes and rents of the empire, giving little or nothing in return; it lacked all the elements identified as progressive in the medieval town. Yet, like other giant cities in medieval China and early modern Europe, its effects on the economy of its hinterland were far-reaching, and can indeed be described as progressive. It would appear that, far from being a distraction from higher pursuits, the belly's hunger is what forces the rest of the body to rouse itself and exercise its strength and ingenuity. Freed from the burden of supporting a capital city, the country would happily slumber until doomsday.

The city of Rome thus became a driving force in the development of the Italian economy. However, this process could not continue indefinitely. Rome's population stabilised at around a million; perhaps there were insufficient migrants to sustain a higher level, perhaps the city's supply infrastructure (especially the Tiber, the bottle-neck in the system) could support no more. The market was not infinitely expandable, and so limits were set on the extent to which the metropolis could promote changes in its hinterland. The chief constraint on development in the Roman economy was not the consumptive nature of Rome or other cities but the limits set on surplus production, and hence on the level of demand, within a pre-industrial economy.

The phenomenon of urbanisation cannot be separated from its historical context; it is not an independent, cross-cultural variable. As we have seen in the contrast between London and Madrid, the effort required to maintain a metropolis in a pre-industrial economy can have very different effects on the country that has to support it. Social and political factors cannot be ignored. The city's influence is often channelled by existing structures of power – indeed, the emergence of such cities is the result of a decision by the elite to spend part of society's surplus in a particular way, as a means of maintaining their dominance. The growth of the city of Rome and the changes which it brought about in the economy of the peninsula must be seen in the context of changing structures of power in Italian society, just as the social and political impact of 'Romanisation' cannot be fully understood without reference to the impact of the city's demands on its hinterland.

Bibliography

Abrams, P. (1978a) 'Introduction', in Abrams and Wrigley, eds., 1–7.

(1978b) 'Towns and economic growth: some theories and problems', in Abrams and Wrigley, eds., 9–33.

Abrams, P. and Wrigley, E. A., eds. (1978) *Towns in Societies: essays in economic history and historical sociology*, Cambridge.

Abulafia, D. (1981) 'Southern Italy and the Florentine economy, 1265–1370', *Econ. Hist. Rev.* 33: 377–88.

Aerts, P. and Clark, P., eds. (1990) *Metropolitan Cities and their Hinterlands in Early Modern Europe*, Leuven (Papers from the Tenth International Economic History Conference).

Alcock, S. E. (1993) *Graecia Capta: the landscapes of Roman Greece*, Cambridge.

Alcock, S. E., Cherry, J. F. and Davis, J. L. (1994) 'Intensive survey, agricultural practice and the classical landscape of Greece', in Morris, I., ed., *Classical Greece: ancient histories and modern archaeologies*, Cambridge: 137–70.

Alvares, C. A. (1979) *Homo Faber: technology and culture in India, China and the West, 1500–1972*, Bombay.

Amouretti, M. C. *et al.* (1984) 'A propos du pressoir à huile: de l'archéologie industrielle à l'histoire', *MEFR* 96.1: 379–421.

Amphores (1989) *Amphores Romaines et Histoire Economique: dix ans de recherche*, Rome (*CEFR* 114).

Ampolo, C. (1988) 'La città riformata e l'organizzazione centuriata. Lo spazio, il tempo, il sacro nella nuova realtà urbana', in Momigliano and Schiavone, eds., 203–39.

Andreau, J. (1974) *Les Affaires de Monsieur Jucundus*, Rome (*CEFR* 19).

(1984) 'Histoire des métiers bancaires et évolution économique', *Opus* 3: 99–114.

(1987) *La Vie Financière dans le Monde Romain: les métiers de manieurs d'argent (IVe siècle av. J.-C. – IIIe siècle ap. J.-C.)*, Rome (*BEFAR* 265).

(1987–9) 'La cité antique et la vie économique', *Opus* 6–8: 175–85.

Arias, P. E. (1939) 'Villa repubblicana presso la Cecchignola', *NSc*: 351–60.

Arthur, P. (1982) 'Roman amphorae and the Ager Falernus under the Empire', *PBSR* 50: 22–33.

(1991a) 'Territories, wine and wealth: Suessa Aurunca, Sinuessa, Minturnae and the Ager Falernus', in Barker and Lloyd, eds., 153–9.

(1991b) *Romans in Northern Campania: settlement and land-use around the Massico and the Garigliano Basin*, London (Archaeological Monographs of the British School at Rome 1).

Ashby, T. (1927) *The Roman Campagna in Classical Times*, London.

(1935) *The Aqueducts of Ancient Rome*, Oxford.

Aston, T. H. and Philpin, C. H. E., eds. (1985) *The Brenner Debate: agrarian class structure and economic development in pre-industrial Europe*, Cambridge.

Attolini, I. *et al.* (1982) 'Ricognizione archeologica nell'Ager Cosanus e nelle valle dell'Albegna: rapporto preliminare 1981', *ArchMed* 9: 365–86.

(1983) 'Ricognizione archeologica nell'Ager Cosanus e nelle valle dell'Albegna: rapporto preliminare 1982/1983', *ArchMed* 10: 439–65.

(1991) 'Political geography and productive geography between the valleys of the Albegna and the Flora in northern Etruria', in Barker and Lloyd, eds., 142–52.

Bagnall, R. S. (1985) 'The camel, the wagon and the donkey in late Roman Egypt', *BAPS* 22: 1–6.

(1993) *Egypt in Late Antiquity*, Princeton.

Bagnall, R. S. and Frier, B. W. (1994) *The Demography of Roman Egypt*, Cambridge.

Baldacci, P. (1967–8) 'Alcuni aspetti dei commerci nel territorio Cisalpini', *Atti del Centro Studi e Documentazione sull'Italia Romana* I: 7–50.

Barker, D. G. N. (1993) 'Gold and the Renascence of the Golden Race: a study of the relationship between gold and the "golden-age" ideology of Augustan Rome', Ph.D. thesis, Cambridge.

Barker, G. (1982) 'The animal bones', in Whitehouse, D. *et al.*, 'The Schola Praeconum I', *PBSR* 50: 81–91.

(1989) 'The archaeology of the Italian shepherd', *PCPhS* 35: 1–19.

(1991) 'Approaches to archaeological survey'. in Barker and Lloyd, eds., 1–9.

Barker, G. and Lloyd, J., eds. (1991) *Roman Landscapes: archaeological survey in the Mediterranean region*, London (Archaeological Monographs of the British School at Rome 2).

Barker, G., Lloyd, J. and Webley, D. (1978) 'A classical landscape in Molise', *PBSR* 46: 35–51.

Barnish, S. J. B. (1987) 'Pigs, plebeians and *potentes*: Rome's economic hinterland c.350–600 A.D.', *PBSR* 55: 157–85.

Bassett, S., ed. (1992) *Death in Towns: urban responses to the dying and dead, 100–1600*, Leicester.

Beloch, J. (1886) *Die Bevölkerung der griechisch-roemischen Welt*, Leipzig.

van Berchem, D. (1939) *Les distributions de blé et d'argent à la plèbe romaine sous l'empire*, Geneva.

Bergqvist, S. (1992) 'Considerations on yields, the distribution of crops and the size of estates: three Roman agricultural units', *C&M* 43: 111–39.

Bernardi, A. (1977) 'Sul popolamento dell'Italia antica', *Athenaeum* 55: 88–106.

Bintliff, J., ed. (1991) *The Annales School and Archaeology*, Leicester.

Bolton, J. L. (1980) *The Medieval English Economy 1150–1500*, London.

Boserup, E. (1965) *The Conditions of Agricultural Growth: the economics of agrarian change under population pressure*, London.

(1981) *Population and Technology*, Oxford.

Bottomore, T. (1985) *Theories of Modern Capitalism*, London.

Bradley, K. R. (1984) *Slaves and Masters in the Roman Empire: a study in social control*, Brussels.

Braudel, F. (1972) *The Mediterranean and the Mediterranean World in the Age of Philip II*, Vol. I. 2nd edn, tr. S. Reynolds, London.

(1973) *Capitalism and Material Life, 1400–1800*, tr. M. Kochan, London.

(1981) *Civilization and Capitalism, 15th-18th century, Volume I: The Structures of Everyday Life. The Limits of the Possible*, rev. S. Reynolds, London.

(1982) *Civilization and Capitalism, 15th-18th century, Volume II: The Wheels of Commerce*, tr. S. Reynolds, London.

Brenner, R. (1985a) 'Agrarian class structure and economic development in pre-industrial Europe', in Aston and Philpin, eds., 10–63.

(1985b) 'The agrarian roots of European capitalism', in Aston and Philpin, eds., 213–327.

Brockmeyer, N. (1968) *Arbeitsorganisation und ökonomisches Denken in der Gutswirtschaft des römischen Reiches*, Bochum.

(1979) *Antike Sklaverei*, Darmstadt.

Brown, F. E. (1980) *Cosa: the making of a Roman town*, Michigan.

Bruhns, H. (1985) 'De Werner Sombart à Max Weber et Moses I. Finley: la typologie de la ville antique et la question de la ville de consommation', in Leveau, Ph., ed., *L'Origine des Richesses Dépensées dans la Ville Antique: actes du colloque organisée à Aix en Provence*, Aix: 255–73.

(1987–9) 'La cité antique de Max Weber', *Opus* 6–8: 29–42.

Brunt, P. A. (1971) *Italian Manpower 225 B.C. – A.D. 14*, Oxford.

(1980) 'Free labour and public works at Rome', *JRS* 70: 81–100.

Bücher, K. (1968) *Industrial Evolution*, tr. S. M. Wickett, New York.

Busalla, C. (1988) *The Evolution of Technology*, Cambridge.

Bussi, R. and Vandelli, V., eds. (1985) *Misurare la Terra: centuriazione e coloni nel mondo romano. Città, agricoltura, commercio: materiali da Roma e dal suburbio*, Modena.

Butlin, N. G. (1971) *Ante-Bellum Slavery: a critique of a debate*, Canberra.

Caird, G. B. (1984) *The Revelation of St John the Divine*, 2nd edn, London.

Cannadine, D. (1984) 'The present and the past in the English Industrial Revolution 1880–1980', *P&P* 403: 131–72.

Capogrossi Colognesi, L. (1990) *Economie antiche e capitalismo moderno: la sfida di Max Weber*, Rome and Bari.

(1995) 'The limits of the ancient city and the evolution of the medieval city in the thought of Max Weber', in Cornell and Lomas, eds., 27–37.

Carandini, A. (1980) 'Quando la dimora dello strumento è l'uomo', preface to Kolendo (1980), ix–lv; reprinted in Carandini (1988a), 287–326.

(1981) 'Sviluppo e crisi delle manifatture rurali e urbane', in Giardina and Schiavone, eds., Vol. II: 249–60; reprinted in Carandini (1988a), 327–38.

(1983) 'Columella's vineyard and the rationality of the Roman economy', *Opus* 2: 177–204.

(1985a) 'Da villa perfecta', in Carandini, ed. (1985b), 107–37; reprinted in Carandini (1988a), 19–108.

(1985b) 'Racconto di una villa', in Carandini, ed. (1985b), 138–85; reprinted in Carandini (1988a), 109–224.

(1985c) 'Schiavitù antica e moderna a confronto: il sistema della piantagione in America', in Carandini, ed. (1985b), 187–206.

(1985d) 'Le ville nell'antico territorio di Vulci: il sorgere delle ville', in Carandini, ed. (1985a), 145–7; reprinted in Carandini (1988a), 225–34.

(1988a) *Schiavi in Italia. Gli strumenti pensanti dei Romani fra tarda repubblica e medio impero*, Rome.

(1988b) 'Orti e frutteti intorno a Roma', in Carandini (1988a), 339–57.

(1989) 'L'economia italica fra tarda repubblica e medio impero considerata dal punto di vista di una merce: il vino', in *Amphores*, 505–21.

(1994) 'I paesaggi agrari dell'Italia romana visti a partire dall'Etruria', in *Italie*, 167–74.

Carandini, A., ed. (1985a) *La Romanizzazione dell'Etruria: il territorio di Vulci*, Milan.

(1985b) *Settefinestre. Una villa schiavistica nell'Etruria romana: la villa nel suo insieme*, Modena.

Carandini, A. and Settis, S. (1979) *Schiavi e padroni nell'Etruria romana: la villa di Settefinestre dallo scavo alla mostra*, Bari.

Caroselli, M. R. (1984) 'Aspects of the economic history of the Roman "Campagna" in the modern and contemporary world', *Jnl Eur. Econ. Hist.* 13: 591–8.

(1987) 'The economic development of the region of Lazio in the Middle Ages', *Jnl Eur. Econ. Hist.*16: 101–43.

Cartledge, P. (1993) *The Greeks: a portrait of self and others*, Oxford.

Casson, L. (1971) *Ships and Seamanship in the Ancient World*, Princeton.

(1980) 'The role of the state in Rome's grain trade', in D'Arms and Kopff, eds., 21–33.

Castells, M. (1976) 'Theory and ideology in urban sociology', in Pickvance, C. G., ed., *Urban Sociology: critical essays*, London: 60–84.

Celuzza, M. G. and Regoli, E. (1982) 'La Valle d'Oro nel territorio di Cosa', *DArch* n.s. 4: 31–62.

Champion, T. C., ed. (1989) *Centre and Periphery: comparative studies in archaeology*, London.

Champlin, E. (1982/5) 'The suburbium of Rome', *AJAH* 7.2: 97–117.

Chao, K. (1986) *Man and Land in Chinese History: an economic analysis*, Stamford.

Chartres, J. (1990) 'The marketing of agricultural produce, 1640–1750', in Chartres, ed., 157–253.

Chartres, J., ed. (1990) *Agricultural Markets and Trade*, Cambridge.

Chaudhuri, K. N. (1985) *Trade and Civilisation in the Indian Ocean: an economic history from the rise of Islam to 1750*, Cambridge.

(1990) *Asia Before Europe: economy and civilisation of the Indian Ocean from the rise of Islam to 1750*, Cambridge.

Cherry, J. F. (1983) 'Frogs around the pond: perspectives on current archaeological survey projects in the Mediterranean region', in Keller, D. R. and Rupp, D. W., eds., *Archaeological Survey in the Mediterranean Area*, Oxford (*BAR* Int. Ser. 155): 375–416.

Chevallier, R. (1983) *La Romanisation de la Celtique du Pô*, Rome.

Chilver, G. E. F. (1941) *Cisalpine Gaul: social and economic history from 49 B.C. to the death of Trajan*, Oxford.

Chisholm, M. (1968) *Rural Settlement and Land Use: an essay in location*, 2nd edn, London.

Cipriano, M. T. and Carre, M.-B. (1989) 'Production et typologie des amphores sur la côte adriatique de l'Italie', in *Amphores*, 67–104.

Clark, C. and Haswell, M. (1970) *The Economics of Subsistence Agriculture*, 4th edn, London.

Clark, P. (1990) 'Introduction', in Aerts and Clark, eds., 3–11.

Clark, P. and Souden, D. (1987) 'Introduction', in Clark, P. and Souden, D., eds., *Migration and Society in Early Modern England*, London: 11–48.

Clay, C. G. A. (1984) *Economic Expansion and Social Change: England 1500–1700, Volume I: People, land and towns*, Cambridge.

Clemente, G. (1990) 'Dal territorio della città all'egemonia in Italia', in Clemente, Coarelli and Gabba, eds., 19–38.

Clemente, G., Coarelli, F. and Gabba, E., eds. (1990) *Storia di Roma II: L'impero mediterraneo I: la repubblica imperiale*, Turin.

Coarelli, F. (1986) 'L'urbs e il suburbio', in Giardina, A., ed., *Società Romana e Impero Tardoantico, Volume II: Roma Politica Paesaggio Urbana*, Rome and Bari: 1–58.

(1988) 'Demografia e territorio', in Momigliano and Schiavone, eds., 318–39.

Coccia, S. and Mattingly, D., eds. (1992) 'Settlement history, environment and human exploitation of an intermontane basin in the central Apennines: the Rieti survey, 1988–1991, part 1', *PBSR* 60: 213–89.

Cockburn, T. A. (1971) 'Infectious diseases in ancient populations', *CA* 12: 45–54.

Cook, S. (1966) 'The obsolete "anti-market" mentality: a critique of the substantive approach to economic anthropology', *Am. Anthr.* 68: 323–45.

Corbier, M. (1982) 'La place des esclaves dans l'économie romaine aux Ier et IIe siècles après J.-C.', *Opus* I: 109–13.

(1983) 'Fiscus and Patrimonium: the Saepinum inscription and transhumance in the Abruzzi', *JRS* 73: 126–31.

(1984) 'De Volsinii à Sestinum: cura aquae et évergétisme municipal de l'eau en Italie', *REL* 62: 236–74.

(1989) 'The ambiguous status of meat in ancient Rome', *Food & Foodways* 3: 223–64.

Cornell, T. J. (1989) 'The conquest of Italy', in *CAH VII.2*: 351–419.

(1995) 'Warfare and urbanization in Roman Italy', in Cornell and Lomas, eds., 121–34.

Cornell, T. J. and Lomas, K., eds. (1995) *Urban Society in Roman Italy*, London.

Cornell, T. J. and Matthews, J. (1982) *Atlas of the Roman World*, Oxford.

Corradini, P. (1987) 'La città cinese', in Rossi, ed., 181–99.

Corrente, M. (1985) 'Alcuni esempli di forme economiche nel settore Est del suburbio romano', in Bussi and Vandelli, eds., 112–18.

Cotton, M. A. (1979) *The Late Republican Villa at Posto, Francolise*, London.

Cotton, M. A. and Métraux, G. P. R. (1985) *The San Rocca Villa at Francolise*, Rome.

Courtenay, P. P. (1980) *Plantation Agriculture*, 2nd edn, London.

Crawford, M. H. (1970) 'Money and exchange in the Roman world', *JRS* 60: 40–8.

(1985) *Coinage and Money under the Roman Republic*, London.

Crook, J. A. (1967) *Law and Life of Rome*, London.

Curtis, R. I. (1991) *Garum and Salsamenta: production and commerce in materia medica*, Leiden.

Dall'Aglio, P. L. and Marchetti, G. (1991) 'Settlement patterns and agrarian structures of the Roman period in the territory of Piacenza', in Barker and Lloyd, eds., 160–8.

D'Arms, J. H. (1970) *Romans on the Bay of Naples: a social and cultural study of the villas and their owners from 150 B.C. to A.D. 400*, Cambridge (Mass.).

(1974) 'Puteoli in the second century of the Roman empire: a social and economic study', *JRS* 64: 104–24.

(1981) *Commerce and Social Standing in Ancient Rome*, Cambridge (Mass.).

D'Arms, J. H. and Kopff, E. C., eds. (1980) *The Seaborne Commerce of Ancient Rome*, Rome (*MAAR* 36).

David, P. A. *et al.* (1976) *Reckoning with Slavery: a critical study in the quantitative history of American negro slavery*, New York.

David, P. A. and Temin, P. (1976a) 'Capitalist masters, bourgeois slaves', in David *et al.*, 33–54.

(1976b) 'Slavery: the progressive institution?', in David *et al.*, 165–230.

Davis, K. and Golden, H. H. (1954–5) 'Urbanization and the development of pre-industrial areas', *Economic Development and Cultural Change* 3: 6–26.

Degrassi, A. (1962) 'L'esportazione di olio e olive istriane nell'età romana', *Scritti Vari di Antichità* 2: 965–72.

(1963) *Inscriptiones Italiae XIII.2*, Rome.

Delano Smith, C. (1979) *Western Mediterranean Europe: a historical geography of Italy, Spain and Southern France since the Neolithic*, London.

Delumeau, J. (1975) *Rome au XVIe Siècle*, Paris.

Den Boer, W. (1973) 'Demography in Roman history: facts and impressions', *Mnemosyne* 26: 29–46.

Desai, P. B. (1961) *Size and Sex Composition of Population in India 1901–61*, London.

Drachmann, A. G. (1932) *Ancient Oil Mills and Presses*, Copenhagen.

Duby, G. (1976) *Rural Economy and Country Life in the Medieval West*, Columbia.

Duncan-Jones, R. P. (1977) 'Aqueduct capacity and city population', *LibStud* 10: 51.

(1980) 'Demographic change and economic progress under the Roman Empire', in *Tecnologia*, 67–80.

(1982) *The Economy of the Roman Empire: quantitative studies*, 2nd edn, Cambridge.

(1990) *Structure and Scale in the Roman Economy*, Cambridge.

Dyson, S. L. (1978) 'Settlement patterns in the Ager Cosanus: the Wesleyan University Survey, 1974–76', *JFA* 5: 251–68.

(1985) 'The villas of Buccino and the consumer model of Roman rural development', in Malone and Stoddart, eds., 67–84.

Edwards, C. (1993) *The Politics of Immorality in Ancient Rome*, Cambridge.

Eisenstadt, S. N. and Shachar, A. (1987) *Society, Culture and Urbanization*, Newbury Park (Calif.).

Elvin, M. (1973) *The Pattern of the Chinese Past*, London.

(1978) 'Chinese cities since the Sung dynasty', in Abrams and Wrigley, eds., 79–89.

Engels, D. (1990) *Roman Corinth: an alternative model for the classical city*, Chicago.

Erdkamp, P. (1995) 'The corn supply of the Roman armies during the third and second centuries B.C.', *Historia* 44: 168–91.

Evans, H. B. (1993) '*In Tiburtinum usum*: special arrangements in the Roman water system (Frontinus, *Aq.* 6.5)', *AJA* 97: 447–55.

Evans, J. K. (1980) 'Plebs rustica: the peasantry of Classical Italy', *AJAH* 5: 9–47, 134–73.

Everitt, A. (1990) 'The marketing of agricultural produce, 1500–1640', in Chartres, ed., 15–138.

Fentress, E. (1993) 'Field surveyors in northern Campania', *JRA* 6: 367–70.

(1994) 'Cosa in the empire: the unmaking of a Roman town', *JRA* 7: 208–22.

Finlay, R. (1981a) *Population and Metropolis: the demography of London 1580–1650*, Cambridge.

(1981b) 'Natural decrease in early modern cities', *P&P* 92: 169–74.

Finlay, R. and Shearer, B. (1986) 'Population growth and suburban expansion', in Beier, A. L. and Finlay, R., eds., *London 1500–1700: the making of the metropolis*, London: 37–59.

Finley, M. I. (1965) 'Technical innovation and economic progress in the ancient world', *Econ. Hist. Rev.* 18: 29–45; reprinted in Finley (1981a), 176–95.

(1976) 'Private farm tenancy in Italy before Diocletian', in Finley, ed., 103–21.

(1980) *Ancient Slavery and Modern Ideology*, London.

(1981a) *Economy and Society in Ancient Greece*, ed. B. D. Shaw and R. Saller, London.

(1981b) 'The ancient city: from Fustel de Coulanges to Max Weber and beyond', in Finley (1981a), 3–23.

(1985a) *The Ancient Economy*, 2nd edn, London.

(1985b) *Ancient History: evidence and models*, London.

Finley, M. I., ed. (1976) *Studies in Roman Property*, Cambridge.

(1979) *The Bücher–Meyer Controversy*, New York.

Fisher, F. J. (1934–5) 'The development of the London food market', *Econ. Hist. Rev.* 5: 46–64.

Fogel, R. W. and Engerman, S. L. (1974) *Time on the Cross: the economics of American Negro slavery*, 2 vols., New York.

Found, W. C. (1971) *A Theoretical Approach to Land-Use Patterns*, London.

Foxhall, L. (1990) 'The dependent tenant: land-leasing and labour in Italy and Greece', *JRS* 80: 97–114.

Foxhall, L. and Forbes, H. A. (1982) 'Sitometreia: the role of grain as a staple food in classical antiquity', *Chiron* 12: 41–90.

Frank, T. (1924) 'Roman census statistics from 225 to 28 B.C.', *CPh* 19: 329–41.

(1927) *An Economic History of Rome*, 2nd edn, London.

(1933) *An Economic Survey of Ancient Rome, Volume I: Rome and Italy of the Republic*, Baltimore.

Fraser, P. M. (1972) *Ptolemaic Alexandria*, 3 vols., Oxford.

Fraser, P. M. and Nicholas, B. (1958) 'The funerary garden of Mousa', *JRS* 48: 117–29.

Frayn, J. M. (1979) *Subsistence Farming in Roman Italy*, London.

(1984) *Sheep-rearing and the Wool Trade in Italy during the Roman Period*, Liverpool.

(1993) *Markets and Fairs in Roman Italy*, Oxford.

Frederiksen, M. (1975) 'Theory, evidence and the ancient economy', *JRS* 65: 164–71.

(1981) 'I cambiamenti delle strutture agrarie nella tarda repubblica: la Campania', in Giardina and Schiavone, eds., Vol. I: 265–87.

(1984) *Campania*, ed. N. Purcell, Rome.

Friedländer, L. (1928) *Roman Life and Manners under the Early Empire*, Vol. IV, London.

Frier, B. W. (1979) 'Law, technology, and social change: the equipping of Italian farm tenancies', *ZRG* 96: 204–28.

(1982) 'Roman life expectancy: Ulpian's evidence', *HSPh* 86: 213–51.

(1983) 'Roman law and the wine trade: the problem of "vinegar sold as wine"', *ZRG* 100: 257–95.

Gabba, E. (1972) 'Urbanizzazione e rinnovamenti urbanistici nell'Italia centro-meridionale del 1 sec. a.c.', *SCO* 21: 73–112.

(1975) 'Mercati e fiere nell'Italia romana', *SCO* 24: 141–63.

(1987) 'La città italica', in Rossi, ed., 109–26.

(1988) 'La pastorizia nell'età tardo-imperiale in Italia', in Whittaker, ed., 134–42.

(1989) 'Rome and Italy in the second century B.C.', in *CAH VIII*: 197–243.

Garnsey, P. (1970) *Social Status and Legal Privilege in the Roman Empire*, Oxford.

(1976a) 'Urban property investment', in Finley, ed., 123–36.

(1976b) 'Economy and society of Mediolanum under the Principate', *PBSR* 44: 13–27.

(1976c) 'Peasants in ancient Roman society', *Jnl Peas. Stud.* 3: 221–34.

(1979) 'Where did Italian peasants live?', *PCPhS* 25: 1–25.

(1980a) 'Introduction', in Garnsey, ed., 1–5.

(1980b) 'Non-slave labour in the Roman world', in Garnsey, ed., 34–47.

(1981) 'Independent freedmen and the economy of Roman Italy under the Principate', *Klio* 63: 359–71.

(1983) 'Grain for Rome', in Garnsey, Hopkins and Whittaker, eds., 118–30.

(1988a) *Famine and Food Supply in the Graeco-Roman World: responses to risk and crisis*, Cambridge.

(1988b) 'Mountain economies in southern Europe. Thoughts on the early history, continuity and individuality of Mediterranean upland pastoralism', in Whittaker, ed., 196–209.

Garnsey, P. ed. (1980) *Non-Slave Labour in the Greco-Roman World*, Cambridge (*PCPhS* supp. vol. 6).

Garnsey, P., Hopkins, K. and Whittaker, C. R., eds. (1983) *Trade in the Ancient Economy*, London.

Garnsey, P. and Whittaker, C. R., eds. (1983) *Trade and Famine in Classical Antiquity*, Cambridge (*PCPhS* supp. vol. 8).

Garnsey, P. and Saller, R. (1987) *The Roman Empire: economy, society and culture*, London.

von Gerkan, A. (1940) 'Die Einwohnerzahl Roms in der Kaiserzeit', *MDAI(R)* 55: 149–95.

Giardina, A. (1981) 'Allevamento ed economia della selva in Italia meridionale: trasformazioni e continuità', in Giardina and Schiavone, eds., Vol. I: 87–113.

Giardina, A. and Schiavone, A., eds. (1981) *Società Romana e Produzione Schiavistica*, 2 vols., Rome and Bari.

Giovannini, A., ed. (1991) *Nourrir la Plèbe: actes du colloque ... en hommage à Denis van Berchem*, Basel.

Goddard, J. P. (1994) 'Moral attitudes to eating and drinking in ancient Rome', Ph.D. thesis, Cambridge.

Goudineau, Chr. (1983) 'Une réponse de Christian Goudineau', *Etudes Rurales* 89–91: 283–9.

Graham, E. and Floering, I. (1984) *The Modern Plantation in the Third World*, London and Sydney.

Greene, K. (1986) *The Archaeology of the Roman Economy*, London.

  (1990) 'Perspectives on Roman technology', *OJA* 9: 209–19.

  (1993) 'The study of Roman technology: some theoretical considerations', in Scott, E., ed., *Theoretical Roman Archaeology: first conference proceedings*, Aldershot: 39–47.

  (1994) 'Technology and innovation in context: the Roman background to medieval and later developments', *JRA* 7: 22–33.

Grigg, D. (1974) *The Agricultural Systems of the World: an evolutionary approach*, Cambridge.

  (1980) *Population Growth and Agricultural Change: an historical perspective*, Cambridge.

  (1982) *The Dynamics of Agricultural Change: the historical experience*, Cambridge.

Grimal, P. (1943) *Les Jardins Romains: à la fin de la république et aux premiers siècles de l'empire*, Paris.

Grmek, M. D. (1989) *Diseases in the Ancient Greek World*, Baltimore.

Gros, P. (1990) 'L'urbanizzazione dopo la guerra sociale', in Clemente, Coarelli and Gabba, eds., 831–55.

Gross, H. (1990) *Rome in the Age of Enlightenment: the post-Tridentine syndrome and the ancien régime*, Cambridge.

Gualtieri, M. and de Polignac, F. (1991) 'A rural landscape in western Lucania', in Barker and Lloyd, eds., 194–203.

Gutman, H. G. (1975) *Slavery and the Numbers Game: a critique of 'Time on the Cross'*, Urbana (Ill.).

Guzzo, P. G. (1981) 'Il territorio dei Bruttii', in Giardina and Schiavone, eds., Vol. I: 116–35.

Haeger, J. W., ed. (1975) *Crisis and Prosperity in Sung China*, Tucson (Ariz.).

Hall, P., ed. (1966) *Von Thünen's Isolated State: an English translation of 'Der isolierte Staat'*, Oxford.

Halstead, P. (1987) 'Traditional and ancient rural economy in Mediterranean Europe: plus ça change?', *JHS* 107: 77–87.

Harper, J. (1972) 'Slaves and freedmen in Imperial Rome', *AJPh* 93: 341–2.

Harris, A. L. (1992) 'Sombart and German (National) Socialism', in Blaug, M., ed., *Gustav Schmoller (1838–1917) and Werner Sombart (1863–1941)*, Aldershot (Pioneers in Economics 30): 41–71.

Harris, W. V. (1971) *Rome in Etruria and Umbria*, Oxford.

Hartwell, R. M. (1967) 'A cycle of economic change in imperial China: coal and iron in Northeast China, 750–1550', *JESHO* 10: 102–59.

(1982) 'Demographic, political and social transformation of China, 750–1550', *HJAS* 42: 365–442.

Harvey, D. (1989) *The Condition of Postmodernity: an enquiry into the origins of cultural change*, Oxford.

Hemphill, P. (1975) 'The Cassia–Clodia survey', *PBSR* 43: 118–72.

Hermansen, G. (1974) 'The Roman inns and the law: the inns of Ostia', in Evans, J. A. S., ed., *Polis and Imperium: studies in honour of Edward Togo Salmon*, Toronto: 167–81.

(1978) 'The population of Imperial Rome: the Regionaries', *Historia* 27: 129–68.

(1981) *Ostia: aspects of Roman city life*, Alberta.

Hesnard, A. (1980) 'Un dépôt augustéen d'amphores à La Longarina, Ostia', in D'Arms and Kopff, eds., 141–56.

Hill, P. (1986) *Development Economics On Trial*, Cambridge.

Hilton, R. H. (1985) 'Towns in English feudal society', in Hilton, R. H., *Class Conflict and the Crisis of Feudalism*, London: 175–86.

Hodge, A. T. (1992) *Roman Aqueducts and Water Supply*, London.

Hodges, R. (1988) *Primitive and Peasant Markets*, Oxford.

Hollingsworth, T. H. (1976) *Historical Demography*, Cambridge.

Holton, R. J. (1986) *Cities, Capitalism and Civilization*, London.

Homo, L. (1971) *Rome impériale et l'urbanisme dans l'antiquité*, 2nd edn, Paris.

Hopkins, D. R. (1983) *Princes and Peasants: smallpox in history*, Chicago.

Hopkins, K. (1974) 'Demography in Roman history', *Mnemosyne* 27: 77–8.

(1978a) *Conquerors and Slaves: sociological studies in Roman history I*, Cambridge.

(1978b) 'Economic growth and towns in classical antiquity', in Abrams and Wrigley, eds., 35–77.

(1980) 'Taxes and trade in the Roman Empire (200 B.C. – A.D. 400)', *JRS* 70: 101–25.

(1983a) *Death and Renewal: sociological studies in Roman history II*, Cambridge.

(1983b) 'Models, ships and staples', in Garnsey and Whittaker, eds., 84–109.

(1983c) 'Introduction', in Garnsey, Hopkins and Whittaker, eds., ix–xxv.

Hoselitz, B. F. (1954–5) 'Generative and parasitic cities', *Economic Development and Cultural Change* 3: 278–94.

Howgego, C. (1992) 'The supply and use of money in the Roman world, 200 B.C. – A.D. 300', *JRS* 82: 1–31.

(1994) 'Coin circulation and the integration of the Roman economy', *JRA* 7: 5–21.

Hudson, P. (1992) *The Industrial Revolution*, London.

Italie (1994) *L'Italie d'Auguste à Dioclétien: actes du colloque international*, Rome (*CEFR* 198).

Jackson, R. (1988) *Doctors and Diseases in the Roman Empire*, London.

Jashemski, W. F. (1979) *The Gardens of Pompeii, Herculaneum and the Villas Destroyed by Vesuvius*, New York.

John, A. H. (1967) 'Agricultural productivity and economic growth in England', in Jones, E. L., ed., *Agriculture and Economic Growth in England, 1650–1815*, London: 172–93.

Jones, A. H. M. (1960) 'The cloth industry under the Roman empire', *Econ. Hist. Rev* 13: 183–92.

Jones, E. L. (1977) 'Environment, agriculture and industrialisation in Europe', *Agr. Hist.* 51: 491–502.

Jones, G. D. B. (1962) 'Capena and the Ager Capenas', *PBSR* 30: 116–207.
   (1963) 'Capena and the Ager Capenas Part II', *PBSR* 31: 100–58.
   (1980) 'Il Tavoliere romana. L'agricoltura romana attraverso l'aerofotografia e lo scavo', *ArchClass* 32: 85–107.

Jongman, W. (1988a) *The Economy and Society of Pompeii*, Amsterdam.
   (1988b) 'Adding it up', in Whittaker, ed., 210–12.
   (1990) 'Het Romeins imperialisme en de verstedelijking van Italië', *Leidschrift* 7.1: 43–58.

Jordan, H. (1871) *Topographie der Stadt Roms in Altertum*, Vol. I, Berlin.

Jouffroy, H. (1986) *La Construction Publique en Italie et dans l'Afrique Romaine*, Strasbourg.

Kahane, A. M. (1977) 'Field survey of an area south and west of La Storta', *PBSR* 45: 138–90.

Kahane, A. M. and Ward-Perkins, J. (1972) 'The Via Gabina', *PBSR* 40: 91–126.

Kaplan, S. L. (1984) *Provisioning Paris: merchants and millers in the grain and flour trade during the eighteenth century*, Ithaca and London.

Käsler, D. (1988) *Max Weber: an introduction to his life and work*, Cambridge.

Kehoe, D. P. (1993) 'Economic rationalism in Roman agriculture', *JRA* 6: 476–84.

Kelly, J. M. (1966) *Roman Litigation*, Oxford.

Keppie, L. (1983) *Colonisation and Veteran Settlement in Italy, 47–14 B.C.*, London.

Kolendo, J. (1980) *L'agricoltura nell'Italia romana: tecniche agrarie e progresso economico dalla tarda repubblica al principato*, Rome.

Kracke, E. A., Jnr (1975) 'Sung K'ai-feng: pragmatic metropolis and formalistic capital', in Haeger, ed., 49–77.

Kunkel, W. (1973) *An Introduction to Roman Legal and Constitutional History*, 2nd edn, Oxford.

Kussmaul, A. (1990) *A General View of the Rural Economy of England, 1538–1840*, Cambridge.

Lanciani, R. (1888) *Ancient Rome in the Light of Recent Discoveries*, London.
   (1909) *Wanderings in the Roman Campagna*, Boston.

Landers, J. (1987) 'Mortality and metropolis: the case of London, 1675–1825', *Pop. Stud.* 41: 59–76.
   (1993) *Death and the Metropolis: studies in the demographic history of London, 1670–1830*, Cambridge.

Langdon, J. (1982) 'The economics of horses and oxen in medieval England', *Agr. Hist. Rev.* 30: 31–40.

(1984) 'Horse-hauling: a revolution in vehicle transport in twelfth- and thirteenth-century England?', *P&P* 103: 37–66.

Laurence, R. (1994) *Roman Pompeii: space and society*, London and New York.

Leighton, A. C. (1972) *Transport and Communication in Early Medieval Europe, A.D. 500–1100*, Newton Abbot.

Lepore, E. (1981) 'Geografia del modo di produzione schiavistica e modi residui in Italia meridionale', in Giardina and Schiavone, eds., Vol. I: 79–85.

Lequément, R. and Liou, B. (1975) 'Les épaves de la côte de Transalpine. Essai de dénombrement, suivi de quelques observations sur le trafic maritime aux IIème et Ier siècles avant J.C.', *Cahiers Ligures de Préhistoire et d'Archéologie* 24: 76–82.

Leveau, Ph. (1983) 'La ville antique, "ville de consommation"? Parasitisme social et économie antique', *Etudes Rurales* 89–91: 275–83.

de Ligt, L. (1990) 'Demand, supply, distribution: the Roman peasantry between town and countryside: rural monetization and peasant demand', *MBAH* 9.2: 24–56.

(1991a) 'Demand, supply, distribution: the Roman peasantry between town and countryside II: supply, distribution and a comparative perspective', *MBAH* 10.1: 33–77.

(1991b) Review of Andreau (1987), *Mnemosyne* 44: 490–7.

(1993a) *Fairs and Markets in the Roman Empire*, Amsterdam.

(1993b) 'The nundinae of L. Bellicus Sollers', in Sancisi-Weerdenburg et al., eds., 238–62.

de Ligt, L. and de Neeve, P. W. (1988) 'Ancient periodic markets: festivals and fairs', *Athenaeum* 66: 391–416.

Lirb, H. (1993) 'Partners in agriculture. The pooling of resources in rural *societates* in Roman Italy', in Sancisi-Weerdenburg et al., eds., 317–42.

Liverani, P. (1984) 'L'Ager Veientanus in età repubblicana', *PBSR* 52: 36–48.

(1987) *Municipium Augustum Veiens: Veio in età imperiale attraverso gli scavi Giorgi (1811–13)*, Rome.

Lloyd, J. (1991) 'Farming the highlands: Samnium and Arcadia in the Hellenistic and early Roman imperial periods', in Barker and Lloyd, eds., 180–93.

Lloyd, J. and Barker, G. (1981) 'Rural settlement in Roman Molise: problems of archaeological survey', in Barker, G. and Hodges, R., eds., *Archaeology and Italian Society*, Oxford (*BAR* Int. Ser. 102): 289–304.

Lloyd, J. A. and Rathbone, D. W. (1984) 'La villa romana a Matrice', *Conoscenze* 1: 216–19.

Loane, H. J. (1938) *Industry and Commerce of the City of Rome (50 B.C. – A.D. 200)*, Baltimore.

Lo Cascio, E. (1981) 'State and coinage in the late Republic and early Empire', *JRS* 71: 76–86.

(1994a) 'The size of the Roman population: Beloch and the meaning of the Augustan census figures', *JRS* 84: 23–40.

(1994b) 'La dinamica della popolazione in Italia da Augusto al III secolo', in *Italie*, 91–125.

Lomas, K. (1993) *Rome and the Western Greeks, 350 B.C. – A.D. 200: conquest and acculturation in southern Italy*, London.

Love, J. R. (1991) *Antiquity and Capitalism: Max Weber and the sociological foundations of Roman civilization*, London.

Lugli, G. (1924) 'Il suburbio di Roma', *BCAR* 51: 3–25.

(1930) 'Scavo di una villa di età repubblicana in località S. Basilio', *NSc*: 529–35.

Ma, L. J. C. (1971) *Commercial Development and Urban Change in Sung China (960–1279)*, Ann Arbor.

MacMullen, R. (1970) 'Market-days in the Roman Empire', *Phoenix* 24: 333–41.

(1987) 'Late Roman slavery', *Historia* 36: 359–82.

Macve, R. (1985) 'Some glosses on Ste Croix's "Greek and Roman accounting"', in Cartledge, P. A. and Harvey, F. D., eds., *Crux: essays presented to G. E. M. de Ste Croix on his 75th birthday*, Exeter: 233–64.

Maier, F. G. (1953–4) 'Römische Bevölkerungsgeschichte und Inschriftenstatistik', *Historia* 2: 318–51.

Malone, C. and Stoddart, S., eds. (1985) *Papers in Italian Archaeology IV: the Cambridge conference. Part iv: classical and medieval archaeology*, Oxford (*BAR* Int. Ser. 246).

Manchester, K. (1992) 'The palaeopathology of urban infections', in Bassett, ed., 8–14.

Mari, Z. (1983) *Tibur III*, Florence (*Forma Italiae*).

(1991) *Tibur IV*, Florence (*Forma Italiae*).

Maróti, E. (1976) 'The vilicus and the villa-system in ancient Italy', *Oikumene* 1: 109–24.

Martin, R. (1971) *Recherches sur les agronomes latins et leurs conceptions économiques et sociales*, Paris.

Martin, S. (1990) 'Servum Merum Mulionem Conduxisti: mules, muleteers and transportation in classical Roman law', *TAPhA* 120: 301–14.

Marx, K. (1973) *Grundrisse*, tr. M. Nicolaus, Harmondsworth.

(1976) *Capital*, Vol. I, tr. B. Fowkes, Harmondsworth.

Mattingly, D. J. (1988a) 'Oil for export? A comparison of Libyan, Spanish and Tunisian olive oil production in the Roman empire', *JRA* 1: 33–56.

(1988b) 'Olea mediterranea?', *JRA* 1: 153–61.

(1993) 'Understanding Roman landscapes', *JRA* 6: 359–66.

McCann, A. M. *et al.* (1987) *The Roman Port and Fishery of Cosa*, Princeton.

McNeill, W. H. (1977) *Plagues and Peoples*, Oxford.

(1980) 'Migration patterns and infection in traditional societies', in Stanley, N. F. and Joske, R. A., eds., *Changing Disease Patterns and Human Behaviour*, London: 27–36.

Meiggs, R. (1960) *Roman Ostia*, Oxford.

Merrington, J. (1975) 'Town and country in the transition to capitalism', *New Left Review* 93: 71–92; reprinted in Hilton, R. H. *et al.* (1976) *The Transition from Feudalism to Capitalism*, London: 170–95.

Mickwitz, G. (1937) 'Economic rationalism in Graeco-Roman agriculture', *EHR* 52: 577–89.

Middleton, P. (1983) 'The Roman army and long-distance trade', in Garnsey and Whittaker, eds., 75–83.

Millett, M. (1991) 'Pottery: population or supply patterns? The Ager Tarraconensis approach', in Barker and Lloyd, eds., 18–26.

(1992) 'Rural integration in the Roman West: an introductory essay', in Wood, M. and Queiroga, F., eds., *Current Research on the Romanization of the Western Provinces*, Oxford (*BAR* Int. Ser. S575): 1–8.

Mitzman, A. (1970) *The Iron Cage: an historical interpretation of Max Weber*, New York.

(1973) *Sociology and Estrangement: three sociologists of Imperial Germany*, New York.

(1987) 'Personal conflict and ideological options in Sombart and Weber', in Mommsen, W. J. and Osterhammel, J., eds., *Max Weber and his Contemporaries*, London: 99–105.

Moeller, W. O. (1976) *The Wool Trade of Ancient Pompeii*, Leiden.

Molho, A., Raaflaub, K. and Emlen, J., eds. (1991) *City States in Classical Antiquity and Medieval Italy*, Stuttgart.

Momigliano, A. and Schiavone, A., eds. (1988) *Storia di Roma I: Roma in Italia*, Turin.

Morel, J.-P. (1981) *Céramique campanienne: les formes*, Rome.

Moritz, L. A. (1958) *Grain Mills and Flour in Classical Antiquity*, Oxford.

Morley, N. (forthcoming) 'Cities in context: urban systems in Roman Italy', in Parkins, H., ed., *The Roman City: beyond the consumer model*, London.

Mounce, R. H. (1977) *The Book of Revelation*, London.

Müller, R. (1972) 'Hegel und Marx über die antike Kultur', *Philologus* 116: 1–31.

Musco, S. and Zaccagni, P. (1985) 'Caratteri e forme di insediamenti rustici e residenziali nel suburbio orientale tra il IV e il I secolo a.c.', in Bussi and Vandelli, eds., 90–8.

Muzzioli, M. P. (1980) *Cures Sabini*, Florence (*Forma Italiae*).

Myers, R. H. (1974) 'Transformation and continuity in Chinese economic history', *Jnl Asian Stud.* 33: 265–77.

de Neeve, P. W. (1984a) *Peasants in Peril: location and economy in Italy in the second century B.C.*, Amsterdam.

(1984b) *Colonus: private farm-tenancy in Roman Italy during the Republic and early Principate*, Amsterdam.

(1985) 'The price of agricultural land in Roman Italy and the problem of economic rationalism', *Opus* 4: 77–109.

Newell, C. (1988) *Methods and Models in Demography*, London.

Nippel, W. (1987–9) 'Finley and Weber. Some comments and theses', *Opus* 6–8: 43–50.

(1991) 'Introductory remarks: Max Weber's "The City" revisited', in Molho, Raaflaub and Emlen, eds., 19–30.

Nissen, H. (1902) *Italische Landeskunde*, Vol. II.1, Berlin.

Nordh, C. A. (1949) *Libellus de Regionibus Urbis Romae*, Lund.

North, D. C. (1981) *Structure and Change in Economic History*, New York and London.

(1990) *Institutions, Institutional Change and Economic Performance*, Cambridge.

Oates, W. J. (1934) 'The population of Rome', *CPh* 29: 101–16.

Oberai, A. S. (1983) *Causes and Consequences of Internal Migration*, Delhi.

O'Brien, P. (1985) 'Agriculture and the home market for English industry, 1660–1820', *EHR* 100: 773–800.

Oliver, J. H. (1953) *The Ruling Power: a study of the Roman Empire in the second century after Christ through the Roman oration of Aelius Aristides*, Philadelphia (*TAPhS* 43).

Ostrow, S. E. (1985) 'Augustales along the Bay of Naples', *Historia* 34: 64–101.

Packer, J. E. (1971) *The Insulae of Imperial Ostia*, Rome (*MAAR* 31).

Painter, K., ed. (1980) *Roman Villas in Italy*, London (British Museum Occasional Papers 24).

Panella, C. (1970) 'Anfore', in *Ostia II: Le Terme del Nuotatore: scavo dell'ambiente I*, Rome (*Studi Miscellanei* 16): 102–56.

(1973) 'Appunti su un gruppo di anfore della prima, media e tarda età imperiale', in *Ostia III: Le Terme del Nuotatore: scavo degli ambienti III, VI, VII*, Rome (*Studi Miscellanei* 21): 460–633.

(1981) 'La distribuzione e i mercati', in Giardina and Schiavone, eds., Vol. II: 54–80.

(1989) 'Le anfore italiche del II secolo d.c.', in *Amphores*, 139–78.

Parker, A. J. (1992) *Ancient Shipwrecks of the Mediterranean and Roman Provinces*, Oxford (*BAR* Int. Ser. 580).

Parkin, T. G. (1992) *Demography and Roman Society*, Baltimore and London.

Pasquinucci, M. (1979) 'La transumanza nell'Italia romana', in Gabba, E. and Pasquinucci, M., *Strutture Agrarie e Allevamento Transumante nell'Italia Romana (III–I sec. a.c.)*, Pisa.

Paterson, J. (1982) ' "Salvation from the sea": amphorae and trade in the Roman world', *JRS* 72: 146–57.

(1991) 'Agrarian structures on the lowlands: introduction', in Barker and Lloyd, eds., 133–4.

Patrick, A. (1967) 'Disease in antiquity: ancient Greece and Rome', in Brothwell, D. and Sandison, A. T., eds., *Diseases in Antiquity: a survey of the diseases, injuries and surgery of ancient populations*, Springfield (Ill.): 238–46.

Patten, J. (1978) *English Towns 1500–1700*, Folkestone.

Patterson, J. R. (1987) 'Crisis: what crisis? Rural change and urban development in imperial Apennine Italy', *PBSR* 55: 115–46.

(1991) 'Settlement, city and elite in Samnium and Lycia', in Rich and Wallace-Hadrill, eds., 146–68.

(1992) 'Patronage, *collegia* and burial in imperial Rome', in Bassett, ed., 15–27.

Peacock, D. P. S. and Williams, D. F. (1986) *Amphorae and the Roman Economy: an introductory guide*, London.

Pearson, H. W. (1957) 'The secular debate on economic primitivism', in Polanyi, Arensberg and Pearson, eds., 3–11.

Pédech, P. (1971) 'La géographie urbaine chez Strabon', *AncSoc* 2: 234–53.

Perkins, D. H. (1969) *Agricultural Development in China 1368–1968*, Chicago.

Pleket, H. W. (1967) 'Technology and society in the Graeco-Roman world', *Acta Historiae Neerlandica* 2: 1–25.

(1983) 'Urban elites and business in the Greek part of the Roman empire', in Garnsey, Hopkins and Whittaker, eds., 131–44.

(1990) 'Wirtschaft', in Vittinghoff, F., ed., *Handbuch de europäischen Wirtschafts- und Sozialgeschichte, Band I: Europäische Wirtschafts- und Sozialgeschichte in der römische Kaiserzeit*, Stuttgart: 25–160.

(1993a) 'Agriculture in the Roman Empire in comparative perspective', in Sancisi-Weedenburg *et al.*, eds., 317–42.

(1993b) 'Rome: a pre-industrial megalopolis', in Barker, T. and Sutcliffe, A., eds., *Megalopolis: the giant city in history*, London: 14–35.

Polanyi, K. (1944) *The Great Transformation: the political and economic origins of our time*, New York.

(1968) *Primitive, Archaic and Modern Economies: essays of Karl Polanyi*, ed. G. Dalton, New York.

Polanyi, K., Arensberg, C. M. and Pearson, H. W., eds. (1957) *Trade and Markets in the Early Empires: economies in history and theory*, New York and London.

Potter, T. W. (1979) *The Changing Landscape of South Etruria*, London.

(1980) 'Villas in South Etruria: some comments and contexts', in Painter, ed., 73–81.

(1991) 'Towns and territories in Southern Etruria', in Rich and Wallace-Hadrill, eds., 191–209.

Potter, T. W. and Dunbabin, K. M. (1979) 'A Roman villa at Crocicchie, Via Clodia', *PBSR* 47: 19–26.

Pucci, G. (1985) 'Schiavitù romana nella campagne: il sistema della villa nell'Italia centrale', in Carandini, ed. (1985b), 15–21.

(1989) 'I consumi alimentari', in Gabba, E. and Schiavone, A., eds., *Storia di Roma IV: caratteri e morfologie*, Turin: 369–88.

Purcell, N. (1983) 'The Apparitores: a study in social mobility', *PBSR* 51: 125–73.

(1985) 'Wine and wealth in Roman Italy', *JRS* 75: 1–19.

(1987a) 'Tomb and suburb', in von Hesberg, H. and Zanker, P., eds., *Roemische Graeberstrasse*, Munich: 25–41.

(1987b) 'Town in country and country in town', in MacDougall, E. B., ed., *Ancient Roman Villa Gardens*, Dumbarton Oaks: 187–203.

(1988) Review of Tchernia (1986) and Carandini, ed. (1985b), *JRS* 78: 194–8.

(1990) Review of Jongman (1988a), *CR* 40: 111–16.

(1994) 'The city of Rome and the *plebs urbana* in the late Republic', in *CAH* IX: 644–88.

(1995) 'The Roman *villa* and the landscape of production', in Cornell and Lomas, eds., 151–79.

Quilici, L. (1974a) *Collatia*, Rome (*Forma Italiae*).

(1974b) 'La campagna romana come suburbio di Roma antica', *PP* 29: 410–38.

(1976) 'Castel Giubileo (Roma) – saggi di scavo attorno a Fidenae', *NSc*: 263–326.

(1979) 'La villa nel suburbio romano: problemi di studi e di inquadramento storico-typografico', *ArchClass* 31: 309–17.

(1991) 'Entre espace urbain et monde rural: le rôle du suburbium dans l'antiquité tardive', in Hinard, F. and Royo, M., eds., *Rome: l'espace urbain et ses représentations*, Paris: 97–110.

Quilici, L. and Quilici Gigli, S. (1978) *Antemnae*, Rome (*Latium Vetus*).

(1980) *Crustumerium*, Rome (*Latium Vetus*).

(1986) *Fidenae*, Rome (*Latium Vetus*).

Ransom, R. L. (1989) *Conflict and Compromise: the political economy of slavery, emancipation and the Civil War*, Cambridge.

Rathbone, D. W. (1981) 'The development of agriculture in the Ager Cosanus during the Roman Republic: problems of evidence and interpretation', *JRS* 71: 10–23.

(1983) 'The slave mode of production in Italy', *JRS* 73: 160–8.

(1991) *Economic Rationalism and Rural Society in Third-Century A.D. Egypt: the Heroninos archive and the Appianus estate*, Cambridge.

(1993) 'Review article: the Italian countryside and the Gracchan "crisis"', *JACT Review* 13: 18–20.

Reece, D. W. (1969) 'The technological weakness of the ancient world', *G&R* 16: 32–47.

Ricardo, D. (1951) *On the Principles of Political Economy and Taxation*, in *The Works and Correspondence of David Ricardo*, Vol. I, ed. P. Sraffa with M. H. Dobb, Cambridge.

Rich, J. and Wallace-Hadrill, A., eds. (1991) *City and Country in the Ancient World*, London.

Rickman, G. (1971) *Roman Granaries and Store Buildings*, Cambridge.

(1980) *The Corn Supply of Ancient Rome*, Oxford.

(1991) 'Problems of transport and development of ports', in Giovannini, ed., 103–15.

Ringrose, D. R. (1970) *Transportation and Economic Stagnation in Spain, 1750–1850*, Duke.

(1983) *Madrid and the Spanish Economy*, Berkeley.

(1990) 'Metropolitan cities as parasites', in Aerts and Clark, eds., 21–38.

Rinkewitz, W. (1984) *Pastio Villatica*, Frankfurt.

Robinson, O. F. (1980) 'The water supply of Rome', *SDHI* 46: 44–86.

Rodriguez-Almeida, E. (1984) *Il Monte Testaccio*, Rome.

Rossi, P., ed. (1987) *Modelli di Città: strutture e funzioni politiche*, Turin.

Rossiter, J. J. (1978) *Roman Farm Buildings in Italy*, *BAR* Int. Ser. 52, Oxford.

(1981) 'Wine and oil processing at Roman farms in Italy', *Phoenix* 35: 345–61.

Rostovtzeff, M. I. (1957) *The Social and Economic History of the Roman Empire*, 2nd edn, rev. P. M. Fraser, Oxford.

Rougé, J. (1966) *Recherches sur l'organisation du commerce maritime en Méditerrannée sous l'empire romain*, Paris.

Rowland, R. J., Jnr (1976) 'The "very poor" and the grain dole at Rome and Oxyrhynchus', *ZPE* 21: 69–72.

Rowlands, M., Larsen, M. and Kristiansen, K., eds. (1987) *Centre and Periphery in the Ancient World*, Cambridge.

Rozman, G. (1973) *Urban Networks in Ch'ing China and Tokugawa Japan*, Princeton.

(1976) *Urban Networks in Russia, 1750–1800, and Premodern Periodization*, Princeton.

(1978–9) 'Urban networks and historical stages', *Jnl Interdisc. Hist.* 9: 65–91.

de Ruyt, C. (1983) *Macellum: marché alimentaire des Romains*, Louvain.

de Ste Croix, G. E. M. (1956) 'Greek and Roman accounting', in Littleton, A. C. and Yamey, B. S., eds., *Studies in the History of Accounting*, London: 14–74.

(1981) *The Class Struggle in the Ancient Greek World*, London.

Sallares, R. (1991) *The Ecology of the Ancient Greek World*, London.

Salmon, P. (1974) *Population et dépopulation dans l'empire romain*, Brussels.

Samson, R. (1989) 'Rural slavery, inscriptions, archaeology and Marx: a response to Ramsay MacMullen's "Late Roman slavery"', *Historia* 38: 99–110.

Sancisi-Weerdenburg, H. *et al.*, eds. (1993) *De Agricultura: in memoriam Pieter Willem de Neeve*, Amsterdam.

Scaff, L. A. (1989) *Fleeing the Iron Cage: culture, politics and modernity in the thought of Max Weber*, Berkeley and Los Angeles.

Schiavoni, C. and Sonnino, E. (1982) 'Aspects généraux de l'évolution démographique à Rome, 1598–1824', *Annales de Démographie Historique*: 91–109.

Schneider, H. K. (1974) *Economic Man: the anthropology of economics*, New York.

Scobie, A. (1986) 'Slums, sanitation and mortality in the Roman world', *Klio* 68: 399–433.

Semple, E. C. (1932) *The Geography of the Mediterranean Region: its relation to ancient history*, London.

Sharlin, A. (1978) 'Natural decrease in early modern cities: a reconsideration', *P&P* 79: 126–38.

(1981) 'A rejoinder', *P&P* 92: 175–80.

Shatzman, I. (1975) *Senatorial Wealth and Roman Politics*, Brussels.

Shaw, B. D. (1981) 'Rural markets in North Africa and the political economy of the Roman empire', *AntAfr* 17: 37–83.

(1982) 'Lamasba: an ancient irrigation community', *AntAfr* 18: 61–103.

(1984) 'Water and society in the ancient Maghrib', *AntAfr* 20: 121–73.

Sherwin-White, A. N. (1966) *The Letters of Pliny: a historical and social commentary*, Oxford.

(1973) *The Roman Citizenship*, 2nd edn, Oxford.

Shiba, Y. (1970) *Commerce and Society in Sung China*, Michigan.

(1975) 'Urbanization and the development of markets in the lower Yangtze Valley', in Haeger, ed., 13–48.

Short, T. (1973) *New Observations on City, Town and Country Bills of Mortality*, Farnborough. Facsimile of 1750 edition; introduction by R. Wall.

Sirks, B. (1991) *Food for Rome: the legal structure of the transportation and processing of supplies for the imperial distributions in Rome and Constantinople*, Amsterdam.

Sjoberg, G. (1960) *The Preindustrial City*, Glencoe (Ill.).

Skinner, G. W. (1977a) 'Introduction: urban development in Imperial China', in Skinner, ed., 5–31.

(1977b) 'Introduction: urban and rural in Chinese society', in Skinner. ed., 253–73.

Skinner, G. W., ed. (1977) *The City in Late Imperial China*, Stamford.

Small, A. M. (1985) 'The early villa at San Giovanni', in Malone and Stoddart, eds., 165–77.

(1991) 'Late Roman rural settlement in Basilicata and western Apulia', in Barker and Lloyd, eds., 204–22.

Smith, A. (1908) *An Enquiry into the Nature and Causes of the Wealth of Nations*, London.

Smith, C. A. (1974) 'Economics of marketing systems: models from economic geography', *Ann. Rev. Anthr.* 3: 167–201.

(1976) 'Regional economic systems: linking geographical models and socio-economic problems', in Smith, ed., *Regional Analysis, Volume I: economic systems*, London: 3–63.

(1985a) 'Theories and measures of urban primacy: a critique', in Timberlake, ed., 87–117.

(1985b) 'Class relations and urbanization in Guatemala: toward an alternative theory of urban primacy', in Timberlake, ed., 121–67.

Snow, J. (1965) *Snow on Cholera. Being a reprint of two papers by John Snow*, New York.

Sombart, W. (1902) *Der moderne Kapitalismus*, 2 vols., Leipzig.

(1916) *Der moderne Kapitalismus*, 2nd edn, 2 vols., Leipzig and Berlin.

(1937) *A New Social Philosophy*, Princeton.

Spurr, M. S. (1985) 'Slavery and the economy in Roman Italy', *CR* 35: 123–31.

(1986) *Arable Cultivation in Roman Italy*, London.

Štaerman, E. M. (1964) *Der Krise der Sklavenhalterordnung im Westen des römischen Reiches*, Berlin.

Štaerman, E. M. and Trofimova, M. K. (1975) *La Schiavitù nell'Italia imperiale*, Rome.

Stambaugh, J. (1988) *The Ancient Roman City*, Baltimore and London.

Standing, G. (1980–1) 'Migration and modes of exploitation: social origins of immobility and mobility', *Jnl Peas. Stud.* 8: 173–211.

Stanley, F. H., Jnr (1990) 'Geographical mobility in Roman Lusitania: an epigraphical perspective', *ZPE* 82: 249–69.

Stefani, E. (1944–5) 'Grottarossa: ruderi di una villa di età repubblicana', *NSc*: 52–72.

Taplin, O. (1989) *Greek Fire*, London.

Tchernia, A. (1982) 'La formule Pane e Vino Adjecto', *Epigraphica* 44: 57–63.

(1983) 'Italian wine in Gaul at the end of the Republic', in Garnsey, Hopkins and Whittaker, eds., 87–104.

(1986) *Le Vin de l'Italie romaine: essai d'histoire économique d'après les amphores*, Rome (*BEFAR* 261).

(1989) 'Encore sur les modèles économiques et les amphores', in *Amphores*, 529–36.

Tchernia, A., Pomey, P., Hesnard, A. *et al.* (1978) *L'épave romaine de la Madrague de Giens (Var)*, Paris (*Gallia* supp. 34).

Tecnologia (1980) *Tecnologia Economia e Società nel Mondo Romano*, Como.

Thomas, J. A. C. (1976) *Textbook of Roman Law*, Amsterdam, New York and London.

Thompson, D. J. (1983) 'Nile grain transport under the Ptolemies', in Garnsey, Hopkins and Whittaker, eds., 64–75.

Thompson, J. S. (1988) 'Pastoralism and transhumance in Roman Italy', in Whittaker, ed., 213–15.

(1989) 'Transhumant and sedentary sheep-raising in Roman Italy, 200 B.C. – A.D. 200', Ph.D. thesis, Cambridge.

Timberlake, M., ed. (1985) *Urbanization in the World-Economy*, Orlando and London.

Toynbee, A. J. (1965) *Hannibal's Legacy: the Hannibalic War's effects on Roman Life, Volume II: Rome and her neighbours after Hannibal's exit*, Oxford.

Treggiari, S. (1969) *Roman Freedmen during the Late Republic*, Oxford.
(1980) 'Urban labour in Rome: mercenarii and tabernarii', in Garnsey, ed., 48–64.

Vallat, J.-P. (1987a) 'Le paysage agraire de Piedmont du Massique', in Chouquer, G. et al., *Structures Agraires en Italie Centro-Méridionale: cadastres et paysages ruraux*, Rome (*CEFR* 100): 315–77.
(1987b) 'Les structures agraires de l'Italie romaine', *Annales ESC* 42.1: 181–218.
(1991) 'Survey archaeology and rural history – a difficult but productive relationship', in Barker and Lloyd, eds., 10–17.

Vera, D. (1995) 'Dalla "villa perfecta" alla villa di Palladio: sulle trasformazioni del sistema agrario in Italia fra Principato e Dominato I', *Athenaeum* 83: 189–211.

Ville, S. P. (1990) *Transport and the Development of the European Economy, 1750–1918*, London.

Virlouvet, C. (1991) 'La plèbe frumentaire á l'époque d'Auguste: une tentative de définition', in Giovannini, ed., 43–62.

Volpe, G. (1990) *La Daunia nell'età della romanizzazione: paesaggio agrario, produzione, scambi*, Bari.

de Vries, J. (1984) *European Urbanization 1500–1800*, London.

Walker, D. S. (1967) *A Geography of Italy*, 2nd edn, London.

Wallace-Hadrill, A. (1991) 'Elites and trade in the Roman town', in Rich and Wallace-Hadrill, eds., 241–72.

Wallerstein, I. (1974) *The Modern World-System I*, New York.
(1980) *The Modern World-System II*, New York.

Ward-Perkins, J. B. (1961) 'Veii: the historical topography of the ancient city', *PBSR* 29: 1–123.
(1962) 'Etruscan towns, Roman roads and medieval villages: the historical geography of southern Etruria', *GJ* 128: 389–405.
(1964) *Landscape and History in Central Italy*, Oxford.

Ward-Perkins, J. B., Kahane, A. and Murray-Threipland, L. (1968) 'The Ager Veientanus north and east of Veii', *PBSR* 36: 1–218.

Watson, A. (1977) *Society and Legal Change*, Edinburgh.

Weber, M. (1958) *The City*, tr. D. Martindale and G. Neuwirth, New York.
(1976) *The Agrarian Sociology of Ancient Civilizations*, tr. R. I. Frank, London.
(1978) *Economy and Society*, 2 vols., ed. G. Roth and C. Wittich, Berkeley, Los Angeles and London.

Westermann, W. L. (1955) *The Slave Systems of Greek and Roman Antiquity*, Philadelphia.

White, K. D. (1959) 'Technology and industry in the Roman empire', *AClass* 2: 78–89.
(1965) 'The productivity of labour in Roman agriculture', *Antiquity* 39: 102–7.
(1970) *Roman Farming*, London.
(1976) 'Technology in classical antiquity: some problems', *Mus. Afr.* 5: 23–35.
(1984) *Greek and Roman Technology*, London.

White, L., Jnr (1962) *Medieval Technology and Social Change*, Oxford.
(1980) 'Technological development in the transition from antiquity to the Middle Ages', in *Tecnologia*, 235–51.

Whittaker, C. R. (1985) 'Trade and the aristocracy in the Roman empire', *Opus* 4: 49–76.

(1987) 'Circe's pigs: from slavery to serfdom in the later Roman empire', in Finley, M. I., ed., *Classical Slavery*, London: 88–120. Reprinted in Whittaker (1993a), section V: 88–120.

(1989) 'Amphorae and trade', in *Amphores*, 537–9.

(1990) 'The consumer city revisited: the vicus and the city', *JRA* 3: 110–18.

(1993a) *Land, City and Trade in the Roman Empire*, Aldershot.

(1993b) 'Do theories of the ancient city matter?', in Whittaker (1993a), section VI: 1–20.

(1993c) 'The poor in the city of Rome', in Whittaker (1993a), section VII: 1–25.

(1994) *Frontiers of the Roman Empire: a social and economic study*, Baltimore and London.

Whittaker, C. R., ed. (1988) *Pastoral Economies in Classical Antiquity*, Cambridge (*PCPhS* supp. vol. 14).

Wickham, C. (1988) 'Marx, Sherlock Holmes and late Roman Commerce', *JRS* 78: 183–93.

Widrig, W. M. (1980) 'Two sites on the ancient Via Gabina', in Painter, ed., 119–40.

Williams, R. (1973) *The Country and the City*, London.

Willigan, J. D. and Lynch, K. A. (1982) *Sources and Methods of Historical Demography*, New York.

Wiseman, T. P. (1969) 'The census in the first century B.C.', *JRS* 59: 59–75.

(1970) 'Roman Republican road-building', *PBSR* 25: 122–52.

Wood, E. M. (1995) *Democracy Against Capitalism: renewing historical materialism*, Cambridge.

Woolf, G. (1990a) 'Food, poverty and patronage: the significance of the epigraphy of the Roman alimentary schemes in early imperial Italy', *PBSR* 58: 197–228.

(1990b) 'World-systems analysis and the Roman empire', *JRA* 3: 44–58.

Wright, G. (1976) 'Prosperity, progress and American slavery', in David *et al.*, 302–36.

Wrigley, E. A. (1967) 'A simple model of London's importance in changing English society and economy, 1650–1750', *P&P* 37: 44–70; reprinted in Wrigley (1987), 133–56.

(1978) 'Parasite or stimulus: the town in a pre-industrial economy', in Abrams and Wrigley, eds., 295–309.

(1987) *People, Cities and Wealth*, Oxford.

(1988) *Continuity, Chance and Change: the character of the industrial revolution in England*, Cambridge.

(1990) 'Metropolitan cities and their hinterlands: stimulus and constraints to growth', in Aerts and Clark, eds., 12–20.

Wrigley, E. A. and Schofield, R. S. (1981) *The Population History of England, 1541–1871: a reconstruction*, London.

Yaron, R. (1959) 'Sale of wine', in Daube, D., ed., *Studies in the Roman Law of Sale*, Oxford: 71–7.

Yavetz, Z. (1958) 'The living conditions of the urban plebs in Republican Rome', *Latomus* 17: 500–17.

(1988) *Slaves and Slavery in Ancient Rome*, New Brunswick and Oxford.

Yeo, C. A. (1952) 'The economics of Roman and American slavery', *Finanzarchiv* 13: 445–83.

de Zulueta, F. (1945) *The Roman Law of Sale*, Oxford.

Index

accounting, 73–4
Africa, exports to Rome, 7, 10, 56, 57, 114
Ager Cosanus, 99, 113, 127, 130–3, 178;
   archaeological survey, 129–31; decline,
   133, 136, 137
Ager Falernus, 129–30, 133–5
agricultural change, 56, 58; in China, 26–7;
   in England, 28, 60–2, 110
agricultural revolution, early medieval,
   118–19, 121
agronomists, Roman: on location theory,
   86–7; on marketing, 159; on slavery, 124,
   139–41; on the ideal villa, 109–10; on the
   suburban villa, 87–8; problems with
   108–9; *see also* Cato, Columella, Varro
Albegna Valley, 131, 133
Alexandria, 2, 65, 95, 183
amphorae, oil, 7, 114, 149
amphorae, wine, 7, 136–7, 149; Dressel 1,
   112–13, 132, 134; Dressel 2–4, 133, 135,
   136, 137, 149; Dressel 6, 150; Greco-
   Italic, 132, 134; Lamboglia 2, 149–50
animal labour, 80, 119–20, 121
Anio, river, 83, 95, 104, 105
Appianus estate, Egypt, 73–4, 76
Apulia, 149–51; desolation, 144, 156–8;
   grain, 70, 147–8; sheep, 154
aqueducts, 2, 38–9, 104–5, 107
archaeological survey, 95–6; definition of
   sites, 99, 130; in central Italy, 130–1; in
   the *suburbium*, 96–7; problems, 96,
   129–30
Aristides, Aelius, 1, 2, 3, 4
army, as market, 71, 150
auction sales and credit, 161–2, 163–4

Babylon, 3, 6
barrels, wine, 136
bookkeeping, 73–4
Bruttium, 72, 149, 154, 155
Bücher, Karl, 14, 15–17

Campagna, Roman, *see suburbium*
Campania, 66, 71, 120, 148; archaeological

survey, 133–5; grain, 57, 70, 114; markets,
   169–74
canals, 66
capital: investment, 58, 117; availability of,
   79–81
capitalism, 17–18, 19
Capua, 173–4, 181–2
Cato: on marketing, 159–62; *see also*
   agronomists
census, Roman, 47–8
central place theory, 170–4
cities: perceptions of, 23; sizes of, 2–3,
   181–2
citizenship: municipal, 174–6; Roman, 36,
   63, 78–9, 175
city, Chinese, 24–6
city, consumer, 5, 13–14, 26, 27–8, 29; in
   Bücher, 16; in Sombart, 18; in Weber, 20;
   in Finley, 20; *see also* Rome, London,
   Madrid
city, early modern metropolitan, 4–5,
   29–31; *see also* London, Madrid, Paris
city, medieval, 16, 18; as progressive, 21–3;
   in Weber, 18, 19–20
city, producer, 13; in Weber, 20
climate, Mediterranean, 69
cloth, 154, 177
coinage, Roman, 78
Collatia, 98, 101, 102–3, 178–9
Columella: economic mentality of, 73, 76;
   on agricultural change, 121; on
   marketing, 87–8; on virtues of
   agriculture, 112; on viticulture, 118, 122,
   128–9; *see also* agronomists
contracts of sale, 78–9, 161–2
Cosa, 178
Crustumerium, 89, 98, 100–1, 102–3, 178–9

demand, *see* pre-industrial economy
dietary revolution, 53
Diocletian, edict of, 63–5, 66, 68, 136
division of labour, 15–16, 18, 21, 23, 122–3
Domitian, edict of, 52, 135, 136
dry-farming techniques, 120